SWAMP

Who Murdered Margaret Clement?

RICHARD SHEARS

SWAMP

Who Murdered Margaret Clement?

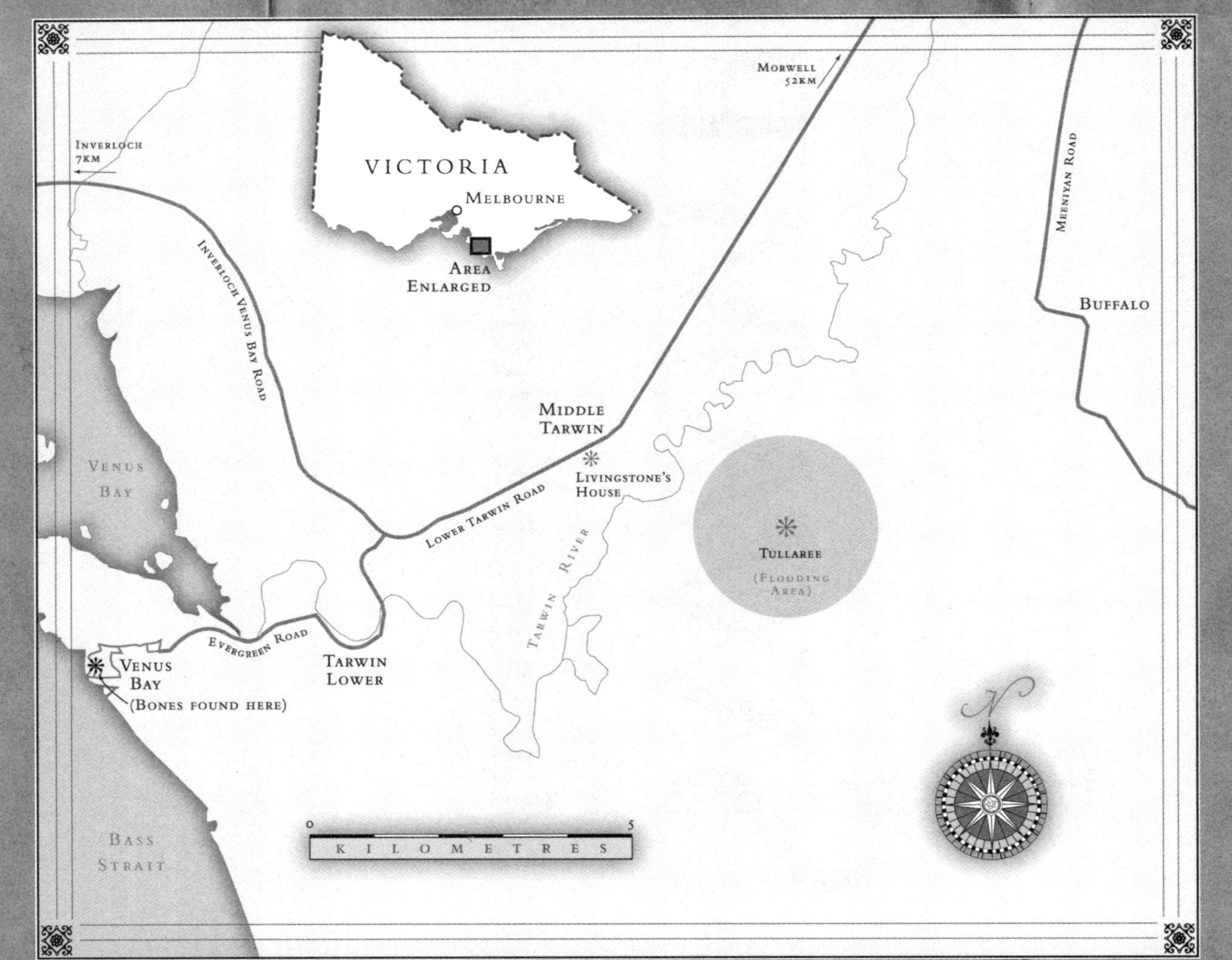

Victoria
Melbourne
Area Enlarged
Inverloch 7km
Morwell 52km
Meeniyan Road
Buffalo
Inverloch Venus Bay Road
Middle Tarwin
Livingstone's House
Lower Tarwin Road
Tarwin River
Tullaree
(Flooding Area)
Venus Bay
Evergreen Road
Tarwin Lower
Venus Bay
(Bones found here)
Bass Strait
0
5
Kilometres
N

CONTENTS

Two faces in one life.
Above: Margaret and her loyal dog Dingo, whose throat was cut.
Right: Margaret, the belle of Melbourne society.

Chapter 1.

~THEN~

There was nowhere more cold, nor bleak, in the autumn of 1952 than the flatlands of South Gippsland, Victoria, at the bottom of Australia, where Antarctic gales turned the waters of Venus Bay black and tore branches from the Mulga bush and ti-tree. And in that sodden, windswept landscape, no place was more joyless than the decayed house standing on a small rise in the middle of a swamp. No-one, then, was more wretched than the old woman who sat inside, hunched against the cold at the kitchen table, her mind full of addled memories.

The shabby, fur-collared black coat in which she was wrapped had seen better days and a wood stove was one of her few means of comfort. The other, a hurricane lamp, was already lit and it deepened the brown in her thick, greying hair. For all that she had been through, her skin, too, was still clear. She had aged surprisingly well. Yet these were the only attributes that hinted that Margaret Clement had once been a beauty.

A dog's bark brought her to her feet.

Her dog.

Dingo.

Unusual. No-one braved the swamp at this hour and in this weather.

Making her way down the hall and onto the front verandah, she called:

'Dingo! Dingo! Here boy!'

Peering around and across the water that stretched like a vast lake ahead and encircled the house, she called the dog again and he came running to her, soaked.

On each side tangled blackberry thickets threatened to swallow the homestead, having over-run the original garden long ago.

'Who were you barking at, Dingo?' she said, patting him. Then looking up, she called: 'Who's out there? Anybody there?'

But the only response was a distant roll of thunder.

It was in this light and in this weather and perhaps even at this hour that the men had come for her sister Jeanie nearly two years earlier. She remembered it as if it were yesterday.

It was the Lord's day at a time when several of them would have been making ready to go to church, but all that fell from their lips were profanities as they pushed through water that was chest deep in places. Dingo had barked and growled then as they approached, but a word from her silenced him.

'My God, it's a witch,' whispered one of the farm hands as her figure materialised through a veil of rain.

Unkempt hair framed the skeletal features of a bloodless face and a bony hand clutched at a hurricane lamp that signalled them towards her.

'And you would be Miss Margaret?' Constable Bert Fry asked, although, of course, he knew the answer.

She greeted them formally in her cultured tones. 'Good afternoon. You've come for my sister.'

She raised the lamp and they followed a muddy and slippery rising path to the verandah. There were seven men, including the police officer, from the district; four who would need to carry the stretcher later and three with poles to prod the murky water for hidden obstacles. Two neighbours had volunteered to help the policeman; Paddy Brennocks and Bernie Buckley, both of whom lived several miles away across the swamp. Goff Jongebloed, licensee of the local pub, the River View Hotel, also gave his services. The undertaker, John Keady, and two farm workers made up the rest of the team.

The property's drainage channels should have been cleared decades ago, Goff had informed the group while they had picked their way through the water. This is what you got when you didn't sort out a little problem at the time.

'Be careful of these steps – they can be quite treacherous in this weather,' the old lady warned, then stood aside for them as they gathered on the verandah. 'My sister is in the back room down there, the one with the door open,' she gestured. Her knuckles were swollen with callouses. 'She has been quite ill and has not been able to leave her room for some time.'

With no regard for the mud on their boots, Margaret Clement led them into the hall. The house was dingy, oppressive and stank of the sickly sweet smell of age, death and urine. There were cats everywhere, asleep or sitting in every nook and cranny. On every side, window panes were cracked or broken but the chilly draught that swept through the house had no effect on the fetid odour that hit each man. Even the experienced policeman wanted to be out of there as soon as was respectfully possible. Somewhere at the rear, a door continuously banged in the wind. Only three of the men, Goff Jongebloed, Bernie Buckley and Paddy Brennocks had been to Tullaree before and knew the run-down state the old homestead was in. For the others it was a house of isolation and dark secrets…uninviting…a place that made you shudder.

'Mind out for the floor,' said Margaret, pointing to a gaping hole in the passageway where the boards had rotted away. Water from the torrent outside poured down stained walls as they followed her to the room where the body of her sister lay. Here, the smell that had engulfed them as they entered the house was even worse. The youngest man, a farm hand, had never seen a dead body before and was so shocked he was almost sick. The old lady's face, frozen in death, was covered by matted hair that looked as though it had never seen a brush or a comb. Jeanie Clement was lying on her left side, knees drawn up to her stomach, covered with just a single, dirty sheet. Her bloated, overweight body hung over the side of the bed, almost rolling off the stained mattress on which she had lain for so long.

'I lost her yesterday,' said Margaret. 'Perhaps last night,' she added. 'She was all I had, you know.'

The undertaker immediately set about preparing the body for its journey out of that rotted old mansion and through the swamp to civilisation. As he went about his work, the policeman took notes while the others tried to make conversation with the surviving sister. However, Margaret appeared too numb to venture little more than say that her sister had become progressively more and more ill. Jeanie knew her time had come, said Margaret, and she wanted to die in the home where she had spent so many long and happy years. Margaret had stayed close to Jeanie until the end. A crumpled blanket lay on a sagging couch near the window and that was where she had slept near her dying sister.

Constable Fry knew of the two old ladies of the swamp, as the community had referred to them, and he asked himself how they had managed to remain so cut off that no-one had been aware that Jeanie Clement was ill. He shook his head slightly as he considered with dismay that it was not until Margaret had waded through the water and passed on the news to her neighbours that anyone knew of Jeanie's sickness and death.

The men lifted Jeanie Clement's body onto the stretcher, covering her with the same sheet she had been lying in. Unlike Margaret, Jeanie, bedridden for so long, was heavy and they grunted as they hauled the litter onto their shoulders.

'You'll need this,' said Margaret, handing the hurricane light to Constable Fry. 'I have others.'

He thanked her, although they had brought torches. Even though Margaret's nearest neighbours knew the extent of the swamp, they had not expected the journey in from the road to have taken three hours and the return was going to be even longer with their extra burden. The more light they could have for the trip, the better.

'And which is the best route to take?' the policeman asked, reflecting on the horrors of the walk in as they had waded through almost a kilometre of water to reach Tullaree, even getting lost.

'There is no best way,' Margaret replied in her refined, clipped voice. 'Things are always shifting about underneath. It's flat land, as you can see, but there's debris everywhere. The trick is to prod the water with a stick and go slowly.'

Constable Fry said he would be back in a day or so to help her with the arrangements for a burial and explained to her the process of what would take place. The doctor at Wonthaggi would first have to ascertain the precise cause of how Jeanie had died and issue a death certificate, following which there would then have to be a short inquest. Was there anything more he could do for her...arrange for someone to be with her... bring supplies...perhaps there was someone she could go and stay with...?

'Thank you,' she replied. 'But I have Dingo here with me' – and her eyes turned to the hallway where her beloved cattledog-cross lay – 'and I have enough now for our needs.'

So proud, the Constable thought.

It was still raining when the men stepped back into the swamp with Jeanie Clement's body. Margaret stood on the verandah, watching, until they moved out of sight and deeper into the marsh, the group struggling to keep the stretcher balanced and out of the water. They had switched on their torches and beams of light randomly stabbed the rapidly descending darkness as they headed towards the road, far away, where the hearse waited.

The witching hour, thought Fry, shuddering from the cold and the ghosts of Tullaree that trailed them, this must be what they call the witching hour. And if it isn't, it damn well ought to be…

In that flash of memory, Margaret saw it all as if it were yesterday. The white veins of lightning streaking over Venus Bay were reminiscent of that sad time 22 months earlier when they had taken her sister away. She turned from the verandah and went back inside, still wondering what had made Dingo bark.

Whatever had disturbed the dog, he was now calm as he followed her to the kitchen table, where she had been perusing a bundle of papers documenting the tortured years. She opened some tins and, lining up some fine bone china saucers, scraped out food for several cats, before tossing the cans out of the window, as was her habit. Seeing the dog sitting there, she opened another tin and gave him some food, too.

She moved to the wood stove and put on a blackened kettle to make some tea. While waiting for the kettle to boil, she turned on a small transistor radio that someone had once given her. It needed new batteries, so she turned it up to its full volume. The programme was about charismatic detective Raymond Kelly, who a little over two years earlier, in February 1950, had arrested armed robbers Darcy Dugan and William Mears for shooting a bank manager after they broke out of jail. Jeannie would have loved that, she thought, if she were alive today – they both shared a love of detective stories.

Pulling the lamp closer, she settled back at the table with her tea to thumb through the paperwork, oblivious to the house creaking and groaning under the weight of the storm that raged around and over it, doors banging off their hinges, the rank air surrounding her and the rotted glory of yesteryear. Tullaree had been falling into ruin for decades.

In a room to the side of the hall an iron bed remained neatly made up: Margaret's old bedroom, which she had abandoned long ago. When Jeanie had first become ill, Margaret had made her bed on a couch in her sister's room, remaining there until she died and then moving to another couch in a front room.

A single dining chair occupied a corner of the old lady's former bedroom and from it stretched spiders' webs, speckled with flies and small white moths, the tiny insects, trapped for years, turning to dust. Along one wall stood a Victorian dressing table with an oval mirror, slightly angled and locked in its tipped position by the grime that had gathered around its brass hinges. Caps on the jumbled collection of jars of cosmetic creams had seized and the congealed spillages had lost their greens and golds and taken on the colour of the leak stains on the walls. Among the jars, face down, lay a hand mirror with an ornate, tarnished, silver back, unused for years. Hair clogged a cheap plastic comb.

Once, the room had been decorated with lace curtains, crocheted doilies and antimacassars. The embroidered quilt that lay across Irish cotton sheets had been bright and clean and the dressing table had been polished by one of the many servants who glided skilfully and authoritatively throughout the mansion. A painting of the family patriarch, Peter Clement, hung by the door, still as vibrant as it had always been; likewise, the tinted photo of the Clement sisters' mother, gazing from a silver frame on the dressing table, was as perfect as the day it had been placed there.

The dining table, set with gleaming silver cutlery, was capable of seating a minimum of twelve guests. They had sat on high-backed chairs, the young ladies in lace-embroidered evening dresses, the men in wing collars, their eyes flashing admiringly at the women who peeped coyly back under fluttering lashes. The two Clement sisters presided over each end of the table, sophisticated Edwardian society hostesses in long Paris gowns. Specially ordered velvet drapes shut out the night beyond the long windows and oil lamps cast soft, wavering shadows, creating an atmosphere of ease and wealth. Wine flowed freely from Italian cut-glass decanters as the guests conversed with each other.

Remnants of Japanese embroidered wall hangings had somehow survived theft and the water that poured in under the rotting eaves, but the images of Samurai warriors were now fading behind a tapestry of mildew. A filigreed hallstand with delicate fretwork leaned against the wall for support, two of its legs collapsed inwards.

The drawing room was a forgotten museum of Victoriana and specimens of natural history. A scruffy stuffed owl with dusty startled eyes still perched on a shelf. In a corner the hands of a carved grandfather clock had stopped, freezing time, and a cluster of bulrushes in a large alabaster jar had shed seeds onto the satin ottoman beside it. All the books on the shelves, Wordsworth, Keats, Longfellow, Tennyson, were thick with dust, stained and ragged from the onslaught of bookworms. A brass tiger Margaret and Jeanie had brought back from Asia many years previously had lost its brilliant shine and now wore a tainted coat of green.

The floor was covered by a huge Persian carpet that had been laid down during that carefree extravagant period leading up to World War I. Now it was filthy with the excreta of nature, but it served to cover the loose rotting floorboards. In that room, also, was the Lipp grand piano, untouched and out of tune for years. And there was the armchair that Margaret had once posed in, straight-backed, for a formal portrait, with Jeanie and her other sisters gathered around. Now its floral covers were torn and faded, the springs rusted through and broken.

Tullaree, like Margaret Clement, was in the final stages of decline. Its corrugated roof had rusted, split and lifted. Cracks divided the walls allowing the rain to gush in. The attic, awash from the rains that swept in from Venus Bay, was a reservoir for the water that dripped through the ceilings and streaked down into every room. The mansion was weeping, shedding tears for its lost glory; for long-gone ladies in their finery and men in their evening jackets who stepped out the Pride of Erin and waltzed at fashionable gatherings hosted by the Clement sisters and who by day had played croquet in the sunshine on the green lawn. The house was grieving for its decayed treasures, for the elite who had lived and laughed there, for the parties the magnificence of which compared only with those of the Governor in far-away Melbourne…

Sometime in the night the old lady thought she heard Dingo barking outside again, but then he stopped so she decided against calling him in. She rose early as usual. Curiously, the dog was not beside the couch where he was always to be found when she woke. She went to the verandah to bring in wood, at the same time calling him.

Dingo was on his side, his body rising and falling in quick bursts. His glazed eyes stared back at her helplessly. A dark stain had spread around his head.

'Oh Dingo, dear Dingo, what has happened to you?'

His throat had been cut.

She took his head in her lap. It was hopeless, she knew, to walk through the swamp to seek help. What could anyone do? She cradled him tenderly for the remainder of that day until his life ebbed away. Then, before nightfall, she went to the shed and found a spade and dug a shallow grave near the house, out of reach of the water.

She carried the dog to the place she had dug for him, laid him down gently and showered the earth over him.

'So you have gone, too, Dingo,' she said and, turning, eyes blinded with tears, made her way back to the homestead. Her heart was breaking.

For the first time in all the years that she had fought to hold on to Tullaree, throughout the attempted inducements, despite the harassment, her kidnapping and the sinister threats, Margaret Clement felt truly alone – and afraid.

Not long after Dingo's death the heavy autumn rains began to fall on the Gippsland plains, stirring up the swamp water and flattening the mound that marked his grave.

Margaret always loved to watch the turn of the season from the verandah. She took comfort in the icy blasts that accompanied the storms – it made the homestead seem warm and inviting whenever she stepped back inside.

This time, as the wild weather battered Tullaree, the Lady of the Swamp was not on the verandah. Neither was she in the house.

Margaret Clement had vanished.

Chapter 2.

~NOW~

This is where she had stood, under the archway, supported by its two square brick pillars. Above the front entranceway is the shield, bearing the name Tullaree, untouched through the decades. You look out towards the route she had so often taken – across that crumbling old wooden bridge spanning the irrigation ditch running from Fish Creek. Even after the cut had become silted up and the water had spilled up over the banks and spread towards the house she continued to use the bridge rail as a marker, a place to leave her prodding stick.

Tullaree as it is today, drained of water and renovated to its former glory.

It is winter again now and Margaret has been gone for more than half a century but the bite of the wind has not changed, of course. It roars in under a black sky from Venus Bay, eight kilometres to the south, sweeping across the first of the land, the dune brush, then gusting through the streets of weatherboard holiday homes that have sprung up over the decades, bending back the pale grasses lining the edges of the Tarwin River and blowing across the wide open paddocks.

There are cattle, big red-brown Herefords and black and white Friesians, grazing on the lush green plains of Tullaree where once stretched miles of swamp, the animals oblivious to the chill on the wind which is destined to hit the homestead, for there are no hills or enough trees to protect it from the wintry blast. Two dogs chase one another around the verandah, the boards strong and firm. The family who live here have pulled the long windows shut and there is a modern gas fire with fake coals burning in the living room. The fireplace that Margaret, in those terrible years, was unable to burn wood in because the chimney was blocked is no match for today's modern heating, yet its carved wooden surround remains the centrepiece of the room. There is a big wide-screen LCD television beaming in pictures from Hollywood and news from around a world that Margaret would never have dreamed of, but in stark contrast, on the opposite wall, hangs a framed montage of faded newspaper cuttings showing the face of the woman who had laughed and then suffered so much in this very room.

It is a tortured, wrinkled face with no hint of the belle she once was, for that soft-featured countenance, along with her trappings of her wealth, had eroded long before the photographs had been taken.

Where are you now, Margaret?

It was my own whisper as I stared at the pictures and I wondered for a moment, a little embarrassed, if my host had heard me but he was busy in the kitchen, now fitted out with all the mod cons, so very different to the lifeless, cold, quarters the old lady had known in those final years.

A new driveway has been carved through the paddocks, coming in at right angles to the route that the carriages had followed in the halcyon days. But you can still stand there and turn around 100 degrees and hardly see an elevation anywhere. It is long, flat land, over which a flock of ibis now fly south, fighting the wind which brings another rain squall and spreads a sheen on the paddocks. It is easy to imagine, not a thin veneer of dampness, but a vast lake stretching to the horizon. How had she endured the journeys she had made through it in weather like this? For in these wintry mornings there is a blanket of frost but when the deeper water covered the land its surface was coated with ice. It would have cut into her bare legs like sheets of glass.

I look back across the paddocks and there's a hint of the mansion through the stand of trees; a corner of new corrugated roof, a wall, a shed. By today's standards, compared to the huge country homes of England, it is hardly a mansion, but the title was apt for the Victorian period in which it was built. It dwarfed every building in the region.

Here now is the road she took for the next stage of her seemingly impossible trek for supplies. It is still unmade, wet and muddy, falling away at the edges to a ditch in places or lined with fences and hedges erected by farmers who milk their cows with sophisticated machinery and drive powerful tractors across their paddocks. Did she really walk so far – seven miles (a little over 11 kilometres) to the store and seven back? A day's journey for the best of us.

The question I had asked the family earlier – and the answer – is still in my mind as I stare out across the pastures.

'Is it a happy place now?'

'Happy? Oh no,' the wife had said. 'Not happy at all. What is the word I want…? Spooky. That's what I'd say about it. Spooky.' She had her reasons. Deeply private family reasons, which she shared. But said again, with justification, that Tullaree was spooky and no more so than when you are alone in there and the winter winds are howling.

She had no notion of what I had been told earlier that day: the account of two schoolboys – now men - who had once seen the tiny, bent figure of Margaret Clement on this same road on which I now stood. They were adamant it was her; an old woman in her familiar and faded black coat shuffling along, yet moving so efficiently that it seemed her feet were hardly touching the ground. They had heard about her from their parents, a story that had been passed down through the decades by families all around the district, but when they saw her now, gliding away from them through the mist towards her home, they felt a chill run up their spines.

For Margaret Clement had been dead for 35 years.

Chapter 3.

~BEFORE~

There was still some stiffness in his leg as he leaned on the rail, but he hardly noticed it now as he stared out at the massive harbour called Port Phillip. Thirty-five miles wide! He had never seen anything like it, nor, indeed, the armada of sailing ships coming and going from the docks. Vessels from Liverpool, his own port of departure, from London, Europe – America! He had heard his companions talk of the trees that could be found in the new country and now he could see the wattles and gums clearly as the *Ocean Chief* headed towards land, its sails lively with the wind that followed it through the harbour heads. How he was looking forward to seeing his first kangaroo, although that probably wouldn't happen until he reached the goldfields.

Peter Clement, the son of spirit merchant William Clement and his wife Jamima from Crieff, Scotland, was 20 years old and he had travelled to Australia, at his wealthy father's expense, to seek his own fortune – and recover from the accident that had broken his leg when a keg of fine whisky had fallen from a cart and landed on him. That had been six months earlier and it had healed well, although the chill from the sea as the 182 foot wooden ship sailed into the southern hemisphere's winter in that August of 1854 had brought some discomfort. But he'd soon be working up a sweat in the colony that was known as Victoria following its separation from New South Wales three years earlier.

He'd been told before he set out from the old country that there were literally thousands of young men just like him who had sailed to Australia since a Californian, James Esmond, had turned up a nugget at Clunes, north of Ballarat in June 1851. By December, fabulously rich goldfields had opened throughout central Victoria and the cities lost their men to the rush. Flocks of sheep and herds of cattle were abandoned by farmers, doctors left their patients and ministers of religion walked out on the scatterings of congregations they had been left with. In many towns there was not an able-bodied man to be found as with picks, shovels and swags on their backs they had headed out of town on foot or horse and cart following a golden dream.

Peter so accustomed to the cold of wintry Scotland, grinned into the wind that made others shiver as he walked down the gangplank with his fellow passengers, the word gold on every lip. He was not a tall man, but he was muscle-bound, a physique developed from carting casks of spirits around his father's storeroom and he was ready to apply that strength to hours of solid digging in the region where others were striking it rich. Or so it was said.

He booked a seat – £500! – on a stagecoach to take him to the north-west of the colony but first there were several days to wait and with scores of other hopefuls he settled into a crowded tent in 'Canvas Town', a suburb of tents erected near the docks by the government to cope with the thousands who were coming and going from the goldfields with hearts filled with hope or despair. There were six men to a tent, each taking their turn to cook – and often badly burn – meat on an open fire. Opportunistic butchers and grocers had set up canvas stores to cater for the needs of the temporary residents.

Finally the young red-haired Scotsman was clambering into a Cobb and Co coach at the start of his journey to the goldfields in Ballarat, to the north-west of Melbourne, a town of 24,000 citizens that was swelling by hundreds each week. Just seven months earlier the first of the Cobb and Co coaches had set out from the Criterion Hotel in Melbourne for Forest Creek, a gold diggings close to the town of Bendigo, which lay beyond Ballarat. Now, Peter's carriage rumbled along the wide avenue that was Great Collins Street, where pedestrians dodged the horse traffic passing along the dirt road. Peter glanced at the signs on the boarded-up shop fronts declaring: 'Gone to the Diggings'. On the stony tracks closer to the goldfields, he passed men who had crossed mountains and rivers, some by horse, other pushing barrows, all of them, man and horse, coated in the grey-brown dust that blew in their faces.

At Ballarat, Peter stared in amazement at the city that greeted him – a city of canvas, far greater than the cluster of tents that had been erected at the Melbourne port. There were tents on the hills and in the valleys, occupying every inch of space. The ground was full of holes where men had dug frantically for the precious metal. A man-made landscape of mullock heaps hid the true horizon. The prospectors worked like ants and often slept where they fell. Peter, with money to spare from his father despite the high cost of his coach fare, found a room for a few nights in a lodging house, little more than a primitive hut.

He soon fell into a routine. He bought a shovel and started digging into the winter-hard ground in an area taken over by other Scots, just as other gullies had been claimed by Devonians, Cornishmen, Irishmen, Germans, Americans and Chinese. In places, national flags fluttered over the plots. Every man had a vision – the new life that a big strike would bring…a plot of land, a home, a bride, a family. Through rain or shine, Peter and his companions dug, sifted, searched and washed soil, promising to share their finds with others, agreeing it was better to divide the takings of a big strike with ten men than to work alone and miss out on a lucky find by a man in a nearby hole.

At the end of each day, many diggers fired guns into the air to warn would-be thieves that their weapons were in good working order. Robbers were dealt with harshly – they were flogged, tarred and feathered, toasted over a fire or chained to a tree for several days without food or water. But harsher punishment was also handed out at times.

As Peter sat around a camp fire one night, Charlie McLaren, one of his new pals, from Glasgow, recalled an incident that had occurred a few months earlier.

'Two of the men were having an argument while dividing their share of gold,' said McLaren. 'One of them suddenly produced a pistol and shot the other dead straight between the eyes. Before the killer could escape he was caught and begged to be taken before the Commissioner where he said he would get a fair hearing. The men wouldn't hear of it: he'd have the same mercy at their hands that he showed to his messmate. They threw a rope over a branch and soon he was dangling between the heavens and earth. The body of the poor fellow who'd been murdered was then decently interred. The Bible was read out over his remains as four thousand of us bowed our heads. Then we cut down the killer's body, threw the bastard into a hole and covered it up. He deserved nothing less than instant dismissal from this life.'

I, Peter Clement of Prospect Gippsland in the Colony of Victoria
Grazier declare this to be my last Will and Testament. I appoint my frien
John Loyd Roberts of Melbourne in the said Colony Merchant and John Neill of
Walhalla in the said Colony Storekeeper to be Executors and Trustees of this my W
And I declare that the expression "my said Trustees" used throughout this my W
shall be construed to include the said John Loyd Roberts and John Neill and t
survivor of them his heirs executors and administrators. I bequeath to my wi
Jane Clement all my furniture linen plated articles plate wines liquors and
consumable stores and articles of household and domestic use and ornament. I
bequeath to my said Wife the sum of two hundred pounds to be paid to he
within one month after my death for her own use. I bequeath to the sever
persons hereinafter named the several legacies which follow their respective name
that is to say, To my brother William Clement of Maffra in the said Colony
Farmer the sum of five hundred pounds, To my brother James Clement of
Emerald Hill near Melbourne aforesaid Baker the sum of five hundred pound
To my brother John Clement of Emerald Hill aforesaid Baker the sum of
five hundred pounds, To my sister Margaret Clement residing with my sa
brothers James and John at Emerald Hill aforesaid the sum of one
thousand pounds, To my brother Robert Clement of Richmond nea
Melbourne aforesaid the sum of five hundred pounds, and to
Christina Clement of Emerald Hill aforesaid Spinster the daughter
of my said brother Robert the sum of five hundred pounds, To eac
of my three Cousins daughters of James Clement of Perth in Scotland
Writer to the Signet the sum of two hundred and fifty pounds, An
I direct that such legacies shall not become payable until after the
PC expiration of ~~three~~ two years from my death. I devise all my real Estate
(except estates vested in me upon trust) unto my said Trustees Upon trust
that my said Trustees shall within three years after my death at their discr
sell the same either together or in parcels and either by public auction or
private contract and may buy in and rescind any contract for sale
and resell without being responsible for any loss occasioned thereby, an
execute and do all such assurances and acts for effectuating any such sale
as they shall think fit. I bequeath all my personal Estate (except
what I otherwise bequeath by this my Will) unto my said Trustee
Upon trust that my said Trustees shall at their discretion within thre
years from my death call in sell and convert into money such par

The tent city was already badly overcrowded, but still the migrants poured in from England, Scotland, Wales and Ireland. But the young men began to find, just as Peter himself had learned, that striking gold was a lottery. Men a few yards away might haul up a nugget worth hundreds of pounds after just a week or so at the diggings, while others who had been at it for months remained broke. If there was no agreement to share, those who had worked nearby were heartbroken. Peter wrote home to his father telling him that while hundreds of men continued to arrive, just as many were leaving:

'Father, I know that gold fever is running wild all over Scotland, but to all those young men in your employ who are talking of coming, I would tell them to stay where they are. I am contemplating a return myself because good fortune has escaped me. My savings are running out and there is sickness everywhere. The flies drive you mad in these early months of summer and recently there was an outbreak of dysentery. This is not a place for the faint-hearted.'

In Crieff, William Clement greeted his son's news with sadness. He was struggling with ill health – quite simply his body was slowing down and he could hardly walk these days – and he had hoped Peter could have done well for himself in the new country. But he had a proposition. He had read how, in that year of 1856, the ships continued to carry yet more hopefuls from Scotland to Australia, boosting the population of the colony of Victoria to a quarter of a million, English and Irish migrants helping to make up the majority of the remaining numbers. Germans, Americans and Welsh prospectors poured in, too, and there would have been a large Chinese community had a new Act not been introduced to regulate their population. Those who had given up in the goldfields, or had been deterred by the tales of woe, were able to find plenty of work in and around Melbourne, where new roads needed to be cut – and a new railroad, carrying a steam-powered passenger train, the first in Australia, running from South Melbourne to Flinders Street, needed to be maintained.

William Clement believed there could be opportunities for his son in the trade that he knew best – alcoholic spirits – for he had proved himself in the family business in Crieff. Peter collected his father's letter from the post office in Ballarat and read the proposition: don't come back to Scotland. Try something new. A Clement never gives up.

Opposite: Peter Clement's will bequeathed the Clement sisters a legacy of gold mining.

If Peter agreed, his father would arrange for a shipment of spirits to be sent out to Australia and he could set himself up as purveyor.

Two years later, Peter Clement was running a grocery and spirit store in Sale, just over 200 kilometres south-east of Melbourne. Casks of his father's whisky had been sent across from Liverpool and then carted by Peter on the rough 80 kilometres from Port Albert to Sale, where he bottled it. He had initially travelled to Sale with his friend from the diggings, Charlie McLaren, who was going to try his prospecting luck in the Bald Hill region several miles further east. Peter had been tempted to travel on with him to Bald Hill and another goldfield at Stringer's Creek but he did not want to pass up the opportunity his father had created for him. So he opened his small store where he soon found that not only was there a great demand for flour and vegetables, but there was a need for it to be delivered. Peter, then, took on the added tasks of storekeeper, bullock keeper and grocery delivery merchant.

Once a fortnight he would make the arduous journey to the newly opened goldfields that had taken on the appearance of Ballarat when he had first viewed that tent city in the north-west of Melbourne. He became such a familiar figure on the roads, trundling along with his sacks of flour on his bullock cart, that he became known in the district as Peter the Packer. To some, it was a lowly job, but Peter was working the long hours not only for himself but for his father, who had put so much faith in him making good in Australia.

He was viewed by all who met him as a decent, reliable young man now approaching his thirties. For him, though, marriage remained elusive – there was just too much work to be done. In fact the goldfields, east and west, were full of eligible bachelors who were determined to set themselves up financially before they started thinking about finding themselves a wife, although, inevitably, there were wild, bawdy scenes in the pubs that sprang up in the goldfield towns. Young women, hoping to find themselves a wealthy prospector – or have a good time trying – made their way from Melbourne but in many cases the only way they could earn their board and lodgings was by selling sex. Fights, sometimes to the death, broke out among desperate men over theft, jealousy and women. Peter considered he was well out of it, although he was constantly aware that he could be robbed at any time as he drove his bullocks up through the tree-lined tracks to the goldfields. But he remained confident that if there were any hold-ups, it would be by bushrangers after the more valuable hauls of gold being carried under escort for mining co-operatives from the diggings to Melbourne.

Even so, traders like him believed that there needed to be a better road to the diggings than the narrow, treacherous tracks through the gum trees and at a meeting of townspeople and merchants in 1862 it was agreed they would sponsor the exploration of a road from the town to the newly emerged community of Stringer's Creek, where rich deposits had been found. In that year, Sale was entering a new phase of its development. Log homes and stores were being transformed into brick properties as the population doubled and trebled.

Peter wrote to his father describing how the district was now bursting with activity – miners, prospectors, criminals, storekeepers, graziers. With his jovial, open nature, he was rubbing shoulders with them all.

But what a year 1862 was in other respects. The *Ocean Chief* on which Peter had sailed to his new adventures in Australia had become the focus of a drama in New Zealand in January. Early one morning dense smoke was seen pouring from the ship in Bluff Harbour. It had been set on fire by a mutinous crew who believed they could find their fortune in the nearby South Island goldfields more easily than toiling on the vessel. Just to make sure she would never sail again, they also destroyed the fire hoses. The *Ocean Chief* was towed, still burning, further out to sea, where she sank.

'Well, Father,' Peter wrote upon hearing of the fate of the vessel that had carried him to the other side of the world, 'it looks like there's a message in that incident for me – I'm here to stay!'

Peter continued correspondence with his family every month or so, but in 1863 the news from Crieff was bad. His father had died of a stroke at the age of 68 after suffering high blood pressure for four years. His mother, who penned the news on behalf of herself and Peter's brother James, reminded him that time was marching on – and had he found a wife for himself yet? She would die happy, she wrote, if she knew that Peter had started a family of his own.

But the demands of Peter's work in a town that was buzzing prevented any fraternising. There were frequent trips up to Stringer's Creek and back to Sale, fighting his way through the crowds of others walking, travelling by horse and cart, bullock trap and stagecoach. New gold strikes were being reported all around, the name of one new township summing up the mood of the prospectors – Happy-Go-Lucky. Stringer's Creek itself was now bursting at the seams, so the locals liked to joke. The first hotel, the Reefer's Arms, was opened in September 1863 and soon more than a dozen others had thrown open their doors. Such was the prosperity of the hilly region that in 1866 Stringer's Creek was renamed Walhalla after one of the more successful gold mines in the area. The first crushing from the mine had begun a year earlier and in the ensuing years 144,000 ounces of gold were extracted, paying some £286 a share to investors.

In 1870, Peter was driving his cart up to Walhalla on one of his regular runs when he pulled over to make way for a group of miners walking down the hill. As they passed, one of them cried out, 'Well I'll be damned!'

At first Peter did not recognise the haggard face of the man who had spoken. Then the fellow whipped off his hat and there was no mistaking that shock of red hair, so much like his own.

'Charlie McLaren!' declared Peter at the sight of his friend from the Ballarat days. 'My God, I thought you were dead! I haven't heard anything of you for years.'

'Been down the mine, I have, day and night,' said Charlie. 'But I'm doing well. We're all doing well. Except there's a big demand on liquor and flour up there so we're heading down to get some and maybe scrounge a lift back up again with it all.'

Peter looked at his old friend; at his ragged clothes, the wear and tear on his face and hands. Why were they walking, if they were doing so well? The truth was, he suspected, that they were heading away from the mining area to look for cheaper food and accommodation before returning to the daily toil.

'Don't bother going any further,' said Peter. 'You can have my load. And I'll take you back up the hill.'

The four miners jumped onto the cart and Peter took them back to Walhalla. He helped carry his sacks of flour into a lodging house room the men shared, knowing they would be able to sell it on to one of the stores. He threw in half a dozen bottles of whisky.

'You're a good friend, Peter,' said Charlie. 'And if you want a good word in return and you can afford it, listen to this: take out shares in the Long Tunnel Mine. It's looking good.'

As he drove his cart back down the winding track Peter considered his friend's words. Perhaps…

In the weeks that followed he spoke to graziers and well-to-do families in the Sale district who had not settled their accounts. He struck deals. He would be happy to take shares they held in the Long Tunnel Mine at their current market value instead of cash. In many cases his customers, particularly those who were not confident that the mine would continue its high yield, were happy with the arrangement. But the mine flourished. Peter's shares soared. He cashed some of them in, then bought more. He sold his business for a fine profit. He was becoming a wealthy man, almost overnight, it seemed.

One of his first tasks on realising that he would never need to work again was to return to Walhalla and seek out his friend Charlie. Into his hand he thrust £5,000 in crisp notes. His compatriot nearly fainted. 'Now I can find my feet,' said Charlie. 'I can even buy a home! Melbourne, here I come!'

During his many excursions to the bustling township of Walhalla, Peter made deliveries to the Yarras Hotel, where he would often have a beer with another merchant, Arthur Thomson, who had made his way there from Beechworth in northern Victoria. With him was his wife Jane and their young daughter, also named Jane, who was to be among the first group of children to attend the newly opened school. There had been a gold rush in Beechworth, but by 1866 it was virtually over and Arthur took his family to the south-east where, rather than digging for gold, he decided to earn his living by catering for those who were looking for it – just like Peter. The two men got on well together and Arthur often needled Peter about his advancing years and how, if he wasn't careful, he'd end up living alone in some old folks' hostel.

Young Jane had left school by 1874, when she was 14, and had begun helping her father in his grocery store. Just as she had moved on, so had Peter. No longer was he Peter the Packer. He was now a rich man. But a lonely one. Arthur Thomson would joke that if only his daughter was old enough, she'd make Peter a fine wife. Peter couldn't have agreed more. She was a pretty young thing, he told Arthur, quick of mind, and didn't mind getting her hands dirty when there was work to be done. But the age difference... Jane was still only 15; Peter was 41! Yet, the two men agreed, child brides were hardly unusual in the goldfields. If young women were not snapped up as soon as they came of age, they were gone.

'She likes you, Peter,' said Arthur. 'And you do, of course, have the means to care for her.'

Peter and Jane's courtship ran for a blissful year. No-one took any notice of the powerfully built Scotsman and the slip of a girl at his side. They weren't the only father-and-daughter look-alikes who made up engaged couples in town. After all, most young women were mothers two and three times over before they reached the age of 20.

The wedding, before Wesleyan Church Minister Arthur Powell at the Yarras Hotel on 24 October 1876, was a boisterous affair, with friends of the groom, more so than the bride, filling the saloon bar, where beer for the adults and lemonade for the bride and her former school friends flowed. On the marriage certificate Peter declared his 'condition' as a bachelor, adding – perhaps with some pride – that his 'rank or profession' was 'Gentleman'. The bride was described as 'spinster', a title that to those unaware of her tender years, might have suggested a much older woman. Peter was now 42. His wife was 16.

They started married life in a house near Sale, where Peter sat back in comfort and watched his shareholdings continue to soar. Sitting down for dinner, prepared by a housekeeper-cook – such luxury for a man who had once been a humble merchant with a bullock cart – or enjoying balmy summer evenings on the verandah, Peter told his bride what he had learned about the district.

Gippsland, he related, had been the home of the Boonurrong Aboriginal tribe before the arrival of European explorers and in recent years, as new homes were being built and paddocks cleared, the bones of Aborigines killed in long-past battles had been unearthed.

'It sounds terrible,' said Jane as she learned of the early struggles by European explorers, fighting through the swamps and the bush. 'I'm surprised that my father even managed to get us to Walhalla when he did.'

'Oh, you have to thank the prospectors for that,' said Peter, omitting to mention that he had also been partly responsible for ensuring that tracks were opened up in the region. 'There's a river south-west of here called the Tarwin and that was a target for many of the explorers. Get to the river and you had a means of getting to the sea.'

One explorer wrote: 'In the trees we heard the croak of the crows, the scream of cockatoos, the doleful cry of the mopoke, the chatter of parrots, the ridiculous hooting of the laughing jackass and at night the howl of the wild dog.'

'How wonderfully descriptive,' said Jane. 'We're so lucky to live in these modern times. Such a wonderful time and place to raise our children.'

For she had found after two months into their marriage that she was pregnant. Peter was thrilled and gave no thought to how old he would be when even that first child would be Jane's present age of 17.

They called the baby girl Flora, her parents content that Peter's shareholdings assured her of a future without struggle. Many who saw him in the district and remembered his days as a merchant remarked on his incredible change of fortune, for he was now the most wealthy man for miles around. But there were also wild rumours that he had somehow benefited from the theft of 5,000 sovereigns from the P&O liner *Avoca* that had been sailing from Sydney to Melbourne, along the Victorian coast.

What was known was that Martin Wyberg, the ship's carpenter, had made an imprint of the strongroom key in a bar of soap, removed the sovereigns, replaced them with lead to make up the weight and made good his escape into the bush near the Tarwin River.

It was there that he set up a simple wooden house on land that was, years later – and the reason for the unfounded rumours – to become part of the land acquired by the Clement family.

Wyberg was arrested, served time in jail – then recovered the sovereigns he had hidden. Observed by his wife, he set out in a small boat to sail to one of the Glennies Islands, off Wilson's Promontory, with his bounty. But as his wife watched, she lost sight of him in the heavy swell and he was never seen again. It was assumed he had gone to the bottom with his haul, but rumours abounded for years that he had managed to make good his escape. Others believed there was a chance the sovereigns had been washed ashore in the current and for years afterwards large numbers of people could be seen hunting through the sand dunes around Venus Bay.

On another occasion a ship carrying crates of liquor broke up in a storm and its cargo was washed up onto the beach at Venus Bay. How curious, local people were to remark later, that this area where gold sovereigns and crates of liquor were possibly still hidden in the dunes was where the Clement family should buy land. Although he was never to reside there himself, was there something that Peter Clement knew and had passed down to his growing family? It was only rumour, but it stuck.

However, a generation later it was not the discovery of sovereigns in the dunes that turned the attention of the country to the Tarwin region. It was the unearthing of a skeleton.

Chapter 4.

~STYLE~

Jane presented Peter with a new addition to the family every two years – after Flora came Jeanie in 1879 and Margaret in 1881. 'I need a son!' Peter joked after Margaret had come into the world. 'Am I going to have a family made up entirely of women? You will all drive me to my grave!'

Perhaps his humour had led to serious thoughts, for in the year that Margaret was born he made out his will. Significantly, his wealth had not affected his friendship with the people he had dealt with in his days as a merchant. He appointed 'my friends' John Roberts, merchant, of Melbourne, and John Neil, storekeeper, of Walhalla, to be executors and trustees. Now describing himself as a 'grazier', for he had acquired a fine head of cattle, he instructed his executors to hold the trust money and investments until his sons (a clause he had included with hope in his heart) were 21; and his daughters were 21 or until they married. He bequeathed to his wife Jane all his furniture, linen, wines and liquors and the sum of £200 to be paid within one month after his death for her own use. In addition, he instructed his executors to pay to his wife from trust funds and the sale of real estate the sum of £200 a year by equal half-yearly instalments to start from the day of his death.

As for his children's education, he asked that his wife be paid £100 a year for each child. Should his wife or his children not be living at the time of his death, Peter bequeathed his money to the town of Crieff, in the county of Perth, Scotland, and interest arising from it, he instructed, should be used to buy coal, clothing and food for distribution during winter among the poor of the town. He ended his will, witnessed by Henry Jones who was the station manager at the farm he had acquired, by appointing 'my said wife and my said trustees guardians of my infant children.'

Jane duly abided by Peter's wishes and her next two children were sons, William born in 1883 and Peter in 1885.

'Now I think I can celebrate by purchasing us a nice new home,' said Peter, whose wealth had swelled even more. For by now he was a director of the Long Tunnel Mine and he also had interests in the Toombon mine. On 27 February 1886, he purchased a fabulous cattle station, Prospect, at Seaspray, near the coast, south of Sale. Peter and Jane and their older children looked out across the paddocks at the cattle which grazed under a brilliant blue summer sky. It had been a tough start for both of them in their younger days but now, it seemed, life was as perfect as it could be.

In Melbourne, however, it was a different story. The first signs of economic troubles ahead came with men being laid off work, the unemployed walking the streets, hands in pockets, wondering how they were going to feed their families.

Meanwhile, on the banks of the Tarwin, on a stretch of land that would ultimately shape Margaret's destiny, men were at work clearing the ti-tree. Among the first of these, and the man who called the land Tullaree after his birthplace in Ireland, was Francis Longmore, a noted politician who, with his large family – he had several sons – had taken up an area of some 2,000 acres on the eastern bank of the river. He did a great deal of work with his sons in clearing the scrub before selling the land to Charlie Widdis, a grazier.

Charlie brought in a team of men with axes and they hammered into the scrub that Francis Longmore had left. Charlie had a vision, and it was this that drove him onwards.

'When this land is cleared,' he told a group of visiting friends, 'I am going to build a magnificent mansion here. It will be one of the finest – no, the very, very best – in Gippsland and people will travel from miles around to see it.'

Charlie believed that once the house of his dreams was built, buyers would clamour for it. He planned to construct it from bricks made from the mud of the area and he believed he would make a tidy profit, echoing the thoughts of one of the earlier pioneers that there was 'money in mud'.

He called in a gang of Chinese and set them to clawing out the clay from the river banks for the bricks. The mansion Tullaree was on the way.

One morning in the spring of 1889 a small open buggy arrived at the entrance of the Methodist Ladies College in Barkers Road, in the leafy Melbourne district of Kew. It carried a group of excited girls, among them Margaret Clement, aged eight. Her older sister Jeanie was already a boarder and now it was Margaret's turn to live out her father's dream of providing his children with the very best education available. And what better way than to send his daughters to a college whose motto was 'Deo Domuique' – 'For God and for home'. The college stood for education, Christianity and womanhood. It was still very much an experimental establishment, for the first complement of teachers had arrived only seven years before Margaret. It took in the children of the wealthy – its fees for junior resident boarders were 12 guineas a quarter, far more than most families in Victoria could afford, particularly as the economy of the colony was foundering.

Margaret, with the other girls in their new school uniforms, was taken on a tour of the grounds, setting out from the main building, which was already covered with ivy and Virginia creeper. There were sloping lawns edged with flower beds and circular seats embracing the trees.

She settled into college life well and excelled in most subjects. On warm days she sat for classes under the shade of the trees close to where a fountain played water into a pool of goldfish. At 7am the younger students were awakened by a bell although Margaret, fresh from the country, was up an hour before that: she always heard the 6am bell for the senior boarders.

Despite the strict routine of college life, Margaret and her sister succumbed to temptation and were scolded on more than one occasion when prefects caught them smoking in the toilets. They were punished with lines and made to stay behind late in class for not catching up with their homework. Nevertheless, Margaret in particular was regarded as a conscientious student and the staff had little doubt she would turn out to be a model of all that the college stood for. She became actively involved in the 8 o'clock Friday evening social club, giving pianoforte solos and reciting poetry. Performing at the social club was a good test for the young Clement girl, for there was a critical audience of more than 130 students and staff. Margaret also took part in debates on current affairs and impressed the teachers with her widespread knowledge and interests.

Back at the Prospect homestead in Gippsland, Peter Clement, his now-portly figure testimony to the good life he was enjoying, was a happy man. His wife was pregnant with their sixth child and his older children were all doing well at their various schools. In particular, the reports that had reached him about Margaret and Jeanie at the Methodist Ladies College were particularly encouraging. He had looked forward to the end of term holidays in 1889 and when they arrived home, giggling and chatting in the carriage, he proudly showed them off to the Gippsland gentry. The girls played the piano in the large reception room and sang at soirees and other formal gatherings. It was hard for the visitors, themselves living a life of luxury in contrast to the growing unemployment and discontent in far away Melbourne, to imagine that this wealthy gentleman and Peter the Packer were one and the same. Not a vestige of the old hard days remained, as continued astute buying of other land in the arca swelled the Clement fortune even more.

Peter's was now very much a life of ease and luxury. He loved to spend the summer evenings on the verandah, puffing on his pipe, a glass of good whisky in his hand, as he gazed out across the paddocks where the finest cattle in the district grazed. Often he would remain there until after dark, particularly if there was a storm at sea and the spectacle of lightning dancing across the horizon to be enjoyed, swatting lazily at the mosquitoes until they finally drove him indoors. These days, his manager attended to most of his affairs, although occasionally Peter made a business trip to Sale in a horsedrawn carriage that could not be compared in any way to his humble packer's cart of years before.

On Friday 24 January 1890, while Margaret, Jeanie and Flora were home for the summer holidays, Peter travelled into town to enjoy a lunchtime drink with a group of graziers. They jovially chatted about the hot weather and agreed they should make the most of it because winter would be upon them before they realised it, and then they'd all be standing in the pub cursing the cold. The following day, Peter complained of feeling unwell.

'I think I've got a bit of indigestion,' he told Jane.

'Serves you right for eating that pub food,' she joked. 'We have a good cook. You should have waited until you got home. Take some Epsom salts and you'll feel better.'

But his discomfort continued and in the evening a local physician, Dr Macdonald, was called. He advised Peter to take a good rest, although he could find nothing seriously wrong.

The following day, ignoring the doctor's advice, Peter called on neighbours and enjoyed a few more drinks with them, but they agreed later that his face was grey. What happened later that day, 29 January 1890, was recorded in the *Gippsland Times*:

'On Sunday the weather was very oppressive and Mr Clement, who had been out during the day, was in the evening sitting on the verandah of his residence at Prospect, engaged in conversation with the manager of the station, Mr P. Bolger.

'At Mr Clement's request, Mr Bolger was engaged in cutting up some tobacco when the former suddenly stood up, reeled once and fell into Mr Bolger's arms. Drs Watson and Macdonald were sent for immediately but death had taken place before their arrival. The cause of death was apoplexy. The deceased, who was 58 years of age, leaves a widow and 6 children to mourn his loss.'

The report left a slight discrepancy in Peter's age, for he had stated on his marriage certificate, 14 years earlier, that he was 42 at the time. He may have taken two years off his age when he married to narrow the gap between himself and his teenage bride. In any case, his death at a relatively young age – whether he was actually 56 or 58 – was a great shock to the community.

Peter Clement, the newspaper reported, was well known as the proprietor of Prospect Station and as a director of the Long Tunnel Gold Mining Company, in which he was one of the largest shareholders.

Embracing her three oldest daughters in the living room, Jane Clement told them: 'You have lost your father but he has thought of our future and we have not been left wanting. You will continue your education and you will make good your lives. You must do that as if your father were still here to encourage you.'

Few children in the colony could be assured of such a trouble-free future in that year of 1890. It was a time of deep industrial unrest. There was a major strike at the Melbourne docks and thousands of men were laid off from jobs associated with the maritime industry. Wheat slumped to its lowest price in decades and the price of silver fell dramatically. Crowds marched through the streets carrying placards reading 'Work or Bread', such was their desperation. A few remembered the riches that had been gained from gold prospecting 40 years earlier, and, believing that the once popular diggings in the north-west of the city had been thoroughly explored, headed to the goldfields of Western Australia. Soon the trickle of men turned into a flood of more than 100000.

Those left behind, or unable to face the enormous journey across the continent, formed desperate queues at church centres where soup and bread was handed out. Most of them were women and children who were praying that their absent husbands were finding work or gold somewhere out of town.

In Gippsland, Charlie Widdis, the builder who had been among those who went to Peter Clement's funeral in Sale, was soon hard at work again at Tullaree, putting the finishing touches to the magnificent mansion he had envisaged. Although he was proud of the homestead, he expressed some concern to his fellow builders about the sogginess of the surrounding ground. He knew that others who had kept big Shorthorn cattle nearby had complained of stock losses after the animals had become bogged.

Charlie's next task, then, was to work on an efficient drainage system. He had to do much of the job himself after one of the Chinese workers was bitten by a snake and the others refused to step into the reeds. Charlie knew the house was safe from any flood, for he had erected it on a rise, but he still had a niggling concern about the problems strong winter rains might create.

His fears were justified the following winter when torrential rain flooded the land and the house became surrounded by water. Charlie called in his brother John, a grazier from Flynn's Creek, and together they dug drainage channels that led the water away from the mansion and towards the Tarwin River. Next, the Widdis brothers set about landscaping, laying lawns and planting native trees. They worked on it for eight long years before the homestead, the drains and the garden were completed. They stood in a paddock and admired their work. The house was only single storey, unlike many of those springing up in Melbourne, but they could justifiably call it a mansion, for it was a solid structure made from the riverside clay, comprised 17 rooms and was embraced by a wide verandah. It was certainly the finest home between Gippsland and Melbourne, they agreed, and there was no doubt it would attract a great deal of attention and they would easily find a buyer.

Right: A portrait at Prospect Station. From left: Margaret, Flora, Anna, a cousin and Jeanie Clement.

Grazier declare this to be my la
John Loyd Roberts of Melbourne in
Walhalla in the said Colony Storek
And I declare that the expression

thousand pounds, To my b
Melbourne aforesaid the sum
Christina Clement of. Emerald
of my said brother Robert the
of my three Cousins daughters
Writer to the Signet the sum
I direct that such legacies sh
WP PC expiration of ~~three~~ two years from m

Meanwhile, the older children in the Clement family continued their schooling but Jane Clement, enjoying the benefits of her late husband's estate, was determined that when they were old enough – when Margaret was 16 and Jeanie 18 – their education would continue. She made plans to take the older girls, Flora, Jeanie and Margaret, with her on an overseas trip, but Flora preferred to remain at home with her brothers and younger sister, Anna, under the watchful eye of a housekeeper. So it was Margaret and Jeanie who headed off with their mother on their first overseas adventure. They travelled by luxury liner to England, making friends on the way with a wealthy couple called Robson who begged the three women to call on them when they reached London.

But first Margaret, Jeanie and their mother had an appointment with their relatives. They journeyed north through England by train, horse and carriage, travelling eventually through the Scottish Highlands, where the girls tried their hand at trout fishing, a sight which surprised the reserved Scots of the day, for this was the domain of gentlemen! Finally, they arrived at Crieff, the birthplace of Margaret and Jeanie's father.

It was summer, 1897, when the horse and buggy carrying mother and daughters arrived at their relatives' homes – the girls' distant cousins. They were greeted enthusiastically and the two teenage Australians listened to stories of the tough times the Clements had endured when a young Peter worked for his father in the liquor trade. But even then, as the sisters learned of the dark days of the early to-mid 19th century, they could not help thinking how life still seemed hard for the residents of Crieff. They listened, fascinated to tales of how the young Pretender, Bonnie Prince Charlie, had once been quartered in the town in the mid-1700s, and how Rob Roy's outlaw son had been chased through the cobbled streets and killed by soldiers.

The girls chuckled as they heard another story, passed down through the family, of how their father had set off for Australia still recovering from a broken leg, to seek his fortune. For their Scottish relatives, it was strange to think that Peter Clement had embarked on a ship for a far land and now, decades later, these young women and their mother, his 'products' from his new-found life, had turned up on their doorstep. And the girls were so sophisticated! Jane produced a family photograph which was eagerly passed around, the Scottish families they visited gazing in wonderment at the beautiful clothes Peter's children wore.

Word had preceded them that Jane, Margaret and Jeanie were from a highly respected and well-to-do family from the 'new country', so the landed gentry of England were keen to show them the best hospitality. After bidding their relatives' goodbye, Jane took her daughters through the Pennine Chain on their way down through England, staying at stately homes at the invitation of the wealthy owners. When they arrived in London during the early autumn of 1897, they checked into the Ritz Hotel, where Margaret penned a letter to her brothers and sisters – Flora, William, Peter and the last born, Anna, who was now aged seven. Her words reflected how the English hierarchy were ready to welcome those who had done well for themselves in the still-developing nation of Australia:

'We are having a wonderful tour,' Margaret wrote during that month of September, 'and the weather has been very kind to us. Yesterday we went to Buckingham Palace and were presented at court to King Edward VII and Queen Alexandra. There were a great deal of other people there and we met several other girls from Australia. Three were from Victoria and had been boarders at MLC. Tomorrow we have been invited to dinner at the Robsons, who are the people we told you we met on the boat.

'We have been reading the newspapers but have not seen much news about Australia.

'Your loving sister, Mag.'

Their appointments, dinners and recollections over tea and cakes with the other girls from Melbourne finally over, the Clement family sailed from Southampton, down the west coast of France, around the Spanish coast and into the Mediterranean. They played quoits on the sundeck and, one evening, during a birthday ball, the teenage sisters had their first taste of champagne, giggling with the English debutantes who were sailing to Italy to escape the bite of the oncoming northern winter. And then it was on by train through the Italian peninsula to stay at a plush hotel in Sorrento, where rich gentlemen eyed them admiringly as they entered the foyer, a team of porters following with an endless line of trunks. It was not long before the Italian aristocracy were inviting them to balls, but Margaret, in another letter home, recalled that one of the most memorable events was their invitation to participate in local folk dancing:

'We dressed up in traditional costumes with very tight waistbands and danced with four gentlemen who also wore the local costume. They gave us tambourines decorated with painted portraits to shake. It was difficult trying to get the right steps and shake the tambourines at the same time.'

On their arrival back in Gippsland, two horsedrawn carriages rumbled over Prospect Station's long driveway to the Clement homestead – the first carrying the sisters and their mother, the second a host of presents, souvenirs and treasures they had purchased during their tour. The stockmen employed on the station stared in amazement as the trunks of clothing, paintings, cutlery and goblets were carefully unloaded by the household staff.

It was time for a celebration – a new family portrait! A photographer travelled from Melbourne to the homestead and there, in the lounge-room, the four Clement sisters, dressed in their Victorian finery, posed with a visiting cousin. In a flash, the camera captured sisters in their late teens and early twenties. Young ladies who exuded style and wealth and who, through their father's position, money, their own connections and from having attended one of the best private schools in the country, would have had a vast circle of friends and acquaintances. The photograph showed a group of patrician ladies expensively attired yet with a shyness and unworldliness about them. But then, aside from their relatives' homes in Scotland, they were cocooned from the real world – almost unrelated to it with the trappings of the wealth of the landed gentry that had surrounded them all their lives. They were certainly far removed from the misery of Melbourne, where the economic gloom had resulted in the collapse of several major banks even though plans were slowly continuing for the city to become the capital of the newest nation.

On the left for the family portrait sat Margaret, delicately featured, richly attired, yet not ostentatiously, in a tailored velvet outfit, hands clasped on her lap, her auburn hair pulled back into a bun. Next to her sat the youngest of the Clement girls, Anna, her hair falling down over her shoulders and on the right, rigidly poised with an authoritative, forthright expression, was Jeanie. Standing behind Margaret was the eldest sister, Flora, who was soon to marry, while the cousin posed with her hands resting on a filigreed table.

Several weeks later, in December 1898, Margaret and Jeanie were on their way to Melbourne on the train, for it was now possible to reach the city by rail from Sale. Passing through the outer suburbs, Margaret read again the letter that had been waiting when she arrived back from her

European tour. It was from a young well-to-do man called Willie, whom she had met through a college friend when a group of visitors had called at Prospect Station. His father was on the staff of one of the city schools. Willie's parents had invited the three oldest Clement sisters to their home for an Easter visit the previous year but since their mother had been unable to accompany them, the invitation had been politely refused. Now Willie had written again, requesting Margaret, perhaps accompanied by one of her sisters, to spend a few days with his family.

'He's got his eye on you, Mag,' said Jeanie when Margaret shared the contents of the letter with her. 'Tell our mother that I'll be your chaperone.'

Jane had agreed the girls could go, for were they not world travellers by now and respectable, capable young women?

He was waiting at the station, a reserved young man with straight dark hair and dressed in a tweed suit. His greeting was formal, taking the hand of each woman and bowing over it. He was now articled to a firm of Melbourne solicitors and as the open horse carriage trundled off to Kew he spoke briefly of his work.

'But you, Margaret and Jeanie, you have so much more to tell me! A tour of Europe! What sights you must have seen.'

They told him of the Highlands and meeting the King and Queen. Willie quickly dropped his topic of law practice.

His parents greeted them at the entrance of their spacious home and showed them to a room overlooking a park.

'He's jolly nice, isn't he?' said Margaret as they unpacked.

'You'd better watch out, Mag, or you'll be hearing wedding bells before not too long.'

'Oh rot,' laughed Margaret. 'There's so much more to see and do before I turn a mind to settling down. Besides, you'll be wed long before me. Have you heard from Hamish of late?'

Jeanie had met Hamish in Sale when he had travelled with his parents from western Victoria to a relative's home to stay for the weekend and the Clement family had been invited around for dinner. Jeanie and the farmer's son had struck up a friendship which had continued through letters and promises to meet each other again as soon as convenient travel arrangements could be made for either one of them.

At dinner with Willie's family, talk turned to trouble brewing in South Africa. Well read, Margaret and Jeanie concurred with the thoughts of the young man's family that the presence of both Britain and the Dutch there and the fact that gold mines were in the Dutch Boer republics of the Transvaal and the Orange Free State were tinder for a military fire.

'Gold has brought trouble for so many in our own history,' remarked Margaret, recalling stories her father had told her of men being slaughtered in the gold fields.

'But then,' Jeanie reminded her, 'it has brought good fortune too. I think you could say we are witnesses to that fact.'

The prediction of trouble at the foot of Africa proved to be correct, for within a year the Boer War had broken out – and Willie, accepting that Margaret was keen to continue travelling rather than start up any kind of relationship with him, volunteered to join the 16,000 Australian troops to fight the Boers. Hamish was not far behind him, for like so many other young men in the farming districts he could not resist England's call for reinforcements.

As the troop ships left Australian ports for Africa, the liners carrying the carefree rich headed for the Orient and Europe. Among those watching the Australian coastline disappear into the distance were Margaret, Jeanie and Flora, for the youngest sister, Anna, was now receiving her education at an English boarding school. The three young women danced in Leningrad, skied in the Alps and played tennis in Nice.

On their return to the southern hemisphere, they motored through New Zealand in an open car, taking a mountain of clothes that included several pairs of goggles for the road. No sooner were they back in Gippsland, when Margaret and Jeanie began planning to attend another grand occasion – the opening ceremony of the first parliament of the Commonwealth of Australia in the Exhibition Building on 9 May 1901. Guests came from around the world, joining the five Governors from the other States and the Earl of Hopetoun, formerly the Governor of Victoria, who had now been appointed Governor-General.

The Clement sisters stood among the vast crowd as the blare of trumpets announced the arrival of the King's son, the Duke of Cornwall and York, who was accompanied by the Duchess. The Duke formally declared that the Parliament of the Commonwealth of Australia was duly opened. The sisters joined in with the cheering once the formalities, that included the playing of Handel's 'Hallelujah Chorus' and 'Rule Britannia', were over.

A few weeks later, early in the winter of 1901, Jeanie eagerly tore open a letter from Hamilton in western Victoria. Letters from Hamish were usually sent on to her by his parents but this time the envelope seemed thinner. It contained a single page. Margaret watched her sister walk quietly over to a lounge chair and slump down, staring blankly ahead.

'Oh Jeanie, I fear you've bad news,' she said.

'He's dead. Hamish is dead. They haven't told me any more. What more is there to say? What more is there for me to know?'

Willie returned from the war a few months later carrying a limp from a bullet he had taken in his calf, but he assured Margaret and Jeanie, who travelled to Melbourne to see him, that he was 'mentally sound – unlike many of the poor devils who have come back with me. I don't know who is the more fortunate: those who were shot dead or those who have returned but are in a mess.'

Margaret sensed the stiffening in her elder sister's body at his words, but neither woman made mention of Jeanie's loss. Willie did not know Hamish and his death was best left unsaid.

Margaret agreed to visit Willie again, but first she and Jeanie had another trip arranged, this time to China. It would help Jeanie get over her loss, her family agreed.

Within days of arriving in Peking they had become totally enchanted with the teeming country.

'I would love to return to this place or somewhere similar,' Margaret wrote to her family. 'It is such a contrast to all that we have seen. We have been using chopsticks to eat our meals, although I find it more difficult than Jeanie.'

By the time the young women returned, their mother had found for them a beautiful house, Minto, with bay windows and iron lacework in Denbigh Road, Armadale, Melbourne. When the coach rolled up outside, neighbours peered from behind curtains as once again the sisters began unloading trunks of clothes, furniture and other treasures they had purchased on their most recent fabulous journey.

Having travelled together for so long, Margaret and Jeanie were now inseparable and of the Clement sisters it was only they who moved into Minto – Flora had married into the Glenny family from Ballarat and Anna had married into the Carnaghans. So it was just Margaret and Jeanie who, once again, joined in the crowds in Melbourne, this time in the streets, to welcome back to Australia singer Nellie Melba, who had named herself after the city as she carved out a career in the opera houses of London, Paris, Berlin, Milan, St Petersburg and New York. Now, in 1902, she was back to national adulation.

'We are living in such wonderful times,' observed Margaret as the carriage carrying the singer negotiated the crowds in front of the Town Hall.

'But do you not miss the country, Mag?'

'I do,' said Margaret. 'We should talk about it.'

A new phase in the life of Margaret and Jeanie Clement, among the wealthiest and most eligible young women in Victoria, was about to begin.

Chapter 5.

~HOUSEWARMING~

Margaret and Jeanie Clement had inherited £25,000 each from the family trust and they were high on the register of Melbourne's upper crust. They were invited to lavish dinner parties thrown by the city's elite at the finest residences in Melbourne. In turn, the sisters, widely recognised as elegant society hostesses, provided their dinner guests with genuine Russian caviar, freshly shot quail and the most tender of Gippsland beef. At Margaret's side for the most lavish events was Willie, who had by now returned to his father's law firm and was destined to become the principal partner. Jeanie, meanwhile, was accompanied on her rendezvous around the city by numerous suitors, but her heart was cold.

'I had hardly got to know him, but Hamish made such an impression on me,' Jeanie told her sister. 'He was intelligent and good fun. There's no-one I've met since who interests me.'

The young women's social whirl, typical of those wealthy enough to enjoy that Edwardian period, included dinner party after dinner party. And breakfast. And lunch. Breakfast for the Clement sisters, and any overnight guests at Minto, went on until 10.30am, with a variety of fish and fruits being served by a spruce servant. This was followed at one o'clock by a solid lunch and during the afternoon there would be tea and scones, served on the patio. Dinner, even without guests, rarely consisted of fewer than 12 courses and it was surprising the women did not turn to fat for, like many high society Edwardians, they were great nibblers: food was always available.

The women spent many hours dressing and undressing, changing for each meal…frocks for luncheon, sheer tea gowns with slips and petticoats and long dresses with trains for dinner. It was a splendid life for those who could afford it and for the Clement sisters it all seemed so very natural, thanks to the proceeds from their generous father's gold mine shares.

Far away in Gippsland, at the mansion he had named Tullaree, builder Charlie Widdis stood at the edge of a paddock and admired his drainage system. The land was flat, but the drains he had cut ensured that any surface water that came with the winter rains would run away to the river and the sea. The homestead and the land around it would be safe. His eyes swept across the horizon. Strawberry clover grew over what had once been marshes and the land, covering more than 980 hectares, had become one of the richest fattening and grazing areas in Gippsland.

The mansion was officially recorded as standing on Crown Allotment 6 in the Parish of Tarwin South and Charlie was now ready to sell.

Jane Clement and her offspring had never forgotten their privileged, relaxed life at Prospect Station before and after Peter's sudden death and they had often spoken of returning to the land. So many trips abroad had certainly left a dint in their fortune, but they were still extremely wealthy and after much discussion they turned their thoughts once again to Gippsland. When they heard that a mansion was for sale, their interest heightened.

The job of inspecting Tullaree went to the younger of the Clement brothers, Peter Scott junior, who had been educated at Gippsland College and Melbourne's exclusive Scotch College. As the 21-year-old walked through the pastures, old Charlie told him: 'You won't find a finer place in the whole of Victoria, my lad. Just look at the cattle. Examine their quality. Smell the air!'

Peter, who had learned much about the land at Gippsland College, agreed that the river flats with their rich black soil and lush grasses made for perfect grazing. A few days later, as the family was dining at Minto, he said: 'In my opinion, Tullaree will be a perfect home and a fine investment. It should bring in a good income from the land. We'll find a manager and I'll help too. Our father would be proud of us, returning to the area he loved and making our own good fortune, just as he had made his.'

Margaret and Jeanie were delighted. As much as they loved city life, they missed the freshness of the country and, indeed, they had brought back so much European and Oriental furniture from their travels that Minto had always seemed a little cramped. Margaret had been able to recapture some of the feel of the country as she took strolls with Willie through the Botanical Gardens, cockatoos and parrots screeching all about; nevertheless, the thought of moving out of the city had been with her constantly for the past six months.

On 18 November 1907, Margaret and Jeanie Clement, aged 27 and 29, became proprietors as tenants in common of Tullaree and its land. They paid £18,000 to Charlie Widdis, who walked away a happy man. In addition to the 980 hectares of land, a further 117 hectares of neighbouring paddocks were purchased in Jeanie's name only, giving the sisters a total of 1,100 hectares. Jane and her sons had decided to remain in Melbourne for the time being, although the young men knew that one day in the near future they, too, would probably return to the country.

Would life have changed for the women had they remained in Melbourne for one more year? Probably. For in 1908 the Americans came – hundreds of sailors stepping ashore to a tumultuous welcome. They were swamped by the local women, both rich and poor, and one reporter recorded that on the fleet's last night in the city all that could be heard was the 'sibilant sound of kissing' as the sailors said goodbye to their girls, promising to write and meet again one day. From those romances, several marriages stemmed.

At Tullaree, Margaret and Jeanie arranged a staff of two cooks, three maids, two menservants, a butler, a groom and two gardeners, all of whom were waiting at the door as the covered coach pulled by two white horses brought the sisters up the drive. Above the entrance was a shield bearing the name 'Tullaree' – meaning, so politician Francis Longmore had explained to his friends when he had purchased the land, 'little hill' – embossed on an angle. The sun shone down as the sisters stepped from the coach in their long white dresses, the men bowed and the women curtsied and in turn they politely murmured: 'Good morning, Miss Jeanie; good morning, Miss Margaret.'

The sisters gazed at the landscaped garden with its fountain, stone angels and flowers. The furniture had already arrived and the plush carpets laid. Despite the wealthy surroundings to which they had been accustomed all their lives, the women could not help but stare in admiration at the opulence of their new home.

The Gleeson family enjoys a day with their friends at the abandoned Tullarree in the early 1930s.

No expenses were spared in setting up Tullaree and as they wandered from room to room viewing the original paintings, the two Lipp pianos, the Chinese vases, the carved Oriental furniture and the heavy German goblets, they dreamed of the banquets they would host there under the candle chandeliers.

Margaret and Jeanie decided the first event must be a housewarming. Gilt-edged invitations were sent to all the landowners and the doctors, lawyers and aristocrats they had met during their sojourn in Melbourne. And when the day of the great party came, more than 150 guests arrived in a convoy of carriages and early motor vehicles. Liverymen, chauffeurs and horses cluttered the driveway. There was a marquee on the lawn and the finest of embroidered linen-draped tables set with polished silver and delicate china. Red roses nestled among a selection of dainty sandwiches, gateaux, sherberts, Italian ices and strawberries.

Several of the visiting mothers, old college friends, had brought their young children and these were entertained to a tour of the stables at the rear of the house. A game of croquet was in progress while other gentlemen, who had passed through Scotch College, Wesley College and the Melbourne Church of England Grammar School, discussed their common professions, their jackets stripped off, stiff collars and ties removed, shirt sleeves rolled up. Women strolled, twirling parasols or sought the shade of the marquee's awnings, admiring the splendid home and awaiting the chance to speak to Margaret and Jeanie. When the opportunity for a chat came, no-one dared broach the subject of their unmarried status, although it was plain for all to see that Margaret and Willie – who was one of the guests – were close.

The gentlemen farmers were, of course, more interested in the cattle and sheep that could be seen in the paddocks, but realised there was little point in discussing stock with their hostesses; although brought up in the country, they now seemed to belong to that select group of city people, highly dignified, proficient at entertaining, but oblivious to the ways of the land. Nevertheless, the farmers were able to discuss among themselves the superb animals but did not think it appropriate to take themselves through the pastures examining the excellent feed and the soil.

Most of the important families in the district were there – the Blacks, the Fishers, the Lees, the Cashins and the Singlers – and the Clement sisters, being thoughtful hostesses, had made a point of obtaining a photo-lithograph survey map of the district for one shilling from the Department of Lands and Surveys to hand out copies of the exact whereabouts of the homes of their guests. The land down to the Tarwin River was still marked as being in possession of the former Lands Minister Longmore, but most of the other ownerships were correct and the sisters knew that the Stewarts and the Ambroses were their closest neighbours, while the Waides had travelled some distance from Pound Creek at the wide mouth of Anderson's Inlet. Many of their guests had never travelled beyond Gippsland, so they listened with disguised envy as the sisters recounted their travellers' tales, by request, for it was not their nature to boast.

That evening a select number was invited to stay for dinner. The long dining room table was adorned with Worcester plate and fine cut-glass goblets. An array of the best French wines stood on the sideboard and in silver-plated ice buckets. There was game soup and fresh venison, carved at the table. Rich farmers' sons admired the elegance and beauty of their hostesses whose wide knowledge of world affairs made them appear unattainable. In any case, they had gathered that Willie was Margaret's suitor. One of the young men mentioned to the others that he had even seen Willie and Margaret together at a garden party at Government House.

During dinner Willie, who had been invited to stay for a few days, asked Margaret if she would ride with him in the morning. He had brought his gun from Melbourne and they might bag some game. Perhaps later that evening, when all the others had retired, he suggested, they might be able to meet, but Margaret shook her head at the suggestion. She was not prepared to risk having a man in her room when the house was so full.

They set out at dawn, spurring their horses across Margaret's newly acquired land.

'You're a splendid horsewoman – and an equally adept hostess, Mag,' he said as they slowed their beasts on the edge of a wooded area. 'I thoroughly cnjoyed your ready wit and your conversation last night. You would certainly grace a man's table each evening.'

Margaret Clement laughed. Was this a proposal?

But Willie was riding on. At times he took a half-hearted shot at a bird but failed to hit anything. Suddenly, close to the edge of the river, he stopped his horse.

'Look, Mag, through there!' he whispered. Amid the ti-tree she saw a paddy melon wallaby, frozen, nervously listening. 'They make a fine meal for the Aborigines, you know, Mag. Perhaps we shall have paddy melon stew tonight!'

Willie dismounted, beckoning Margaret to follow. The wallaby remained immobile. Within 30m and upwind of the little creature, Margaret saw an ear twitch and its nose lift slightly. From her experience of animals at Prospect Station she knew the wallaby was about to flee. She tried to find words to match the sense of horror that had suddenly overwhelmed her but Willie had already raised his gun and, hardly taking the time to aim, pulled the trigger. The wallaby was knocked sideways.

'Got him!' he shouted, running forward.

For a moment Margaret saw an apparition. It was not Willie in his riding clothes. It was Willie in a brown trooper's uniform running after an enemy soldier.

But then she saw the wallaby stagger blindly to its feet. There was a terrible hole in its side and she could see its entrails. It tried to leap away but fell again. Margaret put her hands to her face. Again the wallaby pulled itself up and feebly tried to balance, its fur stained red from where it had dropped in its own blood. It hopped, fell, hopped, towards the river.

'Shoot it!' shrieked Margaret. 'Shoot it for God's sake! End its misery!'

Willie fumbled with his gun and took another wild shot as the wallaby crashed on, whimpering pitifully. Passing through a thick clump of scrub, its entrails caught on a branch. As the panic-stricken, dying animal thrust on, it threw itself into the river. The water reddened around it as it sank, then rose, beatings its paws wildly. And then it disappeared beneath the surface.

Margaret stood shaking, her face ashen.

'Tough little sod that one,' said Willie. He grinned at her, then, seeing her face, walked over to take her arm. She jerked it away and said quietly and determinedly: 'Don't touch me, Willie. Don't touch me ever again.'

Something cold had run through Margaret's body, like an icy wind bringing sudden change to a summer's day. They rode back in silence and, just before lunch, Willie left.

A few weeks after the incident Margaret saw her liveryman, a Scotsman known to the district farmers simply as Jock, throw a stone at a cat slinking through the stables.

'Stop this instant!' she cried. 'If I catch you doing that again, you will be dismissed.'

She crouched and tried to coax the cat to her, but it ran away. Shaking her head, she then gave Jock the strangest of orders: 'I want you to ride into Buffalo and buy a dozen cans of stewed steak. I then want you to open them, empty them out and leave the meat around the stables.'

'But ma'am, that will encourage rats,' said Jock.

'I should hardly think so,' replied the quick-witted woman, 'with the cats around.'

The cats came from nowhere when the food was laid out and soon the property was alive with them. Wealthy guests were astonished to find animals in every room, sleeping on expensive sofas and on the beds. The maids were driven to despair trying to clean up their fur but they had to take care shooing them away, for they heeded Miss Margaret's stern warning: 'Anyone found ill-treating a cat will be instantly dismissed.'

Jeanie raised the subject of the cats with her younger sister. 'Jeanie,' Margaret responded, 'no animal will ever suffer or want while I am living here. I have my reasons. Please respect them.'

She did not tell Jeanie about the wallaby incident. And when her sister inquired when she planned to next see Willie, Margaret simply said that she had not heard from him and she couldn't see any real future with him. Jeanie did not press her, although she guessed that something very wrong had occurred between them.

They continued to pass their days in unashamed luxury, throwing wonderful banquets and parties. They travelled to Melbourne by train with trunkloads of clothing to tide them over during their stay with their mother or wealthy friends.

Their brother Peter had now moved in to Tullaree and he quickly learned the ropes. He ensured that the managers sold and bought stock at the right times. But he was not the only farmer on Tullaree. Margaret and Jeanie were also listed in the Post Office's Victorian directory as Misses Clement, farmers; although a more accurate description would have been 'society hostesses', for the truth was they knew nothing about the land. However, had there been any suggestion that they were idle, wealthy, unmarried women there would have been a danger of encouraging thieves and vagabonds. As it was, they had their share of early problems.

Margaret was in the kitchen one day discussing the wages of Ethel, one of the cooks. Ethel was taking leave and Margaret arranged to send her a cheque the following week. Then Margaret remembered she had several other cheques to pay and, having her bank book with her, remarked to

Ethel that she would write them there while sitting at the kitchen table. She had signed five when there was a knock at the back door, which was open. A rough-looking fellow stood there, tie-less, hat in his hands.

'G'day – wondered if there's any spare work to be done about these parts.'

'I'm sorry, but not here,' said Margaret. 'I'm afraid I have a full complement of staff. But if you need food to help you on your way, I can provide you with some.'

At that moment the butler entered the kitchen and announced that Mr and Mrs Higgins, lunch guests, had arrived at the front door. Margaret asked the butler to give the stranger some food and direct him on his way, leaving her cheques on the table as she made her way through the passageway to the front of the house to greet her callers. The stranger was provided with food and he turned to make his way from the house, while the butler returned to his duties and Ethel went to the storeroom. On returning to the kitchen, she noticed the cheques were missing, but assumed Margaret had collected them.

It was not until the following day that Margaret asked Ethel to give her the cheques. Almost immediately both women realised they had been stolen by the stranger. Margaret tried to stop the cheques, but she was too late. More than £200 had been taken from her account.

'It's a lesson, Miss Margaret,' said Ethel. 'It shows us what we've always known, that the world has its scoundrels.'

Margaret dismissed the incident with a shrug, but sent a message to all her staff that strangers should be watched carefully and never be left alone.

Despite the comforts of home and the success of the farm – for their stock were regarded as prime animals at the sale yards and their bank account remained healthy – the sisters yearned to travel again. They were growing tired of discussing over and over their previous journeys through Europe, China and New Zealand.

'Have you any ideas where we should go?' Margaret asked her sister as they sat in the cool shade of the verandah taking their afternoon tea during the summer of 1908, a dozen cats around them. Margaret was now 28; Jeanie 30. They were in their prime, certainly the most eligible ladies in Gippsland, yet their sophisticated and isolated lives were keeping them apart from any new suitors. The few bachelors remaining in the district considered they had little chance of insinuating themselves into the women's graces. In any case, word had got about that both had suffered some kind of shock with previous boyfriends and they preferred their own company. But as it was, many of the farming sons of Gippsland had already become engaged or were married while Margaret and Jeanie were touring the world. Now, as they sipped their jasmine tea, they were planning to set off again.

'I loved China, Jeanie – what do you say about a return trip?' asked Margaret.

'Perhaps a slight variation, this time,' her sister mused. 'What about Japan? There might be some really nice pieces we might be able to pick up there. And it's so different to anything we're used to here in Australia.'

'Wonderful! I'll arrange for a wire to be sent off to the travel company today.'

As before, there were no financial considerations. It was simply a matter of taking the next appropriate cruise ship.

They sailed from Melbourne at the beginning of April 1909, on the luxury liner S.S. *Aldenham*, built in 1894 for the Aberdeen Line. They left their brother Peter in charge of Tullaree, surrounded by scores of cats and bewildered household staff who had been instructed to kill a sheep a week to feed them. It was overcast and cold as the ship set off and the women, unaccustomed to any kind of hardship, remained in their first-class oak-panelled cabin for most of the short voyage across Port Phillip Bay to Geelong, the first stop. They had not visited the town before, so they decided to take advantage during a two-day stopover to walk about. They hated it. They were buffeted by strong winds and the dust blew into their perfumed faces. The liner offered greater comforts, so they returned and from their cabin Margaret penned a letter to her mother:

'This is a very comfortable boat and they are not so strict about getting up early or anything like that as they are on other boats. We went for a walk in Geelong yesterday, but it was so sickening and windy and the dust was so awful that we stayed on board all today.'

But of course the food for the first class passengers was superb and the sisters soon forgot the unpleasantness of Geelong. As on other voyages, they danced at the ship's balls and were invited to sit at the captain's table, an honour reserved for a select group of passengers. The vessel stopped at Timor and Hong Kong for three days at a time and the women, often attended by a ship's officer in his smart white uniform, strolled or were driven around the interesting areas of the ports. Many treacherous reefs had not been charted and often the ship was forced to anchor at night. And one day the engines broke down close to the equator and the passengers, sweltering on the decks, were supplied with water while a frantic crew worked in unbearable conditions below. Finally, after six weeks cruising with another stop that took in Shanghai, they reached the port of Yokohama. They had to wait at anchor for a day before they were allowed to disembark and it was then that a young officer, who had accompanied the women in Timor, approached them while they sat on the deck.

'I have,' he unexpectedly announced, 'two green Madagascan parrots. Unhappily, I do not know what to do with them and so I wonder if you would accept them from me and despatch them with your luggage to Melbourne.'

His mention of the sisters' luggage was a reference to the curios and furniture pieces they had purchased during their stopovers and which were periodically sent back to Australia. Margaret did not hesitate. She believed the parrots would be far happier in Australia than travelling around on the high seas like some ancient pirate's pets, so she accepted the offer. Then she wrote to her mother, advising her to expect the birds, along with the furniture and souvenirs.

That night, while waiting at anchor, the women were awakened by a tremendous crash. The ship shuddered.

'What is it?' cried Margaret.

'Quickly, into the corridor,' said Jeanie, the vessel still rocking.

They hurried from the cabin in their nightdresses to find the corridor full of anxious passengers, also in their nightclothes.

'We're sinking!' someone cried and at that moment the first officer appeared and told everyone not to panic but to assemble on the deck. There had been an accident, but everything was under control.

On deck, the sisters saw the shape of a huge vessel, its prow against the side of the *Aldenham*. Crewmen were running about and shouting to the Japanese on the other vessel although everyone wondered if that crew could even understand English. Through a megaphone the first officer told the passengers: 'The other ship has broken its moorings and drifted into us. We don't think there's too much damage. An inspection will be made in the morning. In the meantime, I suggest you all return to your beds.'

But Margaret could not sleep. She decided to write to her mother and tell her all about the incident and about the occasion when the engines broke down. The damage to the ship, as expected, was slight and the Clement sisters disembarked the following morning with the knowledge that their cruise would continue on schedule.

They had a two week stopover in Yokohama, where they were taken to the Club Hotel by hand-drawn rickshaw. Recognising their affluence, the staff treated the women to first class service, the manager personally showing them to their suite. Later he invited them to dine with him and his wife at their home and they sat cross legged – as best they could, for this was a most unaccustomed way of eating – while a maidservant poured bowls of steaming sake. Again, the ship's officers were on hand to escort the women about the city and they were invited to a number of official functions, at one of which they were introduced to the mayor.

However, it was not always smooth going. On 11 July 1909, on the Club Hotel's headed notepaper, Margaret described to her mother another incident which frightened her and Jeanie from their beds.

'A little over a week ago there was rather a severe earthquake here. It lasted four minutes, which is a good while for an earthquake. It was in the morning at six o'clock and we were awakened by it.

'Our beds were rocking about and the whole hotel was shaking from side to side. We all got up and got dressed so that we could run out into the street if anything happened.'

However, when the earthquake subsided it was found there had been few injuries and no damage. Shortly afterwards the young women joined thousands of others in the streets to take part in Yokohama's festivities to celebrate the city's 50 years of foreign trade.

'They had all sorts of weird processions in the streets,' Margaret wrote in another letter to Jane Clement in Melbourne. 'The Japanese were in the old costumes they used to wear hundreds of years ago. At night, all the streets were illuminated and there were some splendid fireworks. We took rickshaws and went all over the place both at night and in the daytime.'

Despite their busy schedule, Margaret often thought of Tullaree and the cats, and in one letter to her brother Peter she enquired after her favourite – 'How's Squeaker?' She also mulled over the incident of the stolen cheques and wrote to her mother: 'I can't understand how that man managed to cash those cheques that he took. He must have been somewhere near the kitchen when I told Ethel I would send her cheque. That is the only way he could have found out. Whoever gave that man the money for those cheques must have been very careless.'

In further 'travelogues' from such plush addresses as the Oriental Hotel in Kobe and the Fujiya Hotel at Miyanoshita, Margaret wrote of bathing in hot mineral springs and walking through the hills.

Their life abroad mirrored their idlings at home. They were attended by Japanese beauticians and their diaries were filled with engagements. They went everywhere together and their close relationship, fused by earlier trips and companionship in Australia, made it impossible for would-be suitors they met from around the world to make much romantic headway.

So it was that the Clement sisters, Margaret now 30, Jeanie 32, returned to Tullaree, once again laden with gifts for their friends and relatives. They brought tapestries, more paintings, more furniture, more rugs and more bric-a-brac for themselves. The two parrots that had gone on ahead were now waiting to greet them, along with all the servants, as they arrived.

They were still unmarried – but they were rich young women! And the neighbourhood was filled with talk that surely it could not be long before they found, among that gay carousel of socialites in Victoria, suitable men with whom they would be able to share the rest of their lives.

Chapter 6.

~DECEIT~

Tullaree was a picture. Cattle and sheep from Victoria's finest studs roamed the verdant pastures, their breath steaming out like small clouds in the dawnings. Gardeners tended lawns as smooth as bowling greens, where peacocks strutted. Koalas clambered up nearby gum trees; Cape Barren geese flew overhead. The two Madagascan parrots screeched greetings from their verandah cage whenever visitors approached. There were many callers, many of them notables from Melbourne turning up in carriages pulled by high-stepping horses that had been waiting at the Sale railway station. If ever a place epitomised wealthy Edwardian indulgence it was here, at Tullaree.

Once a week, the women stepped into their own English covered coach and, with Jock the uniformed liveryman at the reins, travelled to Wonthaggi, Buffalo, Leongatha or Meeniyan to do their 'personal shopping', as most of the household needs were attended to by the butler. Margaret enjoyed an after-dinner cigarette in a long silver and black holder so the trips to the local centres meant she always bought a supply of tobacco. Often when she cut and rolled her cigarettes the memory of her father puffing on his pipe on the verandah at Prospect came to her. He had enjoyed a glass of whisky on those warm summer evenings and Margaret's taste was similar.

'I have Scottish blood and Scottish whisky coursing through my veins!' she would often joke as she tasted a quality Highland malt.

Whenever the Misses Clement passed by, the poorer farmers doffed their hats with gentlemanly respect, for these were true ladies in their eyes, although many complained that the women hardly noticed them.

Among those who stared in awe at the splendid carriage and the two graceful ladies who travelled in it was a small boy called Peter McFarlane, who was to remember 65 years later:

'The brass on the horses' reins was so shiny you could see your face in it. The Scottish groom sat on top of the hansom cab in full uniform and a tall hat with a smart leather whip. Whenever he was around with that carriage you knew the Misses Clement were never far away. And when they travelled into Melbourne by train he would take them to the station at Buffalo and be there waiting when they came back. I had never seen a cab like the one they travelled in and I haven't seen one since. I think it was the only one of its kind around.'

But if the local people were amazed by the Clements' extravagance, they were positively stunned by their behaviour at times. With Jock following, Margaret often walked into a grocery store and ordered several boxes of canned fish. Then the groom, staggering under the weight, followed her to the coach and stacked them on the top. Asked by storekeepers and bemused onlookers who was eating all the fish at Tullaree, he whispered: 'The bloody cats!'

Walking through the main street in Meeniyan, Margaret stopped to talk to stray dogs and on one occasion even instructed Jock to open a can of fish in the street to feed a cat. Another starving feline was given the VIP treatment. The liveryman, on his mistress's instructions, caught the animal and it was taken back to Tullaree in the perfume-filled carriage to reside with the other strays. It was a very old cat, at least 15 years everybody guessed, so the sisters named it Old Bob and it took up residence in the front room. . Scores of dishes of meat and fish littered Tullaree so the animals could eat whenever hungry. The staff had their work cut out catering to the whims of cats and wealthy guests. Nevertheless, the business affairs of the property ran like clockwork, thanks to brother Peter and to the attention of an elderly Mr Smith, hired from the auctioneering firm of Pearson, Rowe and Smith, to act as manager. He handled bullock sales and often they fetched the best prices of the day at the local fatstock markets.

Change was coming to Victoria. There was talk of finding a new federal capital in New South Wales and in 1912 a Chicago architect, Walter Burley Griffin, won an international contest to design an entirely new capital city, where the federal parliament would sit. They would call the capital Canberra and in 1913 the first peg was driven home by the Minister of Home Affairs, King O'Malley.

In that same year, Jock the liveryman was leading one of the horses around the side of Tullaree when he heard an extraordinary roar. The horse reared and bolted. Jock stared down the drive.

'Good Lor',' he exclaimed. Coming towards him was a black English Wolseley motor car belching smoke, despite its apparently brand new condition. It stopped at the front door and out jumped a chauffeur in a grey uniform.

'Mornin',' he said. 'I'm the new man. Blenkinsop's the name. Personal driver to the Misses Clement.' He patted the bonnet. 'Bit of a bother with the motor on the way from Melbourne but I'll soon fix that. Carbie, I'd say.'

The 'new man' was there to stay. He and his Wolseley were a gift from the ever-modern sisters to themselves and brother Peter. Jock was dismayed, fearing for his job as horse and trap driver, but Margaret told him not to worry about another addition to the staff. She assured him his appointment was safe – and would be for a long time to come – because she and her sister so much enjoyed the clip-clop of the horses, rather than the bangs and groans from the car's engine. And as it turned out, after a few trips to nearby community centres and into Melbourne, the sisters developed a distinct dislike for the vehicle. It was partly due to the chauffeur. Blenkinsop turned out to be a bit of a madcap who enjoyed swerving from side to side and hitting bumps at top speed to 'test the springs'. To add to their distaste, the vehicle broke down on the Melbourne road one day when they were already running late for a Government House garden party. The chauffeur managed to fix it while the sisters sat as patiently as they could, sweating in their fine clothes in the heat of the midday sun. When they finally arrived at the gates of Government House, Blenkinsop handed over the sisters' invitation cards smudged by his greasy fingers.

But the grand lifestyle went on. Margaret and Jeanie's social calendar was full from January to December and huge stocks of gourmet foods continued to be delivered to the tradesmen's entrance of Tullaree. There were marquees for the lawns in the summer and roaring fires in the grates for winter parties. The mighty, imposing home was always a haven, no matter how kind or cruel the weather.

Yet as surely as the storms would gather far beyond the horizon before hitting southern Gippsland, clouds of misfortune began to draw in around Tullaree.

In 1914, Peter, who had bought his own, smaller farm at Wurruk Wurruk, near Sale, and was now managing both properties, received a letter from a friend who was volunteering to fight for England in the war that had broken out in Europe. They had already heard of events in Austria and the ultimatum to Serbia which led to the outbreak of war. The Prime Minister of Australia, Andrew Fisher, declared that his countryfolk 'will stand beside our own to help and defend her to our last man and our last shilling.' Peter's friend wrote how he had joined the crowds gathered outside the offices of the Melbourne newspapers, *The Age* and *The Argus*, hoping to hear the latest news first hand and they had sung 'Soldiers of the King' and 'Rule Britannia'.

'I must join them,' Peter told his sisters. 'They're calling for volunteers. The streets are filling with men ready to fight. I can't stay behind.'

'Oh dear,' said Margaret, recalling the bullet that had struck Willie and remembering the death of Jeanie's beau in South Africa. 'But of course you must go, Peter. You cannot ignore the call. Just make sure you come back to us safely.'

'Don't worry,' he grinned. 'You girls need me here. I'll be back home before you've even noticed I've gone.'

Their older brother, William, was unable to take Peter's place on the property because he was tending a farm away from the district. The only man on whom they could still rely for faithful management was old Mr Smith. It worked out well – until he dropped dead within a year of Peter's heading off to war.

The sisters' reputation for knowing little or nothing about the running of the farm was widespread, and on the death of Mr Smith they were inundated with offers of management. There were still servants, cooks and handymen, but what did they know about running a sprawling farm?

'Who on earth should we choose?' Margaret asked Jeanie as they sifted through the pile of application letters.

'Well, we don't know any of these people. Perhaps it would be wise to select a man who is already working here as one of the general hands. At least he would know his way about the place and he must know something about cattle.'

And that was what they did. Unknown to the sisters, the newly appointed manager, a fellow called Smythe, did not have the cleanest record for honesty and the women, unfamiliar with property and livestock management, became caught in his web of deceit.

'If you'll pardon my mentioning it, Miss Clement,' said George Williams, one of the house servants, 'but I'd keep an eye on Smythe.

There's something about him that worries me. He's not keeping the other men under much control out there and the stables are in a mess and some of the fences are down.'

'Oh, when we see him we'll mention it to him,' said Margaret. 'He seems a nice enough man.'

Margaret did raise the question of the upkeep of the land with Smythe and he explained that there was so much to be done that the work was always catching up with him. But he would make sure their concerns were attended to.

The animals of which Smythe was given charge were of the highest quality. Copies of the newspaper *Stock and Land* for the years 1914–1915 record that Tullaree bullocks averaged top sale prices of all animals handled by Pearson, Rowe, Smith and Co.

But his promises to the sisters were hollow. He began to sell the best cattle privately and replace them with poorer beasts to ensure that, when the women gazed out across the paddocks, they saw the same number of animals that had always been there. Smythe received good prices for the quality stock and paid only a minimum for their replacements, the profits going straight into his pocket. This insidious whittling away of the property's assets worsened when rustlers blatantly stole bullocks before they were branded with the Tullaree mark. On other occasions, the sisters paid out high sums for pedigreed animals that never arrived at Tullaree, although they were checked in at Buffalo railway station. Bills came flooding in for cattle the sisters had not ordered and, because they had been brought up in a world removed from the actuality of business dealings, they indiscriminately signed cheques to unknown creditors. The more they were cheated, the faster word spread among unscrupulous and criminal elements that the two isolated women were ripe for the picking.

In the early weeks and months following the death of old Mr Smith, the decline in the fortunes of the two dignified yet inept women was imperceptible. Staff, occupied with the demands of the household and its interminable guests – for they still arrived for lunch and dinner and the occasional party to talk of news of the war – were unaware of the deception that had begun.

Eventually cattle and sheep were being sold at a faster rate than that at which they could be replaced and with fewer animals to keep it in check, the grass and the weeds grew. Tullaree was slowly and quietly losing its profitability.

It was only when the sisters received their statement of account from the bank in 1916 that they noticed a serious decline in their finances.

'This is ridiculous,' said Jeanie. 'I think there's been some mistake at the bank. We are thousands of pounds down. What on earth is happening?'

They arranged for a wire to be despatched to the bank in Melbourne and the news they received was bad. The books were in order. The farm was running at a serious loss.

They called in Smythe.

'Our income is drastically reduced,' Jeanie said. 'Why are we losing money when we were doing so well before you took over?'

'You can put a lot of it down to rustlers, ma'am,' said the manager, nervously brushing back his thick grey hair. 'Not much you can do about that, unless you employ extra men to patrol the paddocks.'

'Well, that's exactly what we shall do,' said Margaret – and once again their naivety led to a blunder in judgement. The new men drafted in from outlying areas included some of the very fellows responsible for the rustling. They loosened fences and made theft easier for themselves and their co-conspirators.

And all the time, weeds grew in the soft pastures, creeping in from the creek and the river, choking the good grasses.

Yet still the sisters entertained and kept their social engagements, for it was impossible to consider any other lifestyle. It was all they knew.

They read Peter's letters from Europe, thankful that he had survived the terrible events at Gallipoli in 1915, but worried about his presence in the prolonged war.

On a warm morning in the autumn of 1917, Margaret and Jeanie sat in Chinese wicker chairs on the verandah and watched the rain sweep across the paddocks and run down the backs of the thin cattle that remained.

'Has it been raining all night?' asked Jeanie.

'I think it started early this morning. Why do you ask?'

'Well, look at that far paddock. There seems to be a lot of water lying about in it. I've never noticed that before. It must have been raining particularly heavily. Oh well, it will go away when the weather clears up.'

But those first rains at the end of the summer were a sign of what was to come. For without the trusted workers of the past, many having gone off to war in the troop ships and not returned, the drainage ditches laid by Charlie Widdis years before had begun to clog up, preventing rain water from running away.

'I've been looking at our affairs,' said Jeanie, as one of the maidservants refilled their tea cups. She waited until the woman had gone back indoors before adding, softly: 'I think we are going to have to lay off some of the household staff for a while. We've lost thousands and gained nothing.'

'Oh dear, but I'm sure it will be all right when Peter comes home. At least we'll be able to continue to hold our gatherings…won't we?'

'It doesn't look so good, Mag. I'll send a wire to Petty' – a reference to their younger sister Anna, who was now Mrs Carnaghan. 'She may be able to help with an idea. And you're right. When Peter returns he'll get us back on our feet. We just need someone reliable to take charge.'

Anna responded to the distress call and arrived to stay, bringing her two-year-old son, Clement. She looked at the farm's record books and, horrified at the gloomy state of affairs, said: 'You must free all your staff. Get rid of that man Smythe. And you must stop entertaining.'

'But we can't just stop,' protested Jeanie. 'We have a vast number of engagements to fulfil. Just have a look at our diaries. We even have people coming for dinner tomorrow. We can't cancel now.'

In the next few weeks, at Anna's insistence and against her older sisters' protests, the domestic staff were given their notices. And even though some had whispered that the sisters were 'funny', what with the cats being allowed to run everywhere, they left with tears in their eyes. There was something endearing about the two women and none of the staff wanted to go. Smythe and the other farm workers, too, were sacked, with the exception of one man the women thought they could trust and whose job was to fatten the cattle in order to make them profitable. He tried to clear the blocked drains, but it was an impossible task. It took almost a week to clear 50 metres of ditch and the drains ran as far as the eye could see.

That winter of 1917–18 was dire. The rains were heavy, the river flooded and water spread across the paddocks. Several cattle fell into one of the hidden ditches, broke legs and drowned while a large number of sheep developed foot rot and had to be destroyed. Most of the remaining cattle had to be sold at a loss to prevent further disaster, the return hardly covering the cost of their transportation to market.

'Peter's coming home!' declared Jeanie, opening a letter from the Army. 'There's hope that the war will soon be over. Everything's going to be all right, Mag!'

On 11 November 1918, crowds poured into the streets of Melbourne to celebrate the Armistice, unfurling flags, cheering to brass bands and dancing in the streets. The soldiers began to return home. Margaret and Jeanie stood at the docks waiting for their brother. They had been forewarned that he would not be on one of the regular troop carriers – but on a hospital ship. What did it mean?

Before a word had been spoken as he walked unaided ashore they realised he was not the same vibrant man who had set off so enthusiastically to fight for the Empire. He was severely shell shocked. He had lost much of his hair, his hands trembled incessantly and the deep blue of his eyes had turned glassy. He assured them he was doing all right, but on returning to Tullaree, told his sisters the property was too big for him to handle and he was going to stay at his old place at Wurruk Wurruk. Don't worry, he reassured them, don't worry; he would be all right. Yes, he would be quite all right in time and then he would come back to Tullaree.

Bills for cattle the sisters had never bought – or at least never seen – continued to arrive in their postbox at the end of their driveway, delivered by the dairy cart that collected the mail from Buffalo for the local farmers. With no manager and record books missing, the sisters had no alternative but to meet these debts. By arrangement, they left their envelopes with the signed cheques in the same postbox for collection. Then came outstanding accounts for food, wine and clothes. For the first time Margaret and Jeanie were confronted with financial demands normally dealt with by their staff and the list of figures confused and horrified them. They took the train to Melbourne to speak to their bank manager, only to learn that they did not have the resources to meet the demands.

'We had so much,' Margaret said on the return journey. 'It's vanished. I just don't understand it. What of our shares?'

'You heard the bank manager. They were sold up, with our signatures, a long time ago.'

'But we didn't sign anything like that!'

'Well somebody did. And somebody accepted our signatures. It's not a happy state of affairs, Mag.'

That evening they called a family conference with Anna.

'What do you suggest, Petty?'

'It's obvious, isn't it?' replied their younger sister who, having been married for several years, was a more practical woman and had not shared in Margaret and Jeanie's extravagances. 'You are just going to have to sell off some of your land. It's the only way you're going to manage. You should get a valuer up here right away.'

However, it was not until 1919, a year after Anna's advice and when matters had become critical, that Margaret and Jeanie acted. In November, assessor George Martin, from Collins Street, Melbourne, a neatly-presented middle-aged man with a sheaf of papers in an attaché case, arrived at Tullaree. For the next two days he walked around the property taking copious notes, shaking his head at the emaciated cattle and frowning at the water that had spread out on many of the paddocks.

'If you don't do something soon about the clogged drains you are going to be troubled with very serious flooding,' he warned. 'I'll send you my report. And I wish the two of you good fortune.'

Later, in his official report, dated 25 November 1919, Mr Martin wrote of the excellent soil quality but he questioned the efficiency of the drainage system as a considerable area was subject to periodical flooding. The wells, tanks and windmills were out of repair through neglect and the fencing was in a 'dilapidated condition.'

The two women sat side by side on the verandah as they went through the pages of Mr Martin's appraisal. Occasionally one of them would shake her head. Their position was far worse than they had imagined. Why had the staff they had employed to care for the land and the cattle let them down so badly?

The bad news continued in the report:

'Unless immediate steps are taken to arrest the depreciation now going on, the earning power of the property will be considerably reduced and the cost of reclamation increased. I estimate the cost of clearing at £2 to £4 an acre.'

A warm breeze shuffled the pages as Jeanie let them fall to her feet.

'Even if we cleared only half of the land,' she remarked, 'it would cost nearly £4,000. We just can't afford to pay that.'

'It's not a question of not being able to afford it,' Margaret said gloomily. 'We haven't got it.'

Anna joined them on the verandah. 'I can tell from your faces that it isn't good news.'

'It's disastrous,' said Jeanie.

The three women walked out into the driveway and gazed back at the house, a building which Mr Martin had found to be in good repair internally but which required external renovations. It was true: they could see the brown of rust on the tin edges of the roof and the green paint was beginning to peel from the window sills. A brick was missing from one of the front chimneys.

They went to the rear and looked at the outbuildings – a two-room weatherboard cottage with an iron roof and a weatherboard house with six rooms, both of which had served as staff quarters. They stared at the empty stables, where they had kept four fine horses – sold long ago – and gazed at the chicken house, at the wood sheds, store room and meat shed. Only two years earlier all this was a bustle of activity. Now only the cats and a few chickens remained. The Madagascan parrots had died within weeks of one another, the reason unknown to the women. The nose of the Wolseley poked forlornly from the 'vehicle shed', its tyres flat and cobwebs spreading from the wing mirrors.

'How much does Mr Martin say the total property is worth?' asked Anna on their return to the drawing room.

Jeanie shuffled through the papers. 'If we include my acres, he says £14 an acre. He makes a total valuation of £33,642. The place was worth more than 10 times that a few years ago.'

The older woman looked up from the documents, first at her sisters and then slowly stared around the room; at the paintings, the carved mirrored sideboard, the Chinese vases.

'But I'd never sell the house! Never! We bought this to honour our father's memory. He worked his heart and soul to give himself a good footing in this world and we will not abuse it.'

'Never!' cut in Margaret. 'Jeanie is right, Petty. We can't sell the house. It means too much to us. Everything we loved on our travels came back to Tullaree and it is part of our lives. All our things belong here and so do we. I wouldn't want anyone else to get their hands on it.'

Anna realised her older sisters were not to be moved. 'Well, the only alternative is to do as I suggested and sell off some of the land. At least it will help pay off some of these enormous bills and you should have enough left over to pay some men to work at clearing the drains. That will raise the value of the place.'

That evening Margaret, her dark brown hair piled high, sat in front of the mirror in her beautiful bedroom. She touched her face. Her skin was

that is to say, To my
Farmer the sum of five

Right: Esme and Stan Livingtone at their home in Middle Tarwin.
Below Esme at the fireplace in Tullaree during the search for Margaret.

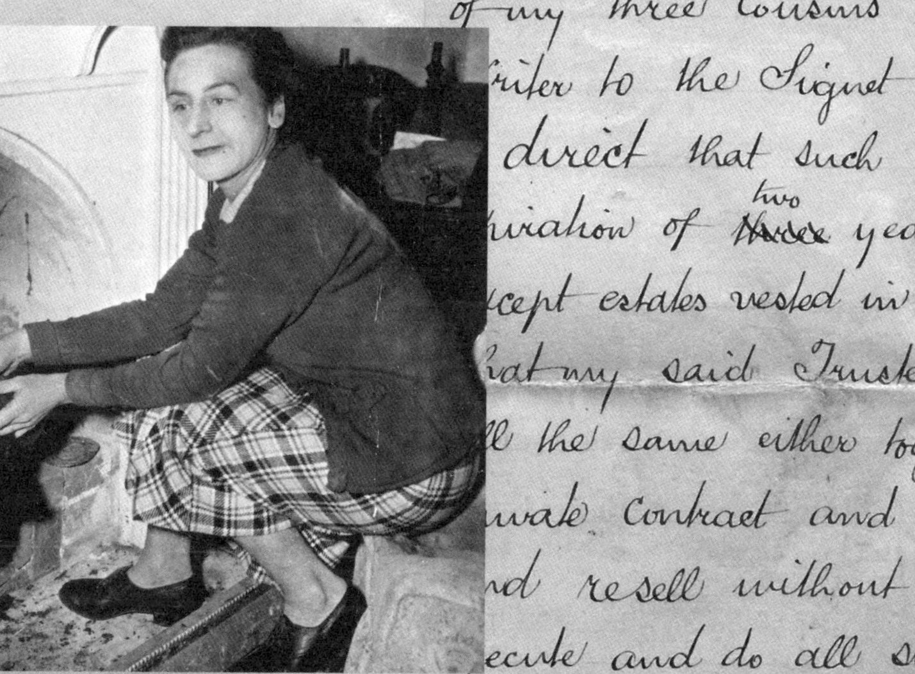

of my three cousins d
riter to the Signet th
direct that such le
piration of ~~three~~ two years
cept estates vested in v
hat my said Trustees
l the same either togeth
ivate contract and m
nd resell without b
ecute and do all such
as they shall think fit
what I otherwise be
Upon trust that my
years from my death

still smooth, although she was now 39. Had it really been 10 years since they had come to Tullaree?

She looked, she believed, like the woman she had always been – a fashionable society belle. But she did not consider as she sat there that she had lived in a cocoon of wealth that removed her from the practicalities of the real world. Now the cocoon was cracking.

Yet it had been only a few months ago that the Harrisons and the Kidds had been down from Melbourne and they'd all laughed together and finished off the sherry. It had not been so long ago that the first hint of doom had entered their protected lives when Peter had returned from the war. Peter, handsome Peter with his once-infectious grin who used to bound in after making his rounds demanding a feed. Now that grin had turned sour, his powerful frame reduced to a quivering wreck. That terrible war had ended it all, Margaret reflected bitterly. What a waste. So many lives, including her dear Peter.

Her hand dropped and she turned listless eyes to look through the window. Even in the purple light of dusk she could see the sorry state of the remaining cattle. Perhaps the fading light, which she noticed now more than at any other time, was a warning of the losses that were to come, unless something was done about their plight.

Margaret Clement fingered her pearl necklace and felt the tears trickle from her lashes and run down her cheeks. Oh Tullaree, Tullaree…

Over the next few months a number of farmers came to the property, by invitation, in the hope that they might buy land, and walked through the paddocks, prodding the ground with sticks, some muttering among themselves. It was a hot summer, but the fields were still soggy in parts and most visitors just shook their heads, climbed into their cars or onto their horses and went away.

Finally, the sisters managed to sell one paddock of 120 hectares and shortly after a 100 hectare lot. But the return barely covered their bills and they knew it would not be long before another batch of demands came in. They discussed selling some of their valuable carpets and furniture, but soon dismissed the idea. Those precious items were part of their lives. They were memories of their fabulous travels with their mother. They would never be sold. They would dig in and they would eventually win the day.

To strengthen their crumbling resources, Jeanie contacted her mother, Jane Clement, who had not remarried and was now living at Baanya,

Waverley Road, East Malvern. She agreed to Jeanie's request to assign to her mother, for £5,100, her sixth share in the residual estate of her father.

Yet in spite of their crumbling world, Margaret and Jeanie could not resist the urge to entertain from time to time, refusing to believe that things could get any worse and trying to cling to their old standards of polite social leadership. Many of their former friends, hearing of the sisters' plight, made excuses and declined the invitations to travel to Tullaree. Those who did turn up could not fail to notice how the property had lost its gloss. They sat at the dining table, ill at ease and were rendered speechless when the sisters left to bring the meals, prepared by a temporary cook, personally from the kitchen. Cats roamed freely, for there was no longer any staff to check them and, fending for themselves nowadays, constantly rubbed against the legs of the seated guests.

Anna had decided to remain at Tullaree for the time being with her young son Clem, who ran playfully from room to room, and the three women worked hard at cleaning the house themselves. Margaret stared in horror at her broken finger nails and the wear on her soft hands. With the cooking and the large number of creditors to whom they hade to write, however, the tasks at hand were greater than the available labour. Anna announced she could not stay at the mansion forever because she had her own family affairs to attend to at Fulham Park, near Sale.

'We are going to have to sell more land,' said Jeanie, opening yet another account, this time from W.J. Farrell, general storekeeper of Meeniyan, for the relatively small sum of £14. 'The bills are still pouring in and we just cannot meet them. Did none of our staff ever pay anyone at all?'

'They told me we had a great deal of credit in the district because we were so well off,' said Margaret. 'But I think we know now that a lot of our money went into the wrong pockets. I realise this is a bother, but we must not sell. If we continue to do so, we will be left with nothing.'

'In that case,' said the business-like Anna, 'the answer is to mortgage the property. You ask the bank for a loan and put the property up as collateral. That way you'll be able to keep Tullaree and have cash. It will give you time to straighten out your affairs.'

Anna returned to Sale, leaving her older sisters in the mansion that by the early part of 1922 had become a towering liability.

'Petty's right,' said Jeanie. 'We shall have to mortgage. Things will work out well for us, because we can use the money we borrow to set the place in order again and make it profitable.'

Reluctantly, Margaret Clement sat down that evening by candlelight and, dipping her pen into the inkwell, began writing letters to their solicitors asking them to act for them in the mortgage negotiations.

She and her sister, she explained, were in need of about £13,000 and she felt that Tullaree, despite its continued decline since valuer George Martin had been there three years earlier, was worth about £35,000. That, she felt, was sufficient security to warrant a first mortgage for £13,000.

Eventually the National Bank agreed to loan the sisters just £8000 on a first mortgage at an interest rate of six and a half per cent. Two other mortgages brought the sisters close to the total amount of cash they needed. The second mortgage, for £3,500, was obtained from William McCullock Nash, an accountant who worked for the legal firm of Francis Grey Smith and McEachern, who were, in fact, the bank's solicitors.

It was during this same year, 1923, that Nash was admitted to the Bar, but his career was to be short-lived for, according to records at the Law Institute of Victoria, he was to be removed from the Roll by Sir William Irving on 15 April 1929, for failing to account for clients' money. Nevertheless, Nash came to the sisters' aid by putting up some of the money they so desperately needed at an interest rate of 10 per cent.

The third mortgage also came from within the bank's solicitors. One of the firm's partners, Frank Grey Smith, put up £900 at an interest rate of seven per cent. So Margaret and Jeanie Clement, the women who once had the world at their feet, had now fallen heavily into added debt to the tune of £12,400. But, they told themselves, everything would be all right as soon as they repaired Tullaree and the drains.

'It's a nuisance, but if we raise an income by leasing the property for grazing we will clear ourselves,' said Margaret, when all the papers had been signed.

'I pray so, Mag,' said Jeanie. 'I sincerely pray so.'

Despite the increasing swampiness of the ground, some farmers found parts dry enough to put cattle on and a number of hectares were leased. The sisters had a few animals of their own, but they had no idea how to care for them, so the milking was done by sympathetic neighbours who called by from time to time.

'Thank heaven we still have friends,' said Margaret as she waved goodbye to a farm hand who lived in the district and who had come by on his bicycle to help.

'What is his name?' asked Jeanie.

'I don't know,' said Margaret. 'I never thought to ask. He was just one of the ordinary people from the district.'

In the early 1930s, Margaret and Jeanie left Tullaree in the hands of a temporary caretaker.

Chapter 7.

~DESPAIR~

Winter wrapped itself around the homestead. Ill-prepared for their plight, the Clement sisters carried in bundles of logs from the woodshed. It was 1924. Once a happy house, Tullaree was now a bleak shelter, confining its spinster owners to the warmth of a few flames in the sitting room grate. The other fireplaces stood empty behind closed-off doors. Bird nests clogged several of the unused chimneys. The women had no clothes for working the land or cleaning the mansion and were forced to wear the fashionable dresses in which they had once entertained; garments that were now frayed and patched.

As they stacked the last of the wood in the hearth, Jeanie suddenly cried: 'It's no good! We'll never manage on our own. We shall have to pay people to come and help full time.'

'We can't afford it,' said Margaret. 'We're already stretched.'

'We shall have to afford it!'

Late in July, as the cruel winds swept across the Gippsland paddocks, Margaret wrote to Hanson's Labour Agency in Bourke Street, which advertised as the 'Oldest Established and Most Reliable Licensed Registry Office for Male and Female Servants.' She wanted a general help, she wrote, and he would have to come to Tullaree immediately. As usual, she left the letter in the property's postbox but they had to wait for three weeks before they received a reply.

The agency found a man: Percy Bush, who was signed into their registry on 22 August 1924. His employment agreement stated that he agreed to serve Miss M. Clement of Buffalo, in the capacity of 'milker, driver, chop wood'. He would obey 'all lawful commands' and would be paid at the rate of 30s a week. It was agreed he would do his own cooking.

On the back of the agreement, the agency's proprietor, Mr H.G. Hanson, wrote:

'Dear Madam, We have engaged you a man whom we think will suit you – to leave Melbourne on Monday 25th, by the 7.25am and have already wired you advice to meet him on arrival at Buffalo…thanking you for your order and hoping he gives every satisfaction.'

Hanson charged Margaret and Jeanie an eight shilling fee and a shilling for the wire.

Percy Bush, a stocky, powerfully built man in his mid-30s, whose appearance lived up to his name as a worker from the country, duly arrived at the railway station but there was no-one to meet him. As he was the man who would be driving the now-faded coach, and perhaps the car if he could ever get it to start and there was money for petrol, the Clement sisters had no means of making their own way to Buffalo; they had not been able to arrange a lift. So the rugged Percy Bush walked the seven miles to Tullaree in driving winter rain, carrying his meagre bag of possessions, wondering what he had let himself in for. Margaret and Jeanie apologised, gave him afternoon tea and went through his expected duties.

Even Bush, who had spent most of his life outdoors and had endured all kinds of hardships, shuddered as the women took him through the mansion. Despite its opulent furnishings, the like of which he had never seen before, it was…creepy. But he didn't like to say so.

Percy Bush was offered the two-room weatherboard cottage at the back.

'You should be comfortable here,' said Margaret, but there was something about the place he just did not like. It was damp and the grimy windows allowed little light through. Paint was peeling from the ceilings. The musty smell of the blankets on the single bed filled his nostrils. It either feels right or it doesn't, he thought to himself; and this place doesn't.

Margaret and Jeanie saw it still as it had always been, for gradual change is never noticed by those to whom it occurs, like the subtle greying of hair. Percy Bush walked in on Tullaree not as it had been, not as the sisters still saw it; but as it was now, an enormous house where, it seemed to him from the dust and the unidentifiable smells, somebody might have died 10 years before and nobody had lived since.

The new man was put to work hacking down trees and mending fences, although in the wet paddocks in mid-winter it was all rather unpleasant, even for a man of his calibre. He was able, however, to start fires burning again in about six rooms and the doors were opened to circulate the heat. The sisters wore long gowns for added warmth and gloves that had once clutched delicate parasol handles. Bush, in stark comparison, wore a short jacket with a scarf and a thick pair of woollen mittens. As appearances went, he belonged more to the property than the owners.

He worked hard trying to restore the old coach, but it required a craftsman to bring back its original gleam. Nevertheless, Percy did manage to get the wheels rolling behind a couple of horses a neighbour loaned to the sisters. It was a strange contrast to see Percy in his jacket and scarf sitting atop the coach where once the smartly uniformed Jock had perched with his whip. But for Margaret and Jeanie it was the past relived. How they chuckled as they climbed aboard and the carriage rocked its way into Leongatha's wide main street. Life was not so bad after all! And look at the men taking off their hats with a nod of respect as they passed by! As they stepped from the carriage, the pair were not even aware of the glances of the women at their patched and outdated clothes. Nor did they hear the whispers about how sad it was to see them like this.

Rent was collected from farmers whose cattle grazed on the land and with the income, averaging £1,250 a year, the women were able to meet the interest payments on the mortgages. They did not eat splendidly – game was definitely off the menu – but they ate reasonably well, cooking meat and potatoes for themselves in the kitchen on the wood stove. Once in a while they even treated themselves to a bottle of sherry.

Percy Bush kept himself to himself, as indeed he was expected to, and as he sat alone at night in his small bungalow, listening to the wind howling and the rain spattering on the roof, he was overcome with a loneliness he had never felt before. Through the window he'd cleaned he could sometimes see the sisters in the kitchen and he wondered why they never invited him in for a glass or two. After all, it was only the three of them there. And then he would think about how creepy the house had always seemed and he decided he was, after all, better off here in the bungalow, solitary though his existence was.

Out in the paddocks, the cruel hand of fate was undermining the sisters' confidence that all would be well one day. Rain was washing earth from the sides of the drains and the loose soil became mixed with pieces of grass, sticks and leaves and debris was trapped behind tussocks that grew in the drains. Small dams started to build up, preventing the water from flowing to the river. With nowhere to go, it insidiously crept out over the land and the farmers who were renting the acreage grew concerned for their cattle. One by one they came to the Clement sisters and told them they were taking the animals away and not paying any more rent.

With their income reduced and in danger of coming to nothing, the women worried about meeting the interest payments on the mortgages.

'We shall have to sell,' said Jeanie.

But again Margaret resisted. 'Don't you care about our home, Jeanie? Don't you care what it has stood for; what it still stands for? We have managed until now. We are still here aren't we? We must try to keep it in the family – we must!'

Jeanie conceded. But she could see no immediate way out of the financial mists that swirled around them.

'We are getting no return from the land,' she said. 'We have to meet the interest repayments. Even if we found some form of work for ourselves, what we could earn would not be sufficient to meet our debts. And what could we do anyway? Speaking for myself, I didn't learn anything from our cooks or our servants so even that is not work I could offer to do anyway. Things are going to get worse, Mag. We will have to sell up. And I mean the house. Perhaps then we can get a smaller place in the city, be closer to our mother, because she is not getting any younger.'

'And neither are we,' retorted Margaret. 'But we must remain strong. Whatever happens, we must hold out to keep the house. Sell all the land if we must, but Jeanie, let us keep our lovely home.'

She began to sob. Jeanie picked up the tea cups and walked to the kitchen. She did not want her younger sister to see the tears that fell down her own face.

On 25 August 1925, Margaret wrote to their solicitors saying they had reluctantly agreed to sell the land and proposed an auction sale in Leongatha in December that year. The women now had less than £20 in cash between them. But they were able to borrow £500 from another member of the Grey Smith legal family.

Tullaree, once an architectural ornament of its time, was now ensnared by creditors, mortgagers, soggy pastures and spreading blackberry thorns. Brambles stretched towards the doors and Percy Bush, the odd job man, realising the task of beating them back was impossible, the environment too lonely to endure, packed up his little bag and walked out.

Once again Margaret and Jeanie Clement were left to cope. And they knew they could not. It was too late to learn common household repairs.

On 27 September, Margaret began a letter to a Queen Street firm of employment agents:

'Dear Sirs, I want to engage a man to do generally useful work. He must be a good driver, able to drive a strong pair of horses over bad roads and able to milk. He must also be prepared to live in a hut by himself and batch for himself. It is no use sending a man who will not stay in a quiet place. Wages 30 shillings.'

But the letter was never sent. Jeanie interrupted and asked:

'What is the use of getting another man in when we shall be selling most of the land soon? He will only be trouble like the last one. With less property to care for, we should be able to manage.'

Because of legal delays the land sale did not go ahead in December , as the sisters had hoped. They now lived under financial siege on a deteriorating property surrounded by mortgagers whom they had no hope of paying. And they knew it was only a matter of time before new and final demands were made...before Tullaree was taken from them.

Ross Grey Smith sat the ball on the tee, pulled the No.1 wood from the bag and cracked a beautiful drive down the middle of the fairway at Melbourne's exclusive Commonwealth Golf Club. He was only 21, but the former Church of England Grammar School boy and Melbourne University graduate had already made it into the club's Pennant Team. He was a confident young man, as sure of his future as he was of his golf, and his dreams did not fade, for later in life he was to be listed in *Who's Who*, became chairman of the Victoria Racing Club and receive a knighthood.

The year 1926 was to be interesting and fruitful for him. It was to hold some unexpected developments for the Clement sisters, too. For in January they made a sudden decision to move out of Tullaree.

'The only way we can get any income is to rent the whole place,' Jeanie had suggested as they sat on the verandah sipping tea that they had become well accustomed to making for themselves.

'But where would we go?' asked Margaret.

'Do you not recall old Mr Osborne at Fish Creek said his house would

persons hereinafter na
that is to say, To my
Farmer the sum of f
Emerald Hill near

Stan Livingstone during the search.

be vacated at this time? We could stay there and lease Tullaree while we wait for the sale of the land. The rent we get from Tullaree would pay for the lower rent at Fish Creek and leave us a little cash to keep us going. When the land is sold, we will have sufficient to move back into Tullaree and be comfortable again.'

For once, things happened quickly. Through local enquiries the sisters discovered a Mr T.G. White was looking to rent a property where he could graze cattle. Areas of the land surrounding Tullaree had dried out that summer and he was ready to move in right away. Within a week the Clement women, set off in the back of a hired motor car, for the few miles to Fish Creek to stay at 'Pop Eye' Osborne's, a former baker, whose wife ran a tearooms in Railway Crescent. Many of the sisters' more valuable pieces of furniture and paintings followed in other vehicles, to be stored in Pop Eye's outhouses.

A month later the sisters, trying to come to terms with their humble abode, learned they were being charged for a surveyor who had inspected the property.

'This is outrageous,' cried Jeanie. 'We did not ask them to inspect the place. They didn't even consult us about it. What has our agreement to rent to Mr White got to do with sending a surveyor down there? We must get the money back.'

'I don't think they will part with it,' said Margaret.

Letters flowed between the sisters and their solicitors, but the net was tightening. There was talk of foreclosure.

At Fish Creek, Margaret Clement opened an official-looking envelope.

'It looks as though terrible things are happening, Jeanie,' she said, her eyes running down through the threatening words. 'It says they want us to take notice that Francis Grey Smith requires us to pay all moneys due under the mortgage. Well, they know we haven't got it.'

'But that's only one mortgage,' said Jeanie. 'It's not over yet.'

'There's more,' said Margaret. She picked up another letter. 'It's from the same people. They're also calling for payment on the second mortgage.' She slumped back in her chair, the letter on her lap.

'We are lost,' she whispered. 'They'll just walk in and take our home now. There's no alternative now but to sell up and get what we can and pay them out. If we don't we won't get anything back from them if they take the first step.'

Resignedly, they wrote to their solicitors to announce they were ready to sell their beloved Tullaree at a convenient date. Broken-hearted, they went to bed.

A reserve of £8,000 was put on the property.

The auction went ahead at Scotts Hotel, Sale. There were some interested onlookers, but no serious bidders.

'It hasn't sold!' exclaimed Jeanie when she opened a letter a couple of days later.

'But that's wonderful news – perhaps we are meant to keep Tullaree after all,' said Margaret.

'The fact that it hasn't sold, Mag, does not release us from our predicament. We still owe money. They won't let us go back there.'

'I still believe we have a chance. Some good is going to come of this.'

But Margaret was wrong. A few weeks later, she read through another letter, gasped, and put her head in her hands.

'I don't believe it, Jeanie. They've sold the place privately after all. And it's been bought by Ross Grey Smith.'

'Ross Grey Smith! But he's one of the bank's solicitors! I know he held one of the mortgages, but can he get so involved that he buys the place? Isn't there something about declaring an interest or something like that?'

'Oh dear, I don't know. I just don't know any more. They've been blinding us with letters and mortgages and demands and it's all become too much. How did it all go so terribly wrong?'

The sisters learned that Ross Grey Smith had bought Tullaree for £13,841 10s 8d, the exact amount, with interest, of the first, second and third mortgages.

'But he's bought our lovely home for next to nothing!' cried Jeanie. 'They didn't even have the courtesy to tell us this private sale was going on.'

'And we have been left with nothing. All that's happened is that the mortgages have been cleared. There's no profit for us. They have taken our property and we have been left with not a penny.'

Jeanie wrung her hands. She was 48, but looked older. Her younger sister was 46 and the strain of recent events was written all over her face. They were destitute. And they had just lost their home. They were bewildered. Their dire position was beyond anything they had ever had to contemplate during the earlier halcyon years.

'Had the sale been more widely advertised there would have been a better chance of getting a good price,' said Margaret. 'Why didn't our lawyers spread the word about?'

'Well, whatever has happened to us, we cannot stay at Fish Creek for ever. We can't even afford the rent because we have no income. We can't go out onto the streets like beggars, either. What are we to do?'

'Perhaps Ma or Petty might take us.'

'But there must be something we can do for ourselves.'

Margaret's lips were tight. 'Yes, Jeanie, there is. We must fight this time. Too many people have got away with too much.'

To add to their immediate problems, Grey Smith lodged a caveat on the property, a legal document which prevented, without his approval, transfer of the title he now held.

Margaret and Jeanie agreed they should approach their local solicitor, even though they did not have the means to pay him.

'You are quite right, ladies,' he said as they sat before him one morning. 'A solicitor acting for a mortgagor cannot buy the property he is dealing with. I suggest you take up the matter with the Registrar of Titles.'

The news brightened them. Although Jeanie was the elder, Margaret was the 'official' letter writer for both of them. She wrote to the Registrar who suggested that the sisters themselves take out a caveat on the title before it actually passed to the purchaser.

Their solicitor, P.J.Wilson, was intrigued: 'Two caveats – one by the previous owners, one by the current owner,' he mused. 'An interesting situation. Which is the more powerful, I wonder? I would suggest that the current owner – Grey Smith – would be in a stronger position, but if there was something out of order in the way he purchased the place, then you would be better off than he. What is in your favour, of course, is that title has still not passed to him. These things take a little time. Well, let's get on with it.'

So Wilson drew up a caveat in the name of Margaret and Jeanie Clement, a move that ensured that even though Grey Smith was the registered owner of Tullaree, he could not take the title. But because he also had a caveat, the sisters could not take the title from him. For the moment it appeared to be a stalemate. But the slender thread that now continued to attach the sisters to Tullaree was enough to lift their gloom.

Word about the curious affair spread through legal circles as far as Melbourne. Lawyers not involved in the action pored through their law books out of curiosity, trying to find out for themselves who legally held the title. Had Grey Smith acted wrongfully in purchasing Tullaree as the solicitor for a mortgagor? Or, having put up the money, did he now have the right to simply move in and claim the property as his?

But there was a distraction from the legal conumdrum – there were problems on the Melbourne waterfront again, businesses were closing, and men threatened with losing their jobs went on strike. Economic gloom seemed just around the corner.

At Fish Creek, Margaret and Jeanie, again desperate for money, appealed to members of their family for help. They wrote to Anna at Fulham Park asking if she could send a small amount of cash to tide them over. Then they wrote to their still-war-shocked brother Peter in Wurruk Wurruk saying they had received the £3 he had sent them earlier and enquiring about some of the jewellery they had asked him to sell.

'If you can't get more than £8 for the things take that and send it, taking out your £3, but try to get as much as you can,' Margaret wrote in a desperate letter to Peter, who was hardly capable of handling his own affairs.

Finally, on 22 April 1927, they turned to the elder of their two brothers, William, with whom Anna was now staying at Fulham Park. They wanted to repeat that something seriously wrong had occurred over the sale of Tullaree, for in expressing it their hopes of holding on to their beloved home were kept alive. But their desperation was also apparent as they begged for whatever money he could spare.

William could not help. He did not have sufficient funds at the time because, being of a generous nature, he had donated large sums to charity – unaware at the time that the most needy charity of all was his own two sisters. The growing cloud of economic gloom also meant that money was short everywhere. Down to their last few pounds, the Clement women wrote to their mother, who had now moved back to Gippsland and taken up residence in Sale, asking her to act as guarantor for them. But Mrs Clement, now aged 67, had become very wary of getting herself involved in her daughters' financial problems and said she could no longer help them.

The hot weeks of summer went by and Margaret and Jeanie fell far behind with their rent to their landlord, 'Pop Eye' Osborne. They could afford only the cheapest food. And Margaret, buying tins of beans from the grocer, found herself weeping for the cats she had left behind. Who was feeding them? She had asked neighbours to call by when they had moved out, but Ross Grey Smith had soon put a stop to that. Perhaps, Margaret thought with an aching heart, they were now running wild in the bush, inept, like herself and her sister, at being able to fend for themselves.

On 13 November 1927, Margaret wrote to her mother again, explaining:

'Our rent is now many months overdue. These people [the Osbornes] cannot afford to let us live in the house for nothing. They have painted it and put a verandah on it and it looks very nice and it is altogether a shame. If we are turned out of the house we will lose all our furniture and have nowhere to go. Also the rent would have to be paid by someone just the same.

'We cannot order any more at the stores and if we go on receiving goods knowing we have no money we could be charged with obtaining goods under false pretences. At any rate, we will have to pay for what we have already received. If we are made insolvent there will be an inquiry in the insolvency court into the whole thing, including the business of the estate and everything we have ever been interested in or entitled to. This would be very unpleasant.'

Margaret reminded her mother that she and her sister had handed to her their shares in the estate. Then, determined to ensure that her mother clearly understood what she was saying, she added:

'It was your business to see that this money was not dissipated or wasted, and if we are not helped in some way the whole thing will have to be put on a different basis. Everything that is being done will have to be done in less than a fortnight or we will be made insolvent and all supplies and food cut off.'

A week later, Mrs Clement, exhausted by the constant demands, sent the sisters a few pounds – nothing like the amount they were hoping for, but it was enough for food. Their mother said she would send more whenever the need arose.

At Tullaree, Grey Smith was arranging for the drains to be cleared and the fences to be mended, although the lawyer was frustrated by the knowledge the sisters had taken out a caveat which prevented the title shifting from their name.

The mansion itself remained empty and when no-one was around on the property boys from the district rode their horses in through the front door and down through the passageway, their laughter echoing through the hall which was once filled with the voices of the well-heeled. The floorboards creaked and groaned under the animals' weight. One of the boys was young John Buckley, son of neighbour Bernard Buckley, and he was to remember it 50 years later.

'The doors were wide open and we were only kids. It was a bit of fun in those days to ride a horse through the front door and out through the back because to us it was simply a run-down empty house.'

John's father was very concerned about the sisters and, calling at Fish Creek one day, he told them if ever there was anything he could do to let him know.

'Well, you could try gambling for us,' joked Margaret. 'It seems that's the only way we are going to get enough money to live on.'

'You never know,' mused Buckley. 'Tell me if you find a good horse for the Melbourne Cup.'

A few weeks later, after the elderly Mrs Clement had forwarded the women more money to help them along, Margaret scribbled a note to Buckley:

'Dear Mr Buckley, I am sending you the money which you said you would put on the Cup for us, three pounds altogether. I hope we are not putting you to any trouble.'

They won a few pounds and, thanks to their mother's occasional contribution, Margaret and Jeanie managed to catch up on their rent, while continuing to receive groceries from Buffalo on credit. Armed with this knowledge, the sisters felt a strong bond returning – a bond they had had years before when they travelled the world together. Born into a 'proper' world, they believed in the power of honesty and remained convinced they would win through.

'We will not let scoundrels get the better of us,' declared Margaret as they ate their evening meal of corned beef and cabbage.

Tullaree remained a curiosity – and playground – for the youngsters of the district, so much so that Grey Smith arranged for caretakers to keep an eye on the place. He employed members of the Gleeson family who had little more to do than keep the locals out. But one summer day a group of Gleeson relatives and friends spent the day on the property and took the opportunity to pose on the side verandah for a sepia group photo. Weeds, evidence of the neglect, grew at their feet and an old iron bedstead stood on the side of the house. Two of the women later gazed into the camera from the front of the homestead while they sat on a rail, knee-high grass all around. They were not smiling this time, as if the building's derelict state had eroded any gaiety from their visit. One more picture was taken, revealing the fence that Grey Smith had erected to keep intruders out and one of the women could be seen standing on it, one last peek perhaps before returning to a brighter world.

Word around the district was that the sisters were now paupers who

Grazier declare this to
John Loyd Roberts of Melb
Farmer the sum of five
Emerald Hill near Melb
To my brother John Cl
five hundred pounds,
brothers James and J
thousand pounds, T
Melbourne aforesaid t
Christina Clement of
of my said brother
of my three Cousins d
Writer to the Signet th
I direct that such le

Above: Tullaree declines in the late 1940s.
Inset: While the search is on for Margaret, the strain shows on the face of her sister Anna, the mother of Clem Carnaghan.

would soon be standing in the soup queues in Melbourne. But they had decided to fight. Inundated with letters from her daughters, the elderly Mrs Jane Clement, already on an overdraft at the bank – for much of her inheritance had long been whittled away in those early extravagances at home and abroad – and longing to spend her last few years in peace, wrote to her son Peter asking for help.

Despite the decade that had passed since he had returned home a physical wreck from the war, he was still not a well man, doing what he could to keep his farm together. Ironically, he had been thinking of writing to his mother for financial assistance. It seemed that all around Gippsland members of the once-fabulous Clement family were turning to one another for support. The fantastic mansion, Tullaree, with which they had been so proudly associated, was now a financial burden, threatening to consume them all.

As the rains swept in from Venus Bay one morning Margaret suddenly declared: 'Do you know what I think Jeanie? I think we should just move back to Tullaree.'

'But we can't do that! It isn't ours any more!'

'It's not Grey Smith's either, as far as I'm concerned. We have the caveat, remember. Ross Grey Smith may have bought the property but we still have the title. Let's not forget what we said about fighting these people.'

It was an audacious plan. But the more the spinsters thought about it, the more determined they were to see it through.

Chapter 8.

~RETURN~

A convoy of cars, pulling trailers piled high with furniture and hired with the last of their money, chugged up Tullaree's long driveway. Margaret and Jeanie sat in the first vehicle peering out across the lands they considered were still rightly theirs. They could see that the far paddocks were covered in water, while in those closer to the mansion cattle agisted from neighbouring properties grazed on dry ground. Several animals were chewing the long grass that had once been a smooth lawn.

The sisters gasped as the front of the home came into view. The caretaker had gone, the windows had been barricaded with corrugated iron and the front door was wide open. They walked slowly up to the entrance, emotions mixed. How glad they were to be back at Tullaree, but the state it was in shocked them. As they stepped in through the door they could see horse manure in the hall and dark, oily scuff marks against the wall where horses had brushed against it. The local boys had been back in there the moment the caretaker left.

Margaret's throat was tight, but she was determined not to weep. They were, after all back in their home. And they were here to stay, come what may.

They directed the men who had come with them where to place the furniture, back in the same positions it had stood for so many years before.

'And we mustn't forget this!' said Jeanie, playfully, and placed on the mantelpiece a jar containing Margaret's appendix, removed when she was a teenager.

'Fancy keeping that!' laughed Margaret. 'It left such a terrible scar.'

The sisters sat in their favourite chairs in the reception room, Jeanie stretching out legs that were beginning to show signs of swelling at the ankles. She was now 49, Margaret 47.

'Do you realise,' Jeanie said with a giggle, 'that we are now a couple of ageing spinsters?'

'Oh don't be so silly, Jeanie. We still have our health and we still have our minds. But yes, it's amazing where our life has gone. Looking back, it seems that those wonderful days were so short. Do you remember the time when Blackie climbed into the linen cupboard and had her kittens and frightened Jane so when she went to get the sheets?'

'Well, I expect you would run through the house screaming if you had put your hand into a dark place and felt something furry.'

'Wouldn't.'

'Would! Look at the time you shrieked when you went out in the car for the first time.'

'That's different. The fellow was mad to drive like that.'

'That may be so, but it was fun, wasn't it?'

'Do you think those things will happen again, Jeanie? Do you think the good days will return?'

'We shall have to get money from people first. I don't think we will be able to go to China or Japan again – not for a while anyway – but we might eventually manage a trip into the city. If we can get compensation for the terrible thing that has happened to us, then we could think about going abroad.'

'Oh, I'd forgotten!' Margaret exclaimed and she hurried from the room, returning with a bottle of sherry.

'I bought it a few days ago when I went to the Fish Creek store to celebrate our return!'

She opened the bottle, then a cardboard box in which their European cut glasses had been packed, and poured. The sisters sipped their sherry. The bottle stood on the mantelpiece beside the appendix jar, the liquor diminishing by the hour…

In Melbourne men had begun to walk the streets again looking for work, but what lay ahead was a prolonged period of economic woe far worse than the country had ever experienced – the Great Depression of the 1930s. Although it affected most nations, Australia was one of the most severely hit with unemployment reaching 29 per cent.

But in Tullaree, the sisters had been more concerned about their own immediate problems as the economic gloom spread around the country. However, in the months that followed their return their morale was fortified. They would fight on – and legal letters flowed in all directions. The sisters were not to know then that the years would go by without any action being taken by the Public Solicitor, on whom they relied to fight for them. But no move was made, either, by Grey Smith to legally establish his £13,841 investment in Tullaree. And the women could not imagine the hardship and the horror that lay ahead.

The storm hit on the night of Friday, 30 November 1934. Rain pounded the iron roof, drumming the Clement sisters from their beds. A roaring wind tore open the front door, racing through the mansion like a crazed intruder, shattering vases and ornaments. Stray cats which had been welcomed to make a home there scrambled terror-stricken from room to room. Pictures crashed to the floor and the force of the gale whipped up the edges of the Belgian rugs. Lightning threw a silver shroud over their neighbour Buckley's sheep and cattle which were in the nearest paddock.

Frightened and bewildered, the women stumbled up the hall, Jeanie clutching a lantern, but no sooner had they stepped onto the verandah when the light was ripped from her grasp and she was blown against the side of the house. Margaret grabbed her as she fell. Both were soaked through; the rain lashed their faces so they could barely open their eyes. Standing in nightgowns pasted to their bodies, the storm, the fiercest in the history of Gippsland, both terrified and enthralled them. Thunder rolled over Tullaree and was lost in the howling wind that hurled twigs and branches onto the roof. Except for the violent flashes of lightning, the countryside was as black as pitch.

They dried themselves off and went back to the room they were temporarily sharing, but it was impossible to sleep. They gathered in the dining room, illuminated by the flashes of lightning.

'Mag, I'm so afraid the house won't stand up to this!'

Margaret, attempting to light a candle but constantly thwarted by the draught, finally succeeded. She turned a worried face to her sister, her reply 'We cannot do anything except pray,' hardly a comfort.

'Then pray with me, Mag! Do you remember how from our school days?'

Jeanie lowered herself achingly to her knees beside her younger sister. The front door, the catch unable to secure it, banged on its hinges and the wind charged through the passage, flinging open the back door.

They put their hands together.

'I don't remember much,' said Margaret. 'Christian values, yes, but prayers, well…I'll try.'

She began inaudibly: 'Our Father who art in heaven, we ask you to deliver us from this storm. Please get us through safely. There is no-one to help; only you – ' Her voice was lost in another burst of thunder. So she began to shout, as if afraid the Lord could not hear. 'We cannot do anything to save the house so we ask you to help.' She paused, then continued yelling: 'We don't remember much about praying but we ask you to put your hand out and guide us through this night. Amen.'

'Amen.'

The rain thrashed the house. The women rose and climbed into their beds. Their candle's leaping flame cast distorted shadows on the walls. Around them, wood creaked and glass tinkled and the house seemed to quiver in the face of the gale. There was no sleep for them that night.

Margaret, in the quiet of dawn, propped herself up on her pillow. She sucked in her breath.

'Jeanie! Don't move too quickly. Our beds are covered in spiders!'

Jeanie saw the black mass on her counterpane. She shrieked and threw it off. Other spiders were scampering across the ceiling. Then she saw more on her pillow and jumped quickly from her bed, horrified.

'Mag, they're on your pillow, too! Where have they come from?'

Her younger sister sat up slowly, gently brushing a large spider from her shoulder. 'It's obviously the storm. It must be very wet outside to drive the insects in. Perhaps they've come down from the attic. I dread to think what it's like up there with the roof in the state it's in . Poor things. We can't really blame them, can we? We were frightened ourselves last night.'

As they shuffled across the room, two hens ran from under Jeanie's bed.

'They must have come into the house for shelter, too,' remarked Margaret. 'I didn't even know we had any chooks left around here.'

They made their way to the back door. The rain had started again and through this translucent veil they saw the remains of the stable roof spread across the paddock. Planks were missing from the walls of the hen house. But the timbers were not lying on grass. They were floating.

Stunned, the women hurried to the front door, which flapped on broken hinges. Even before they reached it they could see the water covering the lawn and the paddocks beyond. The drive had disappeared under the surface.

'We're surrounded by water!' cried Jeanie. 'We can't get out!'

'And look at Buckley's cattle. It's up to their shoulders! If this rain continues I'm afraid they'll drown.'

Margaret and Jeanie turned to go inside and they both saw it together – a large brown snake slithering down the hall. An eastern brown, one of the deadliest on the planet.

'Don't bother it and I'm sure it won't bother us,' said Margaret.

Once the snake had disappeared in a hole by the skirting boards, Jeanie made her way to the kitchen to make tea while Jeanie went into the sitting room with a broom to sweep the insects away, having been warned by Margaret not to kill them. The rain on the roof was incessant and the noise so intense that Jeanie did not hear Margaret's cry from the kitchen. Margaret ran into the room, laughing hysterically.

'Jeanie, come with me!'

The elder sister followed her to the kitchen. Standing on the table was a sheep.

'It must have been here all night,' said Jeanie. 'How it got onto the table I'll never know.'

Between them, they managed to lift it down and off it went up the corridor, disturbing a rabbit crouching under the hall stand.

The sisters made their tea and walked back to the front verandah, noticing two other snakes in the rooms. In the hour they had been away from the front part of the house the water had risen several inches and was very close to the front steps. From there to infinity they saw nothing but water and the heads and backs of miserable cattle. They sat on bentwood chairs on the verandah and looked out on their watery domain 'Water, water everywhere and not a drop – ' they looked at each other, laughing, as they simultaneously recited Coleridge's famous line. Spontaneous humour kept the despair at bay, for each woman was aware that if she did not try to keep her spirits up they would both break down in tears.

By 9 o'clock that morning the water was lapping at the verandah boards. Desperate cattle were now swimming for their lives, heading towards the stables at the back of the house, which were also on a slight rise – old Charlie Widdis had had enough problems with water as he was building the property to realise that all structures should be as high as possible above the surrounding land.

The sisters' feeling of helplessness turned to shock when what seemed to be a tidal surge brought a dead cow past them. Then another and a third, in a procession like a macabre carnival parade. Margaret put her hands to her face and kept them there for a long time until she felt water wash around her bare feet.

'Poor Mr Buckley – he's going to blame us for the loss of his cattle,' moaned Jeanie.

'I shouldn't think so,' Margaret said in an attempted reassuring tone. 'The storm is hardly our fault.'

'But the state of the paddocks is. Perhaps we should have shown more care about the drains years ago.'

'Stop blaming yourself, Jeanie. What has happened has happened. You know we were cheated and robbed. Our immediate plan should be to save ourselves from this flood. We may have to take to the roof. Look, the water is already going in through the front door.'

Margaret volunteered to fetch a ladder from the outhouses. She waded through the floodwater, her nightgown billowing around her. Bringing the ladder back was easy – she floated it along the surface of the water and then leaned it against the outhouse that was attached to the kitchen. At least from there, if it became necessary, they could get onto the roof of that small structure, because climbing up to the roof of the mansion would be a far more difficult task. She hoped it wouldn't have to come to that.

Jeanie had closed the front door and made her way to the kitchen, but already the water was in the hall. They stuffed beautifully embroidered towels they had brought from the Orient along the bottoms of the doors to stop the water entering the side rooms, but as the water rose it easily found its way through the gaps.

By midday the flood water was lapping against the frames of the long windows while the torrential rain poured in through the ceiling and down the walls. It swamped the Persian carpets and Belgian rugs, for to have taken them up would have meant moving tables and heavy chairs, cupboards, sideboards and a piano and they had neither the strength nor the time to do that. The sisters waded about the 17 rooms, helpless, unable to do anything to staunch the flow.

The rain began to ease early in the afternoon and the water level on the outside stopped half-way up the windows. A dead bullock blocked the light into one of the side rooms before floating on towards the distant river.

'Margaret! ' Jeanie cried. 'I do believe I can see a boat coming towards the house!'

Margaret swished over to the front window. It was a boat all right, followed by a second, larger vessel. With the water having dropped down, they were able to look out, two pale and exhausted faces, through a cracked window pane as the motor boats chugged up to the verandah.

'You two ladies all right in there?' called one of the men, who had unhooked their boats from moorings on the Tarwin River to look for people who needed help after the storm. And no-one needed help more than the people marooned in this huge house, they had agreed.

'We are all right if the water doesn't come any higher,' said Margaret. 'Will it rise more?'

'Hard to say, missus. Heard you might be the worst off of anybody in the whole district. Come with us if you'd feel happier.'

'No, but thank you. We won't be leaving here under any circumstances.'

'Suit yourself, missus. Don't know when we'll be back again. G'day. And good luck. Righty-ho Jimmy, back her off.'

The boats set off across the paddocks, weaving around the drowned cattle, a strange scene in the grey collage that was the Tullaree landscape.

'It's a pity we don't have a wireless,' said Margaret that evening as they sat with their legs curled up on their easy chairs, the carpets waterlogged. 'At least we'd know what to expect tomorrow.'

What they didn't expect was scores of bullocks on the verandah the next morning, although they heard them during the night and looked to see what was making the noise. On seeing the first few they had gone back to sleep, exhausted after the disturbances of the first night.

Bernard Buckley, unable to get onto the property to move his cattle – an impossible task in any case – had suffered great losses and all of them on the Tullaree pastures.

The Age newspaper of Melbourne reported under a Leongatha dateline:

'The most serious loss experienced here was that of Mr Bernard Buckley, of Buffalo, who had 4,000 sheep and 180 head of bullocks drowned. He estimates his loss at £6,000.

'The waters of Fish Creek and Tarwin River rose so rapidly that roads leading to the "Tullaree" estate, on which the stock were pastured, were soon ten feet deep. It was therefore impossible to reach the gates to let the stock out.'

The Tullaree homestead was indeed the worst affected by the Gippsland flooding and Margaret and Jeanie Clement were in the greatest danger. Had the mansion not been built on a rise, it would have been half covered in water. The sisters heard planes fly overhead but did not go out. Later, one of the pilots of the RAAF reconnaissance aircraft sent the following report to the Victorian premier:

'Tarwin River, two miles wide between mouth and Tarwin Lower, where twelve houses are isolated but are on islands. They are occupied. Food supplies can be dropped successfully. From Tarwin Lower to Tarwin the river is half a mile wide. One house is isolated but there was no sign of the occupants.'

During that terrible December, with food supplies depleted, Margaret decided to try to walk the seven miles to Neals' General Store at Buffalo, which also served as the district post office. Jeanie said she would go with her, but Margaret said that if there were to be any drownings it would be better to happen to one than both of them.

'Don't say such terrible things,' said Jeanie as her sister prepared to make the long trek.

Tullaree was still flooded and the bloated, decomposing carcasses of cattle drifted about in the breeze. Wearing what was once a beautiful dress, Margaret waded into the water and tried to remember the way the drive had run. It was at least a mile (two kilometres) to the main road by the shortest route and several times she stumbled. The water splashed up into her face and she could taste salt on her lips; such was the spread of the flood that sea water had washed in from the far-away coast. By the time she reached the road, two hours later, she was drenched. Then there was the walk to Buffalo along a sodden, muddy track. Soaked through, caked in dirt and exhausted, she eventually reached the store. Shocked at her condition, Mr Neal and his wife gave her a cup of hot tea and offered her a loan of dry clothes, but she politely declined. She began writing a letter to her mother. There had been no hope of leaving mail in a post box for collection at Tullaree – the dairy van which delivered letters would not be able to negotiate the roads for weeks and in any case the estate's post box had vanished during their absence at Fish Creek.

Margaret's letter began, not about her traumas, but with a thank you for food that had been sent before the storm.

'Dear Ma, We received the last bag safely and everything in it was all right. The butter had not melted. It was quite solid. We enjoyed everything in it very much. Any time you happen to have any spare eggs, even half a dozen, will you send us some. We have only two hens and it is impossible to buy eggs about here.

'I suppose you have read about the flood down here. We are working hard to try and get traces of the flood water out of the house. On Friday there was a terrible wind storm that took the roof off the stable and almost at once the water started rising in the fattening paddock and within an hour the rise the house is on was surrounded by water.

'Next morning it came up over the verandah and dashed against the windows. A number of cattle were standing against the stable up to their backs in water. Later on, other cattle came swimming up past the house and joined them. About the same time a number of dead cattle came floating past and there are eight dead bullocks round the house now and the paddocks are full of them. All the sheep were drowned on this side of Tullaree but one and it was in the house all night with three snakes and a rabbit and thousands of large spiders and the fowls…'

Margaret added a postscript, written just before handing the letter to Mr Neal:

'P.S. I came into Buffalo today to get the pound but it was not there. We have very little left, so be sure and send the pound as soon as ever you get this letter.'

The Neals' own car would not have been able to take her back to Tullaree, so Margaret began the long walk home, arriving cold and wet and hardly able to stand shortly after dusk. She stood shivering in front of the stove as Jeanie warned her not to attempt anything like that again.

But two days later, Margaret waded through the flood waters again. They were in desperate straits and there was no choice but to hope that their mother had sent them some money with which they could buy food. It was raining again as she struggled through the swamp and made her way along the endless straight road to Buffalo. The Neals could not believe she had the strength to return so soon, if at all, but at least they had good news for her. They handed her a letter from the elderly Mrs Clement. Margaret tore it open, smiled, then scribbled the following note in pencil:

'Dear Ma, I walked into Buffalo today and got the ten shillings. The flood has gone down, but there is another one predicted very soon. Will you be sure and send us some more money next week as soon as possible, as we might be cut off again. It is raining again today.

'Buckley has lost six thousand sheep and two hundred cattle. We had the ladder all ready to take to the roof but we did not need to use it. We had about a hundred bullocks on the verandah all night. They were all saved.

'I can get in and out now but if another flood comes on I won't be able to, so please send us some money as soon as possible while I can get out.'

Within days the land began to steam after the sun burst through. But inside the mansion, the carpets were still soggy and the sisters considered it would be too much effort to shift all the furniture to get them up. Sitting in the drawing room as Christmas loomed, Margaret wrote again to her mother.

'Dear Ma, I am going into Buffalo today to get anything that is there. The flood has quite gone down and the roads are very dry now. It doesn't look as if there will be another one and the rats and rabbits are coming back. They left before the flood. We are still trying to clean things up.

'The house is in a terrible state of mud and a lot of cattle are nervous yet and come on to the verandah every night. The aeroplanes only came on Sunday afternoon when the flood was going down fast and the paddocks were all showing, so they did not drop any provisions in this district....

'People down here lost a lot of stock. On Friday afternoon Buckleys could have got all their bullocks off this place but they were pulling sheep out of two feet of water near their own house. They were under the impression that the flood was coming from Fish Creek and the cattle would be all right in a few feet of water over here. But in reality the flood came up from the sea. The sea side of Tullaree was all flooded on Friday afternoon and the cattle were all right on the other side but most were drowned on the Friday night.'

They spent Christmas amid the musty smells of their home, their lunch a tin of soup, their dinner the same. The new year was coming, and with it no hope, just a struggle for survival as they continued to live on the breadline. Neal's general store at Buffalo agreed to keep supplying them, on credit, with a limited number of groceries and tinned foods but the sisters knew this could not go on forever without the bills being paid. Finally, Mr Neal, worried about the rising debt, took it upon himself to write to Jane Clement:

'Dear Mrs Clement, It is with regret I have to write to you re the account due to me by the Misses J. and M. Clement. When they returned to Tullaree they requested me to supply them with goods on a cash basis. I complied and they now owe the amount of £5 10s. When I requested payment, they informed me I would have to wait till the end of the year when they hoped to be successful in a lawsuit they are interested in.

'No doubt you will see how unfair this is, after supplying them with goods on a distinct promise of cash. I do not wish to take extreme measures to recover, and now hope you might assist by the payment of the account on their behalf.'

The arrangement with Neal had fallen down because old Mrs Clement was herself having financial problems. Although her money was tied up in property she was leasing out, she had continued to send her daughters a £3 cheque each week, which Mr Neal cashed for them. But one day the cheque was returned. Their mother's credit was of no value any more.

Within the homestead, trophies from the golden era continued to deteriorate. The legal battle they had initiated obsessed the sisters, consuming their time as, daily, they foraged through the increasing pile of documents and wrote letters to their family and their lawyers. Dust had settled on the two Lipp pianos, balls of cat fur clung to the fading velvet seat covers – for numerous cats had again found a refuge in the place – and the smell of animals' urine reeked in every room. Cobwebs hung in the corners and mould ate into the wall tapestries.

But while they had been shocked at the state of their former grand home when they returned, they had now become accustomed to the decay. So accustomed that they could no longer see it and in a curious way accepted their surroundings as if they had never changed from those halcyon days.

'We must write to the Kidds and ask them down some time,' Margaret said to Jeanie one afternoon as they sat on the dusty chairs on the verandah. 'Once we have won this court case, we will be able to get a large amount of groceries in and fix the place up.'

Having often felt the stab of hunger, their only interest beyond the legal battle was food. But at Buffalo, Mr Neal had said 'No more'. He had not been paid, the debt was high and unless he was paid they would have to look elsewhere.

'If Ma doesn't do something, we are going to starve,' said Jeanie. 'We have a few tins of things left but they aren't going to last for ever and we must also keep the cats fed.'

'It's a pity that the stove is smoking so badly,' said Margaret. 'We might be able to cook things for ourselves and make the money go further. But I think there's a nest or something in the chimney to make it blow back into the kitchen like it does.'

The women were now doing their 'cooking' in the fireplace, opening a can of beans or stewed steak and placing it on the wood.

'Everybody seems to be asking us for money,' said Jeanie after Margaret had returned from Buffalo with a handful of letters. 'I can't understand how all these debts have piled up like this from stores all over the district going back to...well, there's one here from Fish Creek dating back a year.

We can't even afford the luxury of a cigarette. God, how I'd love a smoke.'

'We must write to Ma again and insist she does something to help us. She is our guarantor, after all. When I have finished writing to Mr Wilson, I will tell Ma that she must pay Mr Neal and arrange for him to give us food. Perhaps she can send us some recipes that we can follow.'

A few days later, in response to the letter from Margaret, Mrs Clement, now in her seventies, wrote that she had asked the storekeeper to supply groceries and she would make the payments direct to him. It was also arranged that Mr Neal would drop off groceries at a wooden box the Buckley family had at the end of their property, saving Margaret the long walk to Buffalo.

'Ma's going to help,' declared Margaret, relieved. 'I hope she really understands how desperate things are and that her help must continue. I think I'll write today and make it very clear.'

The ink had run out, so Margaret used a pencil to scribble her letter.

'Dear Ma, I received your letter two days ago. You said in it you were sending a list of things to the storekeeper to send to us every week. It will be a good thing to do if he will do it. We don't get any bread or meat… The price of six tins will only give us enough fresh meat for two meals, one very small. Six tins with potatoes make six meals.

'Everything we get has to be cooked on an open fire. The only little stove in the place is useless. It is impossible to cook anything on it. Any recipes will have to be ones we can cook on an open fire. We have only spent about four pounds a month. Before the cheque was stopped we were getting groceries for thirty shillings of the three pound cheque and the other thirty shillings went towards paying off. But that all came to an end.

'Will you please be as quick as you can in making any arrangement you can make, because we will soon be finished what we have now. It is a fortnight since we got any stores.'

It was as if the sisters still regarded their elderly mother as a much younger woman, still able to cope with the demands of youth. Yet it was not so much greed. Their demands, in their desperation, were a product of their cosseted upbringing. They knew no better.

Despite the ever-increasing hardships. Margaret and Jeanie Clement tried to ensure they kept up with current affairs. Jeanie had insisted on not having a wireless in the house because she considered it an intrusion, but they had managed to get a copy of *The Age* at least once a week and had read with some amusement the antics of Captain de Groot, a former officer of the Irish

Below: The general store at Buffalo, which Margaret walked to for her simple supplies. Right: Shortly after Margaret's disappearance, Mr Neal of the Buffalo store shows her food credit book.

Guards, who cut the ribbon with his sword at the opening ceremony of the Sydney Harbour Bridge in March, 1932.

Although that had happened two years earlier, it had still been a talking point between them

Groceries began to arrive again in Neal's milk van, courtesy of their mother, and the sisters did their cooking on the sitting room fire. But they had absolutely no money between them and, unwilling to sell their furniture and lose the memories it held, Margaret sent to Crawcours, watchmakers and jewellers in Bourke Street, Melbourne, a pair of pearl earrings that she had never really liked. She received a cheque for £1 2s 6d and a note from the firm that they were 'hoping to have the favour of further business from you.'

Encouraged because for the first time in her life she had initiated a financial return, Margaret searched through her dressing table for other items that had had little use. So much had been lost or stolen, she thought, as she hunted. Finally, she sent to Crawcours a Damascene bangle, six Damascene hat pins and a silver brooch. But these were returned by registered post because the firm, which specialised in the purchase of 'diamonds, gold, jewellery, old silver, curious antiques and artificial teeth', considered they were of no commercial value.

Against this struggle to make ends meet, particularly as Australia was suffering badly under the Great Depression and money was hard to come by in any case, Margaret and Jeanie pressured the Public Solicitor to hasten proceedings and take their case against the mortgagers, claiming they had acted wrongly in the purchase of Tullaree, to court.

'If we win it, we will be in clover,' said Margaret one day in 1933, but the waiting went on.

Margaret, particularly, was becoming irritated by the delay and the red tape, which always set the case back.

'What is going on?' asked Jeanie. 'It's almost as if they are waiting for the two of us to peg out so they can take the place again. All these ridiculous questions they keep asking us, too. We don't even know what the other side is up to. It seems to me that the Public Solicitor is almost blaming us for being lax about all this business.'

The sisters travelled to Buffalo by whatever means possible although there was always a trudge through water to get to the road. If they were lucky, a neighbour would give them a lift. But on most occasions they were forced to walk. For Jeanie, far less fit than her younger sister, it was an arduous journey. They had not had the resources to buy any new clothes for years and their shoes were wearing out. Whenever they reached the store they hoped they would find either a parcel of food from their mother or an envelope containing a pound note or two.

Sometimes Mrs Clement sent her daughters a treat like apple cake or jam tart. Pride did not allow them to ask for help outside the family and their dependence on their elderly mother at this stage was complete – they knew that their sisters Anna and Flora did not have money to spare. William had no funds to send to them either, and Peter was still unwell and struggling to keep himself out of debt.

So desperate was the plight of the sisters that they even asked Mrs Clement for two shillings worth of stamps so they could enter a local competition because, as they told their mother, they had thought of ideas similar to those which had won prizes before and they might manage to win a few pounds. But they were unsuccessful and the day by day struggle to get their case to court, the twice-weekly trudge to Buffalo to collect mail, continued.

'If you can manage it without having to spend too much money,' Margaret asked her mother, 'will you send me a pair of shoes? Any old half-worn or mended shoes you don't need will do as long as they will hold together for a while. I have to walk a lot and shoes go to pieces on these rough roads.'

Jeanie's legs began to trouble her more in 1934, so her trips to Buffalo with her sister fell away.

'I don't know what the problem is, Mag, but they seem to be quite stiff nowadays and there's quite a bit of swelling in the ankles.'

'Do you think you should see a doctor?'

'He will want money. We can't afford it. I expect the trouble will go away soon, anyway. It's probably the water I've been walking through.'

And so it came to Margaret to see to most of the chores. She wrote virtually all the letters to the Public Solicitor and to her mother, using black ink for the legal office and pencil for letters to her mother, some of which she composed leaning on the counter in the Buffalo store, having checked that the food parcel had arrived. She had an old plastic shopping bag to carry any food that her mother sent…the potatoes, cans of spaghetti, tinned steak.

The sisters continued to cook on the open fire and ate from the fine plates that had once been wiped and served warm to their high society guests. The water tanks were well stocked, although the flow was slow because the pipes were clogged with leaves and twigs.

Many of their neighbours, recalling the women's grander days, considered them to be still rather aloof and, while they pitied their depressed state, could not bring it upon themselves to call in on them. Apart from those feelings, there were the physical problems of wading through acres of water to get to the decrepit mansion. Those who did make the effort were politely turned away. Pride still controlled the sisters' behaviour , along with private embarrassment at their decline. It was all right to ask for help within the family, but to accept it from outsiders was beyond their ethics.

On hearing of the murder of young girl, Ethel Bradshaw, at a beach a few miles away, Jeanie asked: 'Are we safe, here, Mag? We are so isolated.'

'I don't think we'll be murdered in our beds,' Margaret assured her. 'We have the waters to protect us for a start.'

When the killer, Arnold Sodeman, was finally hanged at Pentridge Prison on 1 June 1936, Jeanie remarked: 'He's just the kind of fellow we might have employed here, like that fellow that worked for us for some time before he went off.'

The murder, in addition to the injustices they claimed were being perpetrated against themselves, served only to convince the sisters of the defencelessness of women living alone and, hearing that newspapers were being stolen from the box at their mother's home in Sale, Margaret wrote:

'It seems strange, the people stealing your papers. It looks as if they were watching and might come in if the place were empty. You should be careful not to stay alone if there are people like that about. Mostly when a house is robbed there are complaints about small thefts beforehand.'

As the months slipped by, a handful of neighbours broke through the sisters' pride barrier and called by, struggling through those areas of the estate that were still covered with swamp water that had failed to drain away, with small food gifts like homemade cakes and puddings. Two neighbouring families, the Blacks and the Buckleys, worked hard at maintaining links with the women on compassionate grounds and one day Mrs Black managed to persuade them to attend a meeting of the Country Women's Association in the hall at Tarwin Lower. Afterwards they spent the night at the Black home, enjoying the pleasures of cigarettes and sherry, although they were painfully aware of their worn-out clothes.

Such rare interludes encouraged Margaret and Jeanie to ask their mother, who had now moved to the Melbourne suburb of St Kilda to live with her youngest daughter Anna Carnahan, to include tobacco and tooth powder among the supplies she arranged for them to pick up at Buffalo. Mr Neal had told Margaret that he could no longer make special trips to drop off her mother's food parcels, so Margaret had begun walking to the store two or three times a week to check if anything had arrived. A few days after receiving Margaret's latest request, Mrs Clement, her handwriting now worsening, informed Margaret she had sent off the following items: two pounds of sausages, butter, bread, tobacco, cigarette papers, tea, apple pies, crumpets, scones, cakes, three tins of cream, corned beef. No tooth paste though and the women were aware of the poor state of their teeth.

Even so, they were delighted to receive the latest parcel. 'Enough for a party!' shrieked Jeanie as she spread the contents out on the kitchen table.

'Yes, Ma is keeping in touch with us and doing as we asked – if only that wretched Public Solicitor fellow would do the same.'

Their attention was diverted from their plight for a while because of the internationally reported relationship between King Edward VIII and Mrs Simpson, which interested the Clement sisters immensely.

'I think it's quite scandalous,' said Margaret, laying aside *The Age*, 'that that woman could ever expect to become queen. As you know, I was rather fond of King Edward until she became involved with him. What a pity he behaved like that and abdicated. But of course they could not have that woman for queen. Do you remember what it was like at Buckingham Palace, Jeanie? Can you imagine her hosting people like those we met when we were once so well treated there? Impossible. Quite out of the question.'

Old Mrs Clement sent her two single daughters a pre-cooked chicken and a pudding for Christmas, 1936, and the women sat at the dining room table and ate it with boiled potatoes and cooked dry peas, watched by an army of cats. They poured cream over the Christmas pudding and followed it with a cup of tea.

'You know, Margaret, that was a very nice fowl. I haven't tasted anything like that since – oh, goodness, haven't the years flown by? I was going to say since we hosted that wonderful party with quail and pheasant on the menu before Peter went off to the war. But now, here is another Christmas and we still haven't settled this business with Ross Grey Smith and the bank.'

Walhalla in the said Colony

And I declare that the ex

inclu

heirs

furn

artic

Wife

ter m

med

y br

hie h

Melbo

Clem

s, To

Job

To

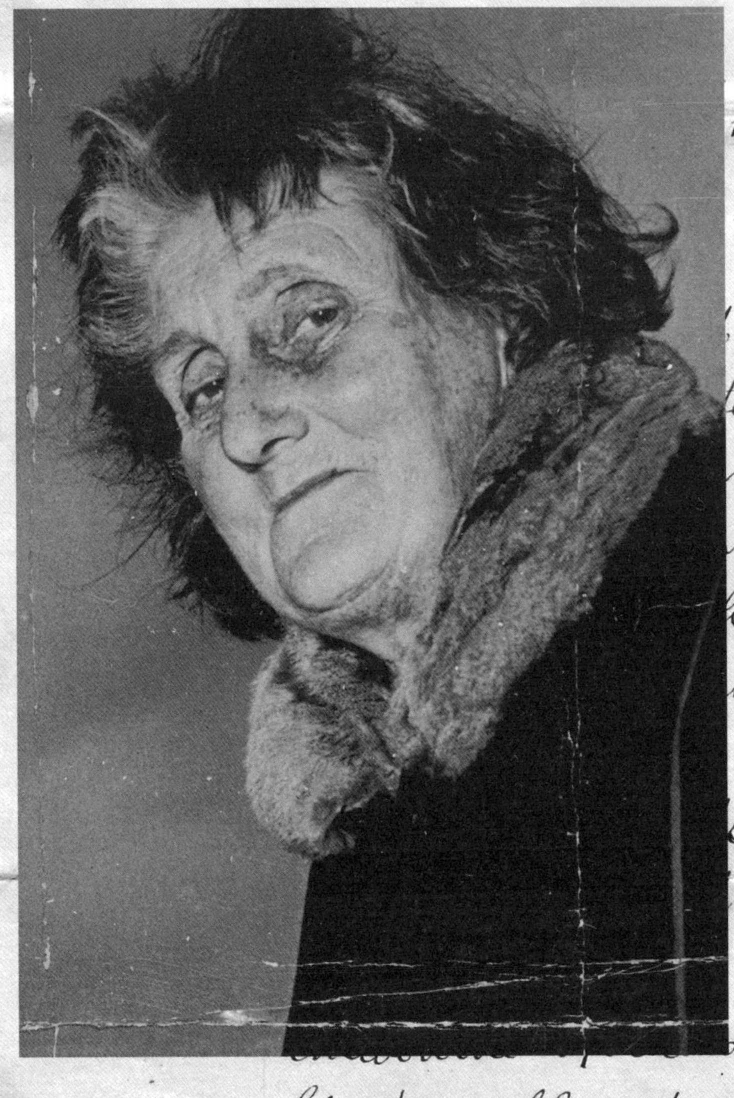

d the

Christina Clement of E

of my said brother R

of my three Cousins da

Writer to the Signet the

I direct that such leg

expiration of ~~three~~ two years

(except estates vested in m

Margaret mourns for Jeanie in 1950. Years of impoverishment have taken their toll. Her once-luxuriant auburn hair is streaked with grey and has been shorn with scissors.

Some of her teeth have broken from the stumps and she has developed a stoop.

WP PC

HJ

'I hope we can sort it out this year. Our Ma hasn't been too well, as you know, and I think she would like to know it has all been cleared up. In the next few months we must really demand that this case gets into court.'

On 17 February 1937, Margaret wrote to Mrs Clement to say she was sorry she had been ill and to be careful not to exert herself in the heat. She also asked her mother to let them know the exact time to boil dumplings – 'we are never sure of just how long to give them and we like them very much.'

But Jane Clement never replied. Instead, Margaret and Jeanie received a rare letter from Flora, their married sister in Ballarat, informing them that a telegram from their brother William told of their mother's passing. She had died at St Kilda at the age of 78, three days after receiving Margaret's letter.

In her own way, wrote Flora, Mrs Clement was 'quite happy, always bright and talkative'. Flora added that she had sent two hat boxes of clothes to Margaret and Jeanie. 'I hope you received them in good order. I am sending some more soon. I hope your affairs are improving...Your loving sister, Flora Glenny.'

A mortgage that Mrs Clement had held was now transferred to Peter, who was still living at Wurruk Wurruk, memories of his wartime experiences still attacking him in his nightmares.

With the death of their mother, Margaret and Jeanie once again worried about their own future. Who was going to provide them with food? Anna had come to their aid 20 years earlier by moving into Tullaree – perhaps she would now help again.

Anna and her son Clement, now aged 22 and a trained radio technician, had already considered the sisters' welfare. There was only one thing she and her son could do – take over where Mrs Clement had left off and continue to send Margaret and Jeanie food parcels.

Clem was not to know it at the time, but the ill fortune that Tullaree had brought to the Clement family – the doomed inheritance from Peter, that young fortune-seeking Scottish immigrant who had arrived in Australia 83 years earlier – was to swallow him, too.

Chapter 9.

~SWAMP~

Tullaree, built to withstand time, crumbled with neglect. The spinsters, raised in refined affluence, aged and fell into further ruin with it. Years of impoverishment had taken their toll. Their once-luxuriant auburn hair was streaked with grey and had been shorn with blunt scissors. Some of Margaret's teeth had broken from the stumps and she had developed a stoop. Jeanie's legs were very swollen and it seemed there was not a part of her body that did not bring her pain. The elder woman's eyesight was fading, too, so that by 1938, when she was 60, she had to ask Margaret to read to her.

For the past two winters, the flood plains around the house had spread and to get to the main road Margaret had to wade through a mile (two kilometres) of waist-deep water, just as she had after the 1934 flood. The drains that Charlie Widdis had dug decades early were now silted up completely and permanently and it was inevitable that after heavy rain the paddocks would vanish beneath a sheet of water. Tullaree was bitterly cold and damp and even the heat of summer seemed ineffective. Windows broken during the 1934 storm hade not been replaced, simply because the women could not afford it. And no offer of repairs came from Ross Grey Smith because he did not want them living on what he considered was his property.

During the cold months, Margaret collected wood from the dry area immediately surrounding the house and at night the sisters sat in the dining room beside the fire and talked of the delays in getting their case to court. A regular visitor might have found the conversation intensely boring, but the women were obsessed with and possessed by Tullaree; but there were never any visitors anyway.

Anna and her son Clem were sending them a pound note or so every fortnight in addition to a box of groceries from their flat in Melbourne's St Kilda, but they were themselves not particularly well off.

Margaret continued walking to Buffalo to pick up the supplies, although sometimes she was able to get a lift with a neighbour if she was seen walking along the narrow road. She used a sugar bag to carry her groceries because her shopping bag had broken. Her clothes were now very shabby, but when she spoke her voice carried all the refinement of those earlier days.

Margaret Clement was an enigma: a dignified lady in a down-and-out's clothes. A woman, once fashionable, who had ridden in style in a polished buggy on country outings, who now trudged through the mud in outsized men's shoes handed over by a sympathetic neighbour. She and her sister were the talk of the neighbourhood. The gossip in the pubs and on the streets was about the sad state of affairs; the obstinate women who would rather live in squalor than ask for outside help. Everyone knew of the sisters' earlier grand lifestyle and there were long debates on whether or not they were responsible for their decline. Whatever views people held, Margaret – or Miss Clement as she was generally known – continued to receive the greatest of respect and, had she asked for help, it would have come from many directions. The local people had stopped offering because they had always been politely turned down. 'No, we can manage quite well, thank you,' was Margaret's usual answer.

But one hot day she was grateful to receive a young neighbour's help. Walking back from Buffalo she suddenly felt dizzy. She fell forward onto her hands and knees on the road, the sugar bag dropping from her shoulder. Trying to stand, she stumbled sideways, head spinning, her breath coming in short gasps. Time meant nothing.

She heard a voice.

'You all right, Miss Clement?'

She opened her eyes. She recognised the man – young Ken Fisher, from one of the nearby properties.

''Ere, let me help you up.'

Margaret Clement struggled to her feet, with the young man's assistance.

'Shall I go and get some help, Miss Clement?'

'No, I am quite all right, thank you.'

She picked up her bag and continued walking home. She felt very weak, but the swamp was down and the soggy pastures were a lot easier to manage. On arrival at the house, she did not tell Jeanie what had happened.

Bushfires swept across country Victoria in January 1939 but at Tullaree, the sisters, hearing of the drama that had sent men from the city rushing to help, could not help seeing the irony in their position. They sat on the verandah and watched the orange glow in the distant night sky. With all that water around them, they were safe from any fires.

A few months later, Anna Carnaghan and Clem, nicknamed 'Knobby' because as a young boy in Sale he had once had a horse of that name, travelled to Tullaree. The four of them gathered in the musty sitting room and Clem, now in his mid-20s, tall, dark-haired and slim, acting as spokesman for his mother, despite her presence, addressed Margaret. With his polite words, Margaret became aware that age had caught up with all the Clement girls, but she had never wanted to accept it.

'Mum hasn't been too well of late, Aunt Margaret, and I'm not earning a fortune fixing up wirelesses,' he said. 'We've been thinking that perhaps you should both go onto the old age pension. Aunt Jeanie already qualifies because she's 61 and you'll qualify next year. We thought that if you received that money – '

'Never! We will never accept charity in this way.'

'But Aunt Margaret, it's not charity. Everyone has a pension when they come of age. It will help both of you and be a relief to us, to be honest.'

'I'm sorry, but we will not go beyond the family.'

Clem and his mother were determined to keep working at persuading the women to take a pension. Their reasons were entirely selfish – with money coming in they would be less inclined to continue asking for help from mother and son. It took Clem and Anna several more months and numerous trips to Tullaree, as well as visits from the Carnaghans' Sale solicitor, Eugene Allman, before the women saw reason and agreed to apply for the pension. Even then, they insisted on receiving the money indirectly because they felt it was too much bother for themselves to keep a check on the payments. So Anna and Clem received the pension cheques, cashed them, and sent the money in the mail.

In Tarwin Lower, the wealthy young sons and daughters who had once dined so well with the sisters were now grandparents. The Clements' neighbour John Buckley, who once rode a horse through the mansion, married and moved into his father's house with his bride, Kathleen. And Ross Grey Smith was chalking up a string of achievements, including being on the committee of the Royal Victorian Aero Club between 1931 and 1932, and on the committee of the Oaklands Hunt Club between

1935 and 1938. He, too, had married. Yet still the case of Misses Clement versus Ross Grey Smith, the National Bank and the Registrar of Titles remained untouched in the files.

The World War II broke out and Australians once again sailed from the ports to support the Allies in Africa and Europe. Ross Grey Smith went into the Royal Australian Air Force and still the women attempted to get the case to court. Margaret Clement waded through the widening swamps to borrow the *Bulletin* magazine from the Buckley family to keep up with the war news. Yet one of her prime concerns was the increasing crime in Melbourne. In a letter to her sister on 19 August 1942 she wrote:

'You better be careful never to go out at night unless with Knobby. There seem to be so many bad characters about and there are cases in the papers of houses being broken into and people knocked about. This sort of thing always happens at war time.'

One day, reading a newspaper she had bought at Buffalo, she saw a picture of Mussolini. It did not look like other photographs she had seen of him, which prompted her to tell her younger sister that she thought 'it must have been someone else impersonating him.' Her sister wondered whether the comment was evidence that Margaret still had a perceptive mind, or whether, in fact, she was losing it.

In any case, Margaret continued to write to Anna with her observations about the war. The Allies, she considered, were getting on better in Italy: 'The Italians seem to be doing far better for the Allies than they did for the Germans,' she reflected.

Italian prisoners were working on some of the Gippsland farms where the local cream wagon called and, noted Margaret, 'I think they are pretty comfortable. They look comfortable and seem to have cigarettes to smoke and everything they need. The ones I have seen wear pinkish-coloured uniforms.'

Throughout the 1940s Margaret and Jeanie Clement refused to budge from their crumbling refuge. Then in February 1944, in the midst of reading good reports from New Guinea where Australian troops were winning battles against the Japanese, they received terrible news.

Their brother Peter was dead.

He had been found at his Wurruk Wurruk farm with a bullet in his head. The enemy had failed to bring him down in the First World War and it was his own hand that had now ended it. The *Gippsland Times* of 3 February 1944, wrote:

'A member of an old Gippsland pioneering family in Mr Peter Scott Clement passed away at the Gippsland Hospital on Monday last. On January 24 he was found at his home at Wurruk with a bullet wound in his head. He was brought into the hospital in a low condition and passed away on 31st January.

'He was the son of the late Mr and Mrs Peter Clement, the owner of Prospect Station, near Seaspray. He was educated at Gippsland College and Scotch College and enlisted for service in World War I. For some considerable time he has lived in complete retirement at Wurruk. He had not for a very long period of years enjoyed good health.

'Born under favourable circumstances, he followed grazing as an occupation for a number of years. He raced a few horses and his principal success was in winning the Adelaide National Steeplechase with Snob. He was a likeable fellow and many years ago his friends regretted the decline in his health.'

Their father had died suddenly and now Peter. Their mother had passed on, too. The sisters wondered who would be next.

In the summer of 1946 Margaret, now 65, saw a cattleman on a neighbouring property kick and curse a dog. The animal cowered in the grass, whimpering.

'Stop!' shouted Margaret. 'Stop hurting that dog!'

'He's no good, Miss Clement. Can't train him to do a thing. Reckon I'll put a bullet in him.'

'You will do no such thing. You will give him to me.'

The cattleman was surprised. 'He's a nasty bit of stuff, Miss. Bitten me a couple of times.'

Margaret called the dog and finally it slunk over to her. It looked, she thought, just like a dingo.

'And that's what I shall call you,' she said, patting it. 'Come on, Dingo.'

The dog followed her to Buffalo and then walked home with her to Tullaree, swimming through the swamp to keep up.

The sisters lost their brother William the following year. He passed away in Melbourne at the age of 64. The *Gippsland Times* of 29 May 1947, said of him:

'Born to the land, he carried on grazing pursuits and also took an active interest in horse racing...In racing as in other walks of life, his code of honour was high and he was greatly respected. He was of a very generous, if retiring, disposition and this was to his own detriment. His only brother,

Peter, died a few years back while his sisters Margaret, Jeanie and Anna (Mrs Carnaghan) reside in Melbourne.'

This last statement was, of course, incorrect. Only the immediate district, it seemed, knew that the decaying, seemingly deserted, house in the middle of a swamp in Tarwin Lower was still occupied by Margaret and Jeanie.

Jeanie was beginning to complain of stomach cramps and she found it difficult to leave her bed. They also heard through their niece, Eileen, in Ballarat that Flora, their oldest sister, was in poor health. She had had a stroke and, wrote Eileen 'she is now able to walk from her bedroom with a crutch and me supporting her on the other side...She can't listen to the wireless as she has got very deaf.'

Margaret, aware that it would probably not be long before she lost Flora, sat beside Jeanie and read the latest correspondence and sometimes a novel, for Jeanie's sight was now very bad. She had not left the house for six years and both women wondered how they could ever ask a doctor to clamber through the spreading bracken in summer or wade through the swamp in winter.

Mrs Kathleen Buckley, John's bride at the nearest property, visited the sisters on several occasions and seeing that Jeanie was very ill one day managed to persuade the women to allow a trained nurse – one of the young Fisher girls – to call. Jeanie was tended but the visiting woman remained concerned about her general appearance.

Mrs Buckley decided to maintain her friendship with the now elderly Clement women, although Margaret and Jeanie seemed embarrassed by gifts of cakes and rarely talked much about themselves. Two visits, she was to recall much later, had caused her a great deal of concern – once she became lost in the swamp and on another occasion, while pregnant, she fell through the floor in the front room when the rotting boards collapsed under her.

But other feet were safe – the paws of the dozens of cats that still roamed the property. The sisters shared whatever food they had with the animals and of course there was now also Dingo the dog, which had finally been accepted by the cats. Often the two elderly women could be seen in the room where Jeanie's bed had been set up surrounded by animals. Thanks to their pension money, it was in that same room that they ate their meals – potatoes, spaghetti, cans of corned beef and eggs. Jeanie was now totally bedridden and it was her sister's added duty to attend to her toilet needs, lifting her onto a pot in the bed.

Her body a constant ache, Jeanie told Margaret: 'I haven't told that nice young nurse, but I'm not good. If I should die – '

'Don't say that, Jeanie. Neither of us has talked about our deaths before. It seems too…sudden.'

'But you know I can't even get up from my bed any more. Look at me. I'm 70. I'm not going to get any better at my age. But at least I know I'll die in my lovely home.'

'It's not right that you should be saying these things. We'll get help. I'll make arrangements for a doctor to come.'

'No, Mag. I don't think a doctor would want to come here. He wouldn't able to do anything either. You know, I never thought I'd find myself lying here like this and the business of the property still not settled. I was only thinking earlier that it's been 20 years – a whole 20 years – that we have been trying to get it all sorted out.'

Jeanie shivered and Margaret, dressed in her old black coat, the one with the fur collar, pulled the blankets up around her sister. It was dusk and another winter was upon them. She could hear the rain hitting the roof and saw the smears of water running down the wall. In the corner of the icy room, Dingo lay curled on a faded rug, one of Tullaree's many cats which had formed a special bond with the dog, lying beside him. Like the sisters, the dog had now accepted seclusion and he growled viciously when neighbours came to the house until he got to know them.

The skies over Gippsland turned grey and the wind whipped leaves from the trees and the rain came down heavy and widened the lake where the paddocks lay and during the third week of July 1950, as Margaret and the animals slept amid the creaks and sighs of rotting Tullaree, Jeanie Swanson Clement gave a short cry in the dark and slumped over the side of the bed, her life of luxury turned to poverty finally over.

Margaret had not heard the cry above the roar of the storm but when she saw the shape of her sister in the faint light of dawn she knew she had lost her. She walked over and felt Jeanie's cold, stiffening hand.

'Oh Jeanie,' she said softly. 'So you have gone. My dear sister and companion.'

Margaret, who had slept in her coat, put on her oversized shoes, and made her way to the front door. And there she stopped, looking out across the swamp, Dingo waiting expectantly at her side. It was not right, surely, to ask them to come and take Jeanie away so soon. Her sister had lived here for most of her life. Was she not entitled to a few hours of absolute peace;

to lie, now undisturbed by the banging of doors, the dampness, the cold; free from the problems that had haunted them for more than two decades?

Margaret Clement nodded slightly, allowed herself a faint smile and walked back into the house, through to the kitchen. There she scraped out food for the cats and Dingo and made herself a cup of tea.

WOMAN ALONE WITH DOG IN RUINED MANSION

IN the dilapidated remains of an old mansion, isolated by swamp, a 68-year-old woman is living with only her dog for company.

MELBOURNE, Saturday.

The 17-roomed home, which has become a legend in the Tullaree district of Victoria's South Gippsland, is nearly 80 years old.

The occupant is Miss Margaret Clement, who, until last week, shared the home with her 70-year-old [illegible] Jenny Swanson Clement.

On Saturday Miss Jenny died and on Sunday police had to walk four miles and wade three miles through the waist-deep swamp to the old homestead.

Poor water supply

They had to carry Miss Jenny's body back over the same route to get it to the nearest point a hearse could reach.

When reporters waded through the swamp to interview her this week, Miss Margaret gave them a gracious welcome.

She has no electricity, no radio. She gets her water from an old well, or from tins placed under the leaking guttering.

Pointing over the swamp only a few yards from the mansion, she said:

"This was a beautiful garden once. There was a bridge and a road. We had a car, but it was a bother."

She added: "Nothing works any more."

Although Melbourne is not much more than 100 miles away, Miss Margaret has not visited the city for more than 20 years.

"There have been men in my life, but they were not very important," she said.

Back in the Tullaree mansion they kept severely to themselves, having very few guests and living quietly on the income from their late father's estate.

Miss Margaret, a striking and handsome woman, said:—"We were very happy. We bothered nobody; nobody bothered us.

"Maybe I will be lonely now my sister has gone, but I have no regrets and no fears."

Miss Margaret has no direct contact with tradespeople.

Wades for food

Twice a week, she takes off her shoes and stockings, pins up her skirts, and wades through the swamps to a neighbor, who does her shopping.

Then she carries her provisions home on her back in a sugar bag.

SUNDAY TELEGRAPH, JU[illegible]

Australia's loneliest woman (in her home amid swamps) reads thrillers

MELBOURNE, Sat.—A 68-year-old woman who lives alone in a swamp-bound, dilapidated mansion said today that she would defeat the terror of loneliness by reading detective thrillers.

The woman, Miss Margaret Clement, is the last surviving member of a wealthy grazing family at Tularee, eight miles from Tarwin Lower, South Gippsland.

"I will stay in my house with my books and my dog for the rest of my life," she said.

Her sister Jennie, aged 70, died in the 13-roomed mansion last Saturday.

On Sunday four men carried her body on a stretcher through five miles of swamps for burial in the family vault at Sale.

After the funeral Margaret returned to the isolation of her home, from which she has banned radio and even electricity.

A reporter who visited her waded through miles of swamps, with [illegible] rank water [illegible]

"My sister and I bought the mansion in 1907," said Margaret Clement.

"In those days cattle grazed on our 1800 acres of rich pastures, which are now swamp.

"Handsome buggies brought parties of guests along a white gravel driveway, which is now buried beneath weeds.

"Managers worked the property for us, while we twice visited Europe and the Far East.

"There was some court litigation, and we were treated harshly.

"The property became a wilderness, and everyone except Jennie and myself left it.

"We were happy in our loneliness. We bothered nobody and nobody bothered us.

"I am alone now, except for my dog Dingo."

Wades To Shopping

[illegible] the ground.

Margaret gets water from an old well or from pots placed under the broken roof guttering.

"Nothing works any more," she said.

"I am not sorry that I never married.

"I shall carry on until my time comes."

In the [illegible] the mansion, its expensive furniture, thick with dust, is a library of detective stories.

Conan Doyle is Margaret's favorite author.

Twice a week, to go shopping, she pins up her skirt and wades through the swamps to her next-door neighbor, Mr. Buckley, a few miles away.

He is her contact with tradespeople.

The mansion's garden, once the best in Gippsland, is buried beneath blackberry scrub, which in places is house high and has entered through broken windows.

[illegible] of empty food tins [illegible]

After Jeanie's death in 1950, the story of the Lady in the Swamp catches media attention.

Chapter 10.

~CONTACT~

The cruel wind took her breath away as she stepped into the swamp on the morning of 23 July 1950, even though she had learned to live with it each winter. She tugged her coat's fur collar tighter as she broached the icy waters. An hour later, her bare legs caked with mud, a streak of blood on one from an unseen obstacle, she walked up the drive of her near neighbour, John Buckley, and tapped on the door.

The farmer was surprised to see her. It was he who usually brought a copy of the *Bulletin* to her whenever he could manage it, for he thought this was what the unexpected call was about.

'I'm afraid we haven't quite got around to finishing the magazine yet, Miss Clement, but as soon – '

'It's Jeanie,' she interrupted. 'She's passed away.'

Buckley froze; then said quietly: 'Come in, Miss Clement.'

As she related to him Jeanie's last few days, describing the feeling she had had that her elder sister was not long for this world, a car pulled up outside the homestead. One of the local horsebreakers, Frank Moore, jumped out, leaving a woman sitting in the driving seat. On hearing the news of Jeanie's death from Mr Buckley, he returned to the vehicle.

'Bad news,' he said to woman. 'We can't do the horses. Miss Clement of Tullaree has died. Her sister is here. They want me to send a telegram off to her relatives.'

At that moment Margaret, accompanied by Mr Buckley, left the house.

The farmer led her to the car and the woman who had been waiting in the front seat climbed out.

'Miss Clement,' he said, 'this is Mrs Livingstone. Mrs Livingstone, this is Miss Clement.'

Margaret smiled at the brown-haired woman, who was in her mid-40s, she thought. Mrs Livingstone's face was delicately made up and she was dressed in a warm woollen coat and scarf and a pair of dark blue suede shoes.

Esme Livingstone grasped Margaret's hand and told her how sorry she was to hear of her loss. With that greeting, a new and turbulent chapter in Margaret's life was about to begin.

'All right, Miss Clement,' said Mr Buckley. 'We'll get things sorted out for you – I'll get some of the boys together and bring the body out.'

Mrs Livingstone appeared to be disturbed by what she might have thought was a brusque comment. And Margaret seemed to hesitate as she turned to walk away. 'I'm not sure I want to go back there at the moment,' she said softly, but continued to make her way down the driveway. Mrs Livingstone had heard the whispered comment and, catching up with Margaret along the ti-tree-lined driveway, drew the car alongside her.

'Is there anything I can do for you, Miss Clement? I'm a trained nurse and would be only too pleased.'

Margaret looked into the younger woman's sharp brown eyes. 'Oh no, thank you. There is so much mud and water to go through and the place is very untidy.'

Mrs Livingstone started to pull away, deciding to call on Margaret later in any case. The old woman had not been unknown to her. She had seen her once before in the heat of summer at the Buffalo store, a stooped pensioner in that same old coat and a hat tied on with string, a sugar bag hooked around a finger by a piece of cord. Mrs Livingstone had smiled at her at the time, admiring her gentle reserve.

Later that day the men, along with the local police, came to collect Jeanie's body, struggling to find a path through the swamp. It was bad enough heading towards the mansion, for the rain had set in and it was even worse going back out with the body. Darkness had descended and the hurricane lamp that Margaret had given to them and their torches were totally inadequate.

'Now I know what those poor buggers, the early explorers, went through when they came here,' groaned Constable Fry under the weight of the stretcher, the rain running down his face, his sodden, thick overcoat adding to the effort. 'It's like the whole place has reverted to the wilderness it once was.'

Several times the bearers almost dropped the body into the blackness of the swamp but they knew that must never happen. To a man they could not help but image the sheer horror of the scene should they stumble and the woman's body splash into the marsh. The corpse was wet through in any case, for the old sheets and bedspreads they had thrown over it were soaked, adding to the weight of the load. When, at last, they reached the road, they laid the stretcher down and caught their breath for a few minutes. Then they slid it into the hearse and drove to Wonthaggi, arriving, as the *Gippsland Times* was to record, at 11.30 at night.

The following day a woman waded through the swamp, screwing up her face at the difficult and cold passage. Unable to find an easy route, Mrs Esme Livingstone, accompanied by two local men who agreed to help her, struggled through knee-deep mud and water for two hours. One of the men, George Baker, was looking for a bridge he once knew, but they became hopelessly lost in dense tri-tree. Finally they found some deep cattle tracks in the bog and they followed them through to the homestead. As they approached the mansion, Dingo snarled and barked from the verandah. Margaret came out, hands clasped in front of her, and watched the three bedraggled visitors approach.

'So you came after all,' she said quietly as Esme offered the basket of food she had asked one of the men to carry for her.

'Oh dear, I can't accept this,' said Margaret. 'I'm going to be quite all right, thank you all the same.'

But Esme insisted, saying it would be too difficult to carry it back out again. Then she made a suggestion.

'Look, Miss Clement, it's probably going to be lonely for you here now, especially in the next few days. Why don't you come and stay with us for a short time? I can cook for you and – '

'No, no. I appreciate your offer, but I will stay here. This is our home.'

Esme realised that Margaret was imagining her sister was still with her.

'Well, if you need anything, anything at all, please try to get a message to me. Stan and I don't live far away.'

Before wading back into the swamp, the men chopped a pile a wood for her. Esme invited Margaret to meet her a week later at the roadside at a point known locally as Buckley's corner. If Margaret did not turn up, she said, she would understand that she was coping.

A few days later one of the stretcher bearers, Goff Jongebloed, was asked by two newspaper reporters from Melbourne to take them through the swamp to interview Margaret, for word of the bizarre trek of the undertaker and his team had stirred the interest of city news editors. Holt Boardman, a writer on Melbourne's *Sun*, found himself on what he was to describe as one of his strangest stories.

He and a photographer pushed through 4 metre-high scrub, so dense it was difficult to see the man ahead. They crossed fresh deer tracks and walked knee-deep in icy cold swamp. Goff Jongebloed said: 'The swamp's even tougher on the route the old lady takes to Buffalo with a sugar sack on her back for provisions.'

Once again, Dingo's growl came from the verandah as the dog watched the visitors approach. Margaret came out in her usual coat, legs bare, her thick hair uncovered. She had no choice but to invite the men in, although she would have preferred to be left alone. They sat in the Victorian drawing room. A swallow flitted through the broken window. The reporter noticed the threadbare carpet but he also recognised the quality that showed through the thick dust veneer on the remaining furniture.

'Everything's spoiled,' said Margaret, the journalist surprised at her cultured tones, just as other newcomers had been. 'I do not know whether I will stay here or not. You cannot make a quick decision like that. After all, my sister has only been dead a few days.'

Boardman cast his eyes around the room and saw the fine, paper-light china on the piano and the mantelpiece. Margaret led him carefully across the rotting floorboards and into a dry part of the garden, where he saw blackberry bushes as high as the house. Piles of empty tins that had contained food for humans and animals littered the ground.

'How do you get through the swamp, Miss Margaret?' the newspaper man asked.

'I carry my stockings and shoes and put them on when I get through.'

'And have you had any bad experiences?'

'I have had some snakes twined around my leg, but they have never bitten me.'

Boardman could not help a sudden shiver at the thought – he had to

Above Top: Tullaree is boarded up in the 1930s to keep out intruders.
Below: Margaret worries about the pressures surrounding her, as she stands on a path of dry ground in 1950, with Dingo.

his h
my p
and
said
after
nam
o my
of fu
ar M
ohn
five hundred pounds,
brothers James and
thousand pounds,
Melbourne aforesaid

walk back through that water and it gave him no comfort to think that snakes would now be hibernating in these winter months.

Margaret noticed that Paddy Brenocks, one of the men who had brought Boardman and the photographer through the swamp, was carrying a rifle.

'I don't like deer shooting,' she said, but kept to herself her experience at watching her boyfriend of decades earlier maiming a small wallaby. 'So many men and dogs after one beast. I don't like this killing of animals. I saved Dingo my dog from a cattleman who wanted to shoot him because he would not work.'

Asked where she got her drinking water from, Margaret said it came from pots placed under the dripping roof guttering. 'Nothing works any more. This was a beautiful garden once. There was a bridge and a road. The traps used to come in here. We had a car, but it was a bother.'

Boardman and the photographer plodded back through what he later described as an 'eerie swamp', wondering how anyone could face a night alone in the house.

Another journalist who visited her, Barney Porter, of the *Argus*, asked Margaret what she thought of the 'modern girl'.

'Oh, she's quite a good type. I smoke myself. I like a drink with my meals and I think that any girl is entitled to wear make-up if she wants to as long as she does not overdo it.'

Did she regret she had never married?

'Not at all. There have been men in my life – but they were not very important.'

Despite the lucidity with which Margaret spoke to the visiting journalists, Goff Jongebloed formed the opinion that Margaret was in a mental daze, brought on, he thought, by the death of her sister. It seemed to him that she was close to not understanding what was going on around her, although the newspaper reporters had not observed this.

In time, others were to form the same opinion as Jongebloed. But was it because her mind was going? Or was she behaving normally for a woman who had lived for many years as a recluse and who believed there were few she could trust?

Margaret, collected by police and driven to Wonthaggi, gave a statement to the district's deputy coroner, Herbert Williams, at Jeanie's inquest on 2 August 1950. She said she had formally identified Jeanie's body and told of how the day before her death she had complained of indigestion and the following day she had drunk only a cup of tea in bed. When, finally, she saw that Jeanie had stopped breathing she knew she had passed away.

Constable Bert Fry told of finding Jeanie in her bed in a room at the rear of house. 'She was lying on her left side with her head overhanging the side of the bed, arms protruding from the edge of the bed and knees drawn up into the stomach. There was scant covering on the deceased and she appeared to have been dead about 12 hours. I inspected the body of the deceased, there was no sign of violence or marks on the body and there were no suspicious circumstances as to the cause of death.'

The doctor who carried out a post mortem examination at Wonthaggi Hospital, Lancelot Sleeman, concluded that Jeanie had died from 'a ruptured gastric ulcer with peritonitis' with the added complication of heart disease and a disease of her coronary arteries.

The coroner recorded that this medical condition, which would have led to Jeanie dying in great pain, was the cause of death.

The inquest over, Margaret was driven back to the edge of the swamp. Constable Fry watched her sadly as she began wading through the water, a defenceless, bent figure in an old coat, walking to – well, he couldn't begin to think what kind of future.

Chapter 11.

~KIDNAP~

Stanley Russell Livingstone, former Footscray and Port Melbourne ruckman and champion axeman, rubbed the dirt from his big hands and watched his wife's Austin lurch up the driveway of their Middle Tarwin property, just a few miles from Tullaree. He had earlier been breaking-in two thoroughbred foals with a friend, George Baker, when they realised they needed straps. Esme had offered to drive to the Buckley homestead to pick some up. She returned now without the straps – but she had some interesting news.

'Stan, you know that run-down place that everyone's been talking about? One of the old women has died. I met the younger sister, Margaret Clement, a short time ago. She has that huge house all to herself now, poor thing.'

Stan Livingstone raised his eyebrows and looked around his land. This was his second Gipplsand home after moving to the area in 1937 to live on a 600 hectare property known as Archers, for which he paid some £6 15s a hectare. An extremely hard worker, he developed the property and then sold it for £9 a hectare. Now he was working away putting a new home on the land at Middle Tarwin, for which he had paid £8,000 and which he hoped to sell for close to double that.

That evening the Livingstones briefly discussed the old lady in the house surrounded by swamp, Esme telling Stan that she felt sorry for her and had made a loose arrangement to meet her again.

Esme travelled along the road between Tullaree and Buffalo several times over the following days, but there was no sign of Margaret, so one morning she decided to call on her. Parking on the roadway, she hesitated as she looked out across the swamp, knowing from her previous experience that to reach Tullaree she would just have to brave those uninviting waters. She took a deep sigh, removed her shoes and began wading through the water. It crept up to the waist of her winter coat and made her shudder. Several times she thought about turning back, but then persevered, although she had failed to pick up the earlier route she had taken and feared she was lost. The water crept higher and at one stage, worried she was on the edge of the river, she was about to start swimming. She changed her mind and tried a new direction. Eventually, she saw the old mansion half a mile away and realised that she had, in fact, waded right past it. As she finally approached, she saw Margaret sitting beside a broken window, watching her, like a portrait on a cracked oil canvas.

Dingo, snarling, raced up to her as she reached the hard ground but Margaret, coming onto the verandah, ordered him off. Dripping wet and a little frightened, Esme said she had called to ask Margaret if she would like to come around to her house. Margaret thought about it for a moment, then, without committing herself, said: 'I have to go for stores anyway, so I'll come out and show you a shorter way to the road.'

The old woman went back into the house, returning with a tea tin tied with rope in which she would bring home the biscuits and the oatmeal she planned to buy. 'The tin keeps them dry,' she said. The string of her sugar bag hung over her shoulder and in her hand she carried a stick. Her coat and skirt were pinned up with safety pins. When the two women reached the edge of the water Margaret said: 'I'll keep my shoes on. I often do.'

But Esme believed Margaret always took her shoes off, so to make her feel at ease she slipped off her own. Margaret then did the same and her visitor could not help noticing her mud-caked feet. She had obviously been walking around like that inside the house.

'I'm sorry they are so dirty,' said the elderly woman, catching Esme's glance. 'With so much mud around, it's a bother to keep them clean. But they'll soon wash off as we walk.'

Esme followed Margaret through the water, the spinster prodding the way with her stick and occasionally grabbing the trunks of ti-tree. She warned Esme to keep right behind her, for with a faltering step sideways she could be up to her neck. After wading through a particularly deep part, they reached the wooden balustrade of an old bridge, just protruding from the water, where Margaret stopped to rest.

As the old woman caught her breath, Esme noticed the lump on her hand from constant use of the stick and the finger that had been disfigured after years of carrying the tin and the sack by the rope.

When they finally emerged from the swamp, they continued barefoot through the slush of the paddocks for a mile to Buckley's corner. Then they walked up the road to check the box outside George Elliot's farm where the milk van from Buffalo was once again leaving Margaret's groceries.

Esme thought: 'Amazing – an old woman trudging through swamps like this in these days. But perhaps no-one has actually seen the problems she has getting out. And if they have, they haven't done anything to help her.'

The younger woman asked Margaret whether this was her routine. And she established that after picking up her groceries, Margaret re-entered the lane at the edge of the swamp, got onto her knees on the grass and sorted through the food. She divided the weight, usually leaving the tinned foods in a ti-tree for collection in following days. As groceries came twice a week, noted Esme, it meant that the old woman probably made four trips through the swamp every seven days. And how old did she say she was…70? Yes, 70.

'Look, Margaret,' said Esme, deciding she was going to sweep formalities aside and address her by her first name, 'why don't you come around to my place and have some tea? It will give you a bit of a company for a while. You don't have to stay long. It might make a change for you.'

'I suppose I could,' said Margaret. It had been years since she had been anywhere new.

Esme drove her to the Middle Tarwin homestead. Stan was not around. They had tea in the sitting room but Margaret, unaccustomed these days to meeting and chatting with strangers, did not speak much. Eventually Esme drove her back to the edge of the swamp, promising to meet her again some time.

In Melbourne, Clem Carnaghan, who had attended Jeanie's funeral in Sale before her internment in the family grave, slowly twisted a screwdriver in the wireless workshop he had set up in the flat as he discussed his Aunt Margaret's future with his mother Anna, who had just turned 60.

'We can't let her stay in that place on her own,' he said. 'And we've got to start talking to her about what's going to happen to Tullaree when she's gone. You're her sister – you ought to be pushing her a bit more about it.'

'It's not the time,' said Anna.

'Well, we've got to be practical here. If something happened to her you wouldn't know for days, perhaps weeks. I think we should bring her down to Melbourne and find out what she wants to do.'

Anna watched her son remove a valve from a bakelite radio as she considered his words – not that there was anything new in what he had said. He was constantly raising the question of Margaret now that Jeanie had died. How he had changed, she thought. He was always coming back late at night and she was unhappy about the people he was mixing with. She'd heard talk that he would spend his evenings drinking with members of the underworld – at best they were unsavoury people, a neighbour had told her, but she could never get the truth out of him. In any case, he was an adult and what he did with his life was his business.

'I suppose you're right, Clem,' she said to his suggestion that Margaret should be brought to Melbourne. 'But she might not want to listen. You know how stubborn she can be. I really can't see you persuading her to come down here to St Kilda.'

'Don't worry,' he said. 'I'll persuade her.'

A week later Clem walked in through the door of the first floor flat in Lambeth Place. At his side was Margaret, clutching the hurricane lamp she had brought with her, her lips tight.

'Mag – so you decided to come!'

The old lady bit her lip. 'I made no such decision. He dragged me here with his confederates. I've been kidnapped.'

Anna spun on her son. 'You brought her here against her will? What have you done?'

'I did no such thing,' he snapped. 'She couldn't decide and I talked her into it, telling her it was for the best. I had a couple of fellows with me to keep me company on the way down. Do you really think I could drag someone through that bloody swamp if they didn't want to come? Besides, there's that dog of hers. Be sensible. We wouldn't have got anywhere near the house if she hadn't told it to shut up.'

Above: The house that Stan Livingstone built for Margaret. She refused to move in there.
Below: Letters from opportunists were found in Tullaree after Margaret's disappearance, including one from a Swiss man. Biblical texts were also found – did they contain hidden meanings?

Santjohanser Carl
c/o Mr. A. F. Young
Darnum. Gippsl.

Dear Miss. Clement.

J'm was just seading jour story again in the Sun-Paper. It must be very hard for jou Miss. Clement, tu stay up there after jour sister is dead.
J'm a joung Swissboy 31 year old and should lake to bay a farm. Well, J don't know if you want to sell your 2500 acres. Now, if jou want J should be very interestet to bay jour plays.
J beg to ask you how much per acres jou want.
J hope that you can read this letter. J'm very sorry but still J can't write very well.
J lake Australia very much, but to learn the language is very hard.

jours faithfully

C. Santjohanser

THURSDAY

These things I command you, that ye love one another.

John 15: 17.

TUESDAY

These things have I written unto you that believe on the name of the Son of God; that ye may know that ye have eternal life.

1 John 5: 13.

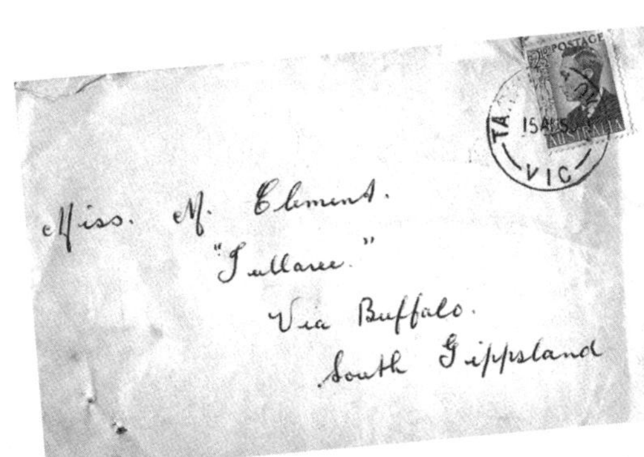

Margaret slumped down onto a chair. 'Dingo and the cats will be relying on me to return. You must take me back this instance.'

'A couple of days, Aunt Margaret,' said Clem. 'A couple of days rest for you and then I'll take you. The animals will manage without you for that short time.'

Clem waited until the following day before he began questioning his aunt. He understood that Tullaree was still the subject of an unresolved legal tangle, but as everyone who had been involved in the struggle over the property in years gone by had apparently washed their hands of it, what did she intend to do about the homestead? Was she planning to stay there, alone and uncared for, until the day she dropped dead, just like Jeanie?

Margaret shook her head dismissively at the questions, then said quietly:

'I have been asked to go and live with a Mrs Livingstone and her husband. They want to buy Tullaree.'

'What!' Clem's face hardened.

'But how can they buy it from you?' asked Anna, reaching for her older sister's hand. 'You don't actually own it.'

'I'm well aware of that,' replied Margaret. 'Ross Grey Smith is still the owner, although he hasn't had anything to do with it for years. The caveat that's on it is the problem for him. The Livingstones want me to lift my caveat so they can buy the place from Grey Smith and then they'll have the title. Tullaree will become theirs.'

'But this is bloody madness!' growled Clem. 'We don't even know these people and you've been talking to them without consulting us. We're you're family. We're the ones you should be talking to, not some strangers. How do we know what they're up to? You've been hanging on to that bloody place for donkey's years and now in the bat of an eye you're going to hand it over to people we've never met.'

'Clem's right, Mag,' said Anna. 'Why don't you leave all your affairs to us now? You've relied on me pretty heavily in the past and you know you can again.'

Margaret tightened her lips. 'I'm not discussing it any more. Particularly after the way I've been dragged down here against my will.' She turned to Clem. 'You've kidnapped me, that's what you've done, and you know it.'

Clem glanced at his mother, shaking his head. Anna's face was tortured. It was a terrible accusation to make and she tended to believe her sister rather than her son. She knew Margaret well enough for her not to make false claims.

One of Clem's acquaintances, for he had friends on both sides of the social fence, was a local policeman, Constable Leonard Stephenson, stationed at St Kilda. The men had known each other for 15 years and occasionally Stephenson dropped by at the flat. On the third day of Margaret's stay, there came a knock at the door. It was none other than Constable Stephenson. By design.

'G'day Len. Come in. By the way,' Clem added, loud enough for his aunt to hear in the sitting room, 'I have a visitor here. Aunty Margaret from Tullaree in Gippsland. Will you come and see her?'

Margaret was standing, her face grim. 'Aunt Margaret,' said Clem, 'this is Mr Stephenson from the St Kilda police station. I've brought him to say hello, give you a little assurance that all will be well.'

Margaret ignored the introduction. She glared at both men. 'I want to get away from here. Where have you put my lantern?'

'You'd better get to bed, Aunty, and get some rest. We'll get you home soon.'

'I don't want to go to bed. I don't want anything to eat. I have no wish to talk to you. I want to get back up there. I must get back to Dingo and the cats.'

Constable Stephenson wondered whether this old woman in a shabby blue dress was 'losing it', an opinion he was to maintain for months to come.

While his aunt sat on her bed the following day, Clem cast his eyes over the documents he and his mother had gathered over the years, along with more paperwork he had found lying around at Tullaree on his recent trip. He was particularly interested in the ownership of the title. He shook his head as he read again what he already knew – that registration of the transfer had been delayed for the past 20 years. The transfer had been lodged for registration after settlement of the purchase price between Ross Grey Smith, solicitor, and the National Bank on 13 November 1930.

Clem noted that Margaret and Jeanie had issued a writ against the National Bank and that Grey Smith and the Victorian Registrar of Titles were named as co-defendants. One objection to the registration was that the National Bank had not sufficiently advertised Tullaree for sale. Clem saw that by agreement between the parties, the transfer did not proceed pending the hearing of the writ. The action, Margaret's nephew knew, had never been fought. It meant, then, he concluded, that Margaret still held the title.

Continuing to pore over the documents, Clem was reminded that there was one mortgage on the property that Ross Grey Smith did not hold. This was the fourth loan of £500, once transferred to the matriarch, Jane Clement. This mortgage, on Mrs Clement's death, had been passed on once again, this time to Peter Clement, the younger brother who had shot himself. Peter had been dead for some years and he had bequeathed the mortgage to Clem.

Also in the pile of papers he was reading, Clem found an interesting document – a copy of Margaret's will, drawn up in 1925, that critical year when the sisters, in desperate straits, tried to auction off some of their land.

The document, dated 26 June 1925, showed that Margaret 'devised and bequeathed' the whole of her estate to her sister, Jeanie Swanson Clement. If Jeanie died first, money from the estate, Margaret directed, should go to her nieces and her nephew.

'Me!' he whispered to himself.

Margaret stated that money should be held in trust, but used from time to time 'in or towards the education at school, college, university or otherwise, and in or towards the maintenance and advance in business and general other advancement of my nephew John Clement Carnaghan of Fulham Park, Gippsland, son of my sister, Elizabeth (Anna) Carnaghan.'

'Me,' he silently said again. 'When she dies I get £500, at today's value.'

But a grim thought struck him. There was surely nothing left in Margaret's estate except the decaying remains of Tullaree's furniture. The only hope of a cash return from the property would be for Margaret to change her will, giving him a bigger share of the value of the house, and hope that she would be able to retain the title by successfully fighting the outstanding court case. But 20 years had passed and it had remained stagnant. His aunt was losing it, mentally…how much longer could she live?

In the small bedroom they had given her, Margaret could not sleep. Dawn of the third day in St Kilda was breaking. She worried about Dingo and the cats – and made a decision. She found a scrap of paper and a pencil and wrote a note for her younger sister and Clem:

'Gone back to Tullaree.'

Although the street lamps were still on, Margaret, out of force of habit, had taken up her hurricane lamp and lit it. Then, her gaunt face illuminated by the flickering light, she walked along St Kilda Road towards the city centre; a strange, shabby will-o'-the-wisp on the tree-lined thoroughfare at whom passing early morning motorists craned their necks to stare in astonishment. She had last travelled this road in the Wolseley, being driven to Government House and draped in enviable haute couture. Although 30 years and more had lapsed, she remembered the way quite well. At Flinders Street railway station, travellers gaped at the old woman with the lantern. The ticket collector, amazed and pitiful, allowed her through without charge, directing the eccentric-looking figure to the platform for the Gippsland train.

With the lamp still burning, Margaret settled into the corner of a compartment, her travelling companions trying not to seem curious.

Clem Carnaghan yelled out to his mother. 'She's gone!'

'But she's an old woman,' said his mother. 'We can't just let her go wandering around the streets. You'd better ring the police, Knobby.' Anna Carnaghan's son telephoned St Kilda police station and told them of the old woman who had gone wandering away. She was in a ragged coat and probably carrying a hurricane lamp. The police said they would call back when they found her. Patrol cars were radioed and surprised policemen were told to watch for a stooped old woman with an old-fashioned lamplight. They concentrated on the St Kilda beachfront, for there was concern Margaret might have found her way to the beach and might have ended up in the sea. The reasoning from one policeman was that if she was as confused as her nephew had suggested, she might think the sea was the way back to her swampland home. At 11am Clem telephoned Meeniyan police station in Gippsland and spoke to First Constable Ernest Collins and, just in case Margaret had worked out how to get home, asked if a watch could be put on the South Gippsland train.

Collins went to Buffalo and watched for the train. The familiar, bent figure of Margaret Clement stepped down onto the platform.

'We were worried about you, Miss Clement,' he said. 'It's not safe to be taking such long journeys on your own these days.'

'I ran away from them.'

'What do you mean, you ran away?'

'I was detained. He overpowered me and dragged me down to St Kilda.'

It was then that Collins noticed a mark on her face. Like a bruise. 'Did somebody hit you, Miss Clement? And who is the "he" you are talking about? Are you referring to Clement Carnaghan, who has asked me to look out for you?'

Margaret did not reply, repeating only that she had been 'detained'. He tried to sum up her position as he guided her towards his car. If Clement Carnaghan had assaulted her, as she seemed to be suggesting, would he have then called the police with concern in his voice to ask for help in finding her? In any case, Miss Clement did not seem prepared to make a complaint, so he decided to let things go. Even so, he did not think she should return to Tullaree to continue living on her own, but Margaret insisted on being taken home to Tarwin Lower. On the way, she picked up her mail from George Elliot's box and then, clutching an unusually large number of letters in her arthritic hands, waded through the swamp to the refuge of Tullaree.

Two hours later, with Dingo and a large number of cats at her feet, she was sitting in false comfort in her favourite chair opening envelopes. She was stunned to learn that the whole of Australia knew of the recent loss of her sister – more than 20 letters had been posted to her from sympathisers who had read in the newspapers about her extraordinary life. Some of the correspondence was from people who recalled Margaret from the good old days. Ellen and William Benson wrote from Collingwood, Melbourne:

'Dear Miss Margaret, You will wonder who is writing. My husband and I worked for your sister and yourself many years ago. I still retain the memory of the position as married couple we had with you.

'We remember "Old Bob" the cat, who was over twenty years old, who always stayed in the front rooms of the house. We also remember the many cats you had – ' Margaret paused for a moment to smile at the animals at her feet, before continuing with the letter. 'I had a great love for them also. Mr Stammers was manager for you at that time. We also remember Patrick who went into Buffalo for the mail and provisions. He was drowned in the flood.

'You had horses and buggies at that time. You can see that was a long time ago, I think in the beginning of 1913...Something within me made me write as I have not forgotten you and your sister.'

Mrs Leah Graham, writing from North Brighton in Melbourne, said she thought she was Margaret's cousin. She remembered staying at the first Clement home at Seaspray:

'It must be 50 years ago now and I am nearly 58 years old. I remember your mother, two older sisters and Petty (Anna), as I knew her then, and I have never forgotten that she kept a pet spider. You have probably forgotten me, but the time I spent in Sale is very vivid in my memory. You have lived a full life, travelled and gained experience and have a good storehouse of memories to stand you in later years.'

Margaret felt a tear well up as the words took her back to a happy period. Yes, she did remember a little girl called Leah in her white dress and pigtails. And Anna's spider...yes, she remembered that, too. A baby huntsman that she kept in a box with leaves and twigs but which frightened her when it grew big and she let it go. But what of the memories of more recent years? she wondered. She didn't want to recall those. She just wanted things to get better than they were now, although she could not see how that was going to happen.

Many of the other letters she began to open were from people who appeared more interested in the house than in Margaret's welfare. One man, writing from Coburg, Victoria, said:

'After reading of your story in the *Sun*, I was wondering if you have any ideas of selling your property. And if possible, would you give me an opportunity of buying it?'

Another man, describing himself as a truck driver, wrote from Dimboola, Victoria: 'My wife, our six children and myself are living in a four-room house which is, as you can well imagine, far too small for eight people. We are very interested in your house, at least my wife is, my interest lies in the land. Is it at all possible for us to come to some arrangement regarding the farming of the land? Oh, I know there is a lot of work to be done there, but I am young (35) and in the best of health...I would like to come and visit you if you think it's worthwhile so we can talk over arrangements.'

And there was the letter from a Mrs Miles of Redfern, New South Wales, who said she would like to stay at Tullaree for her three-week holiday. Her mistaken impressions were of a property that needed hardly any work on it:

'I would make the place so nice for you. I'd get a go on the drive and get all the weeds away and then start on the garden. In fact, you could help me if you liked. You would be able to see it come back to what it was once. Just because we are women that is not to say we are all useless.

'If you let me come over at Xmas I will be able to bring enough food for us and I am sure I will do my best to cheer you up. When I come back to Sydney you will be able to see how nice the drive looks. I bet you won't find a weed after I'm finished with it. I am sending you a novel to read by your favourite author, Sir Conan Doyle.'

In the next four months, up to Christmas, 1950, Margaret received a number of visitors to Tullaree, a mixture of neighbours and strangers. She was reserved with the neighbours, insisting that she could cope on her own. Newcomers she politely dismissed, even though many had become soaked through to the skin trying to find their way through to her. Clem Carnaghan was a regular visitor, but she was cold towards him. This time there was no attempt to haul her through the swamp, as she claimed he had done before, but he was persistent. Tullaree should stay in the family. He always left disappointed; Margaret remained uncommitted.

The Livingstones called frequently. Margaret liked Esme, for she believed Stan's wife was genuine in her concerns. Esme told Margaret that Stan would help in patching up Tullaree to at least make it safer to walk through and, true to his word, he began by repairing a rotting floorboard which had become dangerous. Esme wiped the damp stains from the walls and got a fire going in the living room, even though Margaret had advised that the chimney had not been swept for years and could catch fire. But soon a warm glow filled the room and no warning smoke billowed from the chimney.

After weeks of visits – the journey through the swamp now more comfortable with the arrival of summer – Esme and Stan finally persuaded Margaret to come and stay with them for the night, if for no other reason than to give her a break and bring a little conversation into her life. But the conversation was one-sided.

Margaret listened to their stories of how they had lived in Melbourne before acquiring land in Gippsland and how Stan, once written off as being of any use with an axe in local competitions, had persevered and become a champion. Margaret could have told them so much about her own life, particularly those glorious early days and all the travel abroad, but she remained uncertain whether to open up to this couple who had so recently come into her life.

One of Margaret's visitors in the weeks leading up to Christmas had been her niece, Eileen Glenny, daughter of Margaret's oldest sister, Flora, who was living in north-west Victoria. Eileen was saddened at her aunt's circumstances and horrified to hear that 'people' had been at her to hand Tullaree over to them one way or another. Margaret did not elaborate, but Eileen could read the anxiety and confusion in her face. Eileen's offer to help was politely turned down. As Margaret had told so many others, she could cope and thank you very much anyway. Eileen told Margaret that her mother had not been well and shortly after the visit she wrote a letter expressing fears for her mother's health – and for Margaret's future. Flora had been very ill and the doctor was afraid she would not get better because her heart was failing.

'Do look after yourself,' wrote Eileen, 'and don't be bullied into doing what you don't want to do.'

Then another visitor waded through the swamp – a Melbourne solicitor, Mr L.P. Goode, who decided he would like to try to buy Tullaree either from Margaret or from Grey Smith, depending on who was legally judged the owner. Goode cut a curious figure, wading through the water alone with his brief case, the mire creeping up the legs of his smartly pressed grey suit. It reached his waist and he was forced to abandon that particular route. Returning in frustration to the road, he set out again and this time, after an hour's wading, he located the house, negotiated a snarling Dingo and, dripping wet, sat with Margaret in the drawing room. He was conscious of his wet clothes on her lounge chair but she insisted he sat, more out of politeness, he felt, than interest in what he had to say to her.

She had, of course, heard it all before. Goode was interested in buying Tullaree. She stopped him, not because she wasn't prepared to sort out her problems but because she had an announcement that shocked him. Friends of hers, she said, were involved in negotiations with Mr Ross Grey Smith and herself and if the arrangement went through she would be provided with a suitable home that would be specially built for her on the property. Goode, who was about to make exactly the same proposition, asked to be given preference if negotiations broke down.

'By the way,' he asked as he prepared to step back into the swamp, 'who are these friends of yours?'

'Mr and Mrs Livingstone,' she replied.

The Livingstones had been showering Margaret with attention. They called for her almost every day and drove her to their Middle Tarwin property. She felt comfortable in Esme's company and began speaking more about her early life while Stan spent the days working on his land. Margaret began stopping over for one or two nights at a time. Esme gave the old lady some of her mother's clothes and showed her how to work the bath – a luxury that had long been denied Margaret since the Edwardian days when servants had taken care of those preparations for her and her sister. Esme played music for her... *The Mikado*, *Faust*, *Aida*, and Margaret Clement, in 'new' clothes, her hair washed, sat back in a comfortable arm chair, sipped sherry and let her mind take her back to similar circumstances 50 years ago.

Gradually, the defences she had built around herself as a recluse fell away. The Livingstones took her shopping in Stan's Land Rover and bought her cakes and bananas, which she had not enjoyed for years. Esme even managed to entice Margaret to the cinema with her and on one trip to Dandenong the old lady ferreted around in her purse for a sixpence, which she put in a juke box in a café and played music from 'The Thing'. Esme grinned as she watched the delight in Margaret's eyes at the loud music and other modern numbers. But Esme knew that it was in the classics that Margaret's knowledge was outstanding.

Esme lent Margaret a portable radio to keep her company in Tullaree and she carried it from room to room. The cats, which had not heard a radio before, fled outdoors when she first turned it on. Margaret mentioned it to Esme later and said she had promised the cats she would keep the sound down. Esme was by now not surprised at Margaret's devotion to animals – she had even seen her stop at the roadside and turn a beetle back on its legs.

Such was the relationship that was building up between the two women that Esme decided to keep a diary, relating their day-to-day experiences and what she had learned from Margaret about the history of Tarwin Lower. Although Margaret had rebuffed many who had shown an interest in getting their hands on Tullaree – including her own nephew – Esme wrote in her diary that Margaret suggested that it might be possible for the Livingstones to buy her out once the caveat had been lifted.

Sitting at the dining room table in their home, Esme put pen to paper, recording how her husband had shown no immediate interest in following up her suggestion: 'Stan, thinking of what he had spent at Middle Tarwin, thought the chances of buying the place were remote, but Margaret thought it the best thing to do if possible.'

It was a curious diary entry, given Margaret's earlier determination to cling on to Tullaree, come what may. But there appeared to be truth in it as the Livingstones continued to discuss the proposition until finally Stan,

Right: Decline of a beauty – Margaret walks across dry ground in 1950.

Below: Clem Carnaghan, Margaret's nephew – claims of underworld connections.

leaving Esme to milk the cows, drove Margaret to Melbourne for a meeting with Ross Grey Smith. The two men spent most of the afternoon discussing the pros and cons in Margaret's presence and the outcome was that Grey Smith agreed to sell the property to Stan.

Esme wrote: 'Margaret was very happy that night, but was always wondering if it would be true and repeatedly asked Stan not to give up. He would be dealing with a bad crowd, etc. We had no idea what this would all mean and result in. At this stage, Margaret signed for Stan to conduct her affairs…'

Word passed around the district and soon reached the ears of Clem Carnaghan.

The message came in a phone call from an acquaintance, a Mr Fravell, in Gippsland. 'Better get down here, Clem,' he said. 'Thought you should know Stan Livingstone's going about the district saying he's now got Power of Attorney from Miss Clement. He's offered £13,000 and it looks like the deal's going through. Looks like he's going to get Tullaree.'

Clem slammed the phone down. 'Those bastards have conned her!' he told his mother. 'How come she's been holding out all these years, not even allowing her own family to have any part of that place, and within a matter of months she agrees to let total strangers have it? They've brainwashed her, that's what those bastard's have done!'

Anna shook her head at the dramatic turn of events. 'When she mentioned those Livingstones to us before, I didn't think she was serious. I just can't understand why Margaret would turn on her family like this.'

'It's not a puzzle,' said Clem. 'They've forced her hand. Livingstone's got a bully boy reputation, don't forget.'

He'd already found out from inquiries in Gippsland that Stan Livingstone had never been a man to turn his back on opportunity. From the time he married in 1939, he and Esme had improved and resold two other properties and were renovating their third at Middle Tarwin. The couple met when Stan was sinking a tank on a property in the Riverina and Esme, then Esme Grubb from Traralgon, Victoria, was working as a private nurse in the district. After their marriage, when Stan was with the Allied Works, they had a flat in the Moonee Ponds suburb of Melbourne before moving to a house in the middle-class seaside district of Sandringham.

Stan, who had shown his prowess as a League footballer, was also to demonstrate his skills as a woodchopper and a shooter after moving to Gippsland. Following months of learning what was an unfamiliar sport, he became a top axeman and a regular winner at local woodchopping competitions.

From there, he went on to compete against the best in the land at the Royal Agricultural Show in Melbourne. He also had a reputation around the district as a 'hard man' of great strength and was said to be able to lift a full 44-gallon drum.

'I'm not going to take him on,' Clem told his worried mother as he prepared to speed down to Gippsland. 'But I'm bloody well going to find out the truth about what's been going on.'

As support, Clem asked a friend, Phil Ellis, a butcher, to travel to Gippsland with him.

'She's not capable of making decisions on her own,' he told Ellis as they drove. 'I ought to know. We had her in St Kilda for a few days and she would hardly talk to her own sister and it's not as if we've done anything to make her that way. My mother really helped her and her other sister along years ago so she owes us...she damn well owes us all right.'

The Tarwin River. Esme Livingstone, a woman with secrets, swam across it fully clothed and drunk.

Chapter 12.

~PERSUASION~

Clem Carnaghan and Phil Ellis arrived in the early evening at Goff Jongebloed's hotel in Tarwin Lower, a 15-minute drive from Tullaree, and booked two rooms for the night. Listening to the talk in the bar over a few beers, Clem realised that the Livingstones were well on the way to buying Margaret's home.

'We'll see about that,' he said to Ellis after hearing it yet again from one of the locals.

In the morning he and his companion found a relatively dry route across the paddocks to Tullaree and, entering quietly through the back door, tricking even the ever-alert Dingo, they walked down through the hallway and found Esme sitting with Margaret in the drawing room

'We've been expecting you,' said Esme. 'We heard that you'd come down from Melbourne.'

Clem glared at her. 'I'd like to see my aunt alone,' he said. But Mrs Livingstone shook her head, turning to Margaret to ask if she wanted her to leave.

'You can stay if you wish,' said Margaret. 'In fact, I would prefer it.'

'And anything you want to say to Margaret, you can say in front of me,' Esme told Clem.

He fixed his dark eyes on hers. 'I hear that you and your husband are trying to buy the property.'

She returned his glare with a soft smile. 'My husband is making all the arrangements. I'm just here to ensure that Margaret is cared for. She's been neglected for far too long.'

'And you're using her. What's this I hear about you offering £13,000 for the place? It's worth a damn sight more than that, and you know it.'

'As I told you, my husband is dealing with the negotiations. I'm more concerned about Margaret's welfare. If the arrangement goes through, Margaret will have a nice little home of her own that Stan will build here for her.'

'Yes, and you'll have her house and her land. Got yourself a nice little deal going, haven't you?'

'If you were offered a better price,' Ellis cut in, addressing Margaret, 'would you take it?'

'Whatever is offered to me would have to go to Ross Grey Smith because he's the one who bought the place years ago, even though it was illegal,' said Margaret. 'Whatever is offered to me is of no consequence. As soon as I lift the caveat, the place reverts entirely to Ross Grey Smith and he can take whatever he asks for.'

'Bloody disgraceful,' said Clem. 'So what are you going to get from the Livingstones? You lift that caveat and you won't be able to stay in Tullaree any more. You'll be giving the place away in exchange for what? Probably a shed in their bloody backyard.'

'I trust them,' said Margaret.

'But you can't call these people friends. You've only known them for six months, for God's sake!'

'I'm free to choose who I like as friends.'

'And neglect your own family at the same time!'

Clem exchanged a glance with Ellis, then said, more softly: 'Listen, Aunt Margaret. I've got an interested buyer who's willing to pay up to £18,000. Why don't you let him offer, say, £14,000 to Grey Smith and the buyer will give you the remaining £4,000. That will be enough to buy a nice little place in Melbourne closer to your sister and me.'

'I won't accept it,' Margaret immediately replied. 'But if you have someone, you should contact the solicitors.'

Esme Livingstone stood and walked over to Margaret, bending to touch her hand.

'I have to go – Stan was expecting me home before now. But don't be forced into anything, Margaret, not by anybody.'

When she had gone, Clem asked his aunt again why she was trusting the Livingstones in a way she had not trusted anyone for years.

'I'm quite capable of managing my own affairs. I wish you would stop interfering.'

'I'm interfering because I think you're selling out at a ridiculously low price. All the years you've been fighting to stay in Tullaree and now you're virtually walking away from it. Tell me, have you signed anything to the Livingstones yet?'

'No,' she replied firmly. 'Not yet.'

After Esme Livingstone arrived home and had prepared Stan's evening meal, she settled down to write in her diary how she had witnessed the angry scene:

'We heard the nephew and company were in the district. Stan sent me at 8am to see if Margaret was all right. At noon, when we thought they were not coming, I heard a voice shout harshly "Margaret!" It was the nephew and Ellis. They came into the lounge and ordered me out. I asked Margaret did she want me to go and she said "No, there is nothing you cannot say in front of Mrs Livingstone."

'I have never heard any two men talk such utter rot as they went on with and if Margaret left the room the nephew would say "She is eccentric – she has been all her life."

'I replied I was quite certain she was not. When I would not leave, he settled himself and said he would not leave until I went out and, looking significantly at Ellis, said, "We can't put you out forcibly." I replied "No, indeed you can't and I am expecting my husband shortly if I am not back." I was bluffing, of course, yet wishing I had arranged it. They tried, with Ellis doing most of the talking, to persuade Margaret from dealings with Stan and said they had a buyer from New South Wales who would give her more. When she asked his name, they would say they could not tell her. Naturally, Margaret was sensible enough to realise that this was no way to conduct business. Then Ellis said he supposed our offer was in order as long as Margaret lived on her interest. Margaret asked him then who he was and he replied "A friend of the family".'

A week later, Anna Carnaghan received a 'courtesy' phone call from the Public Solicitor's office. An appointment had been arranged, she was told, with Grey Smith, Miss Margaret Clement, Mr and Mrs Livingstone and Frank Moore, the Livingstones' solicitor. It was expected a settlement would be reached that morning.

Clem was out visiting a client of his radio repair business, so he did not hear the news. As it was, the arrangements were not concluded during the morning because Mr Moore had been held up on another matter. Arriving home at noon and hearing of the imminent settlement, Clem called the Public Solicitor's office and demanded an adjournment so that he and his mother could be represented.

He left his mother alone while he went about his business in the city. At 3.30pm that day there was a ring at the door of the flat and on answering Anna was surprised to find Esme there with Margaret. She guessed that Stan would not be far away.

'We've come to sort this out once and for all,' said Esme. 'Margaret says you are interfering with her wishes. You've caused a delay by asking for an adjournment and this has added to her distress.'

Anna glared at the woman. 'I have no wish to speak to either you or your husband. Come in Margaret.' She took her older sister's hand and drew her in through the door, closing it in the Esme's face.

Leading Margaret to a sofa, she asked: 'Why are you still doing this? Let me repeat again, Margaret. We are your family. Your only close relatives. Why are you allowing these strangers to take over your life?'

There was an impatient ringing of the doorbell. Anna decided she'd had enough. She went to answer the door to tell Esme to clear off once and for all – but the moment she opened it she was pushed aside and Stan, followed by Esme, stormed into the flat.

'Look Anna,' said Esme, suddenly familiar: 'We're doing everything we can to help your aunt. She's an old lady who has been left dangling. When your sister Jeanie died it was I who had sent you a telegram informing you of her death.'

'I received no such telegram,' said Anna. 'I heard the news from our other relatives. There was nothing from you.'

'Believe what you like, but the fact is that Margaret is now assured of a happy future in her last years. We're going to build a small house for her when we take over Tullaree and she'll also be receiving £4,000 from the sale.'

'Oh yes, I'm sure of that,' said Anna, sarcasm heavy in her response. 'You'd do it up, sell it for a vast profit, and Margaret would be turfed out on her ear.'

As the argument continued, Clem returned and was stunned to find the Livingstones and his aunt in the living room.

It was Margaret who spoke first: 'Why are you going about the district telling people I am mad?' she asked her nephew.

'What the hell are you talking about?' he demanded. 'But now you've raised it, I'd say that the way you've been behaving in recent weeks would lead to a lot of people thinking that was true.'

'Tell me this,' cut in Stan. 'Who was the fellow you brought down to Gippsland recently? A stand-over man to scare the hell out of the old lady? Was that the purpose?'

'Just watch your mouth – and get out of my flat!'

But the Livingstones remained standing. Stan's frame seemed to dwarf the room. 'We've heard from Margaret what you've been doing,' he said. 'You've been stealing things from her home, getting all the good stuff out of there, coming in to take what you can before she dies.'

Clem clenched his fists. 'If you're going to make accusations like that, you'd better go to the police with them. Then we'll find out the truth of the matter. Let's get this sorted now. Come on, if you're so bloody sure of yourself, let's get right down to St Kilda police station.'

But Stan grabbed Margaret's arm. 'Let's go, Margaret. The air in here smells.'

As the Livingstones begun hustling Margaret towards the door, Clem pushed by them, blocking the way.

'Get out of my way, you scrawny rat!' said Stan – and with a sudden and powerful thrust of his fist, he struck Clem in the face, knocking him to the ground. The Livingstones and Margaret were out through the door in a flash.

Clem called the police. He wanted the Livingstones charged with intrusion and assault. Then he followed up his call by driving to the police station and making a statement. It so happened that the duty officer was Clem's friend, Constable Stephenson, who returned to the flat with a colleague to examine the hallway. There were blood specks on the floor.

'It appears you have grounds for a complaint, Clem,' Margaret's nephew was told. 'We'll need to speak to the other side, of course, but you might wish to take this further.'

Clem took no further action but a week after the incident, accompanied by Phil Ellis and a jeweller friend, Alexander Blitz, he drove to Gippsland, calling at Wonthaggi to report to the local policeman there, Constable Stock, that he was going to Tullaree to take items of value from the house for protection because things were being stolen. When the three men reached Tullaree Margaret was absent but, Clem reported later, nearly everything of value had already gone. They removed a few things belonging to the family and returned to Melbourne.

As Anna looked at the silver picture frames and the tainted candlesticks that Clem had brought back, tears came to her eyes. 'I remember these from so long ago. You were right to bring these back, Clem. They belonged to all of us. They weren't just Margaret's. And if you'd left them there, how long do you think it would be before they disappeared?'

'We shouldn't give up on her,' said Clem. 'While the sale is still on hold, we should do all we can to keep the place in the family. We cannot allow the Livingstones to have it. You can see the kind of people they are. They've snuck into her life and are digging away, digging away at her all the time until they get Tullaree. That's going to happen at any moment now. They're just waiting to sign on the dotted line. We should go back down there again. Have one more go at her.'

A few days later Clem and his mother, along with Alexander Blitz, waded through the swamp and found Margaret home alone. They had brought blankets, for they told her they intended to stay for a night or two. Margaret had little choice but to accept their enforced visit. For the next two days the three of them did all they could to persuade Margaret to turn her back on the Livingstones, who, they were glad to realise, had not turned up.

'I trust them,' Margaret told her visitors time and again. But they wondered if she really meant it. There was no conviction in her voice, unlike earlier occasions when she had spoken of them. Due to a shortage of useable beds, Blitz had to sleep in a hammock stretched across one of the rooms. On the second morning he was warned by Margaret not to jump down too heavily when he woke up. When he asked why, she replied: 'Because the floorboards are rotting and right under where you're sleeping are where my seven pet snakes sleep.'

Blitz, however, was to hit back at Margaret's own sleeping habits later, for in a statement he made for a lawyer he recalled that Anna had made a bed up for Margaret but the following morning he saw the old lady sleeping in her clothes on a couch in the bedroom, the bed unused. The Carnaghans, he said, tried to persuade her to go and live with them in St Kilda, but Margaret's reply was: 'I cannot leave my cats.'

Clem, his mother and Blitz eventually decided they were wasting their time. They agreed they might have to try a different tactic, but none immediately came to mind. Meanwhile Goode, the Bourke Street solicitor who had waded through the swamp to make an offer to Margaret several months earlier, had heard nothing from the old lady so he asked his managing clerk, Eric Benson, to call at the Public Solicitor's office to find out what was happening with the Tullaree property. Benson was told that a contract of sale had been entered into between Ross Grey Smith and Stanley Livingstone and was now awaiting consent by the Minister for Lands. Informed of this development, Goode telephoned Clem Carnaghan.

'I'm curious,' he said. 'Are the Livingstones close friends of Miss Clement?'

'They are not, although they claim to be,' Clem replied. 'They're acquaintances who've secured her confidence and I couldn't wish a worse fate upon her. They've taken her to live with them on and off and they're poisoning her mind against her relatives. My mother and I paid for the funeral of Jeanie and we contributed to both their upkeep for a number of years and yet we can no longer see Margaret except in the presence of the Livingstones.'

Clem told Goode that his own inquiries had established that the Livingstones had agreed to buy the property from Grey Smith for £12,500 and the action that Margaret had been trying to get to court – on the grounds that Grey Smith had acquired it illegally – was to be discontinued.

'How much will Miss Clement be getting personally out of the contract?' asked Goode.

'From what I can find out,' said Clem, 'it's around £2,500, which is her pay-off for wiping her hands of the property. The Livingstones say she'll be getting £4,000 but I don't believe a word of it.'

'Well, what I'll do,' said Goode, 'is make an offer of £17,000 for the place and I'll get a home built for Miss Clement there, too.'

Clem was surprised. This was close to the £18,000 he had once told his aunt a buyer in New South Wales was willing to pay. He had later revealed to friends that the buyer had not existed, yet now here was a genuine offer.

Taking a chance that the Livingstones would not be around, he travelled once again to Tullaree and, finding Margaret alone again, told her of the offer by the solicitor she had once met. Once more he left Tullaree frustrated without a commitment from his aunt.

There was further bad news shortly after his arrival in Melbourne. He was informed by the Public Solicitor's office that at 10am on Friday, 19 January 1951, an attempt would be made by Stanley Livingstone and Ross Grey Smith to push the settlement through once and for all and as part of the sale agreement, Margaret would have a small house built for her on the Tullaree land.

Her grip on her beloved Tullaree was finally about to end. And Margaret, despite succumbing to the new friendship and the persuasions that had come with it, was beginning to worry. How she wished she could have the old days back…

Chapter 13.

~PURSUIT~

Flames licked the midnight sky. Farmers, silhouetted against the glow, hacked into the scrub in a desperate attempt to make a firebreak to keep the bush fire from the Middle Tarwin Hall.

The phone rang at the Livingstone house.

'Stan, get down here right away! We need all the manpower we can get.'

'I'm on the way,' said Stan Livingstone. When he climbed into the Land Rover he was not alone – his wife, still in her dressing gown, came with him and so did Margaret Clement, who was staying at their house. Margaret, they had agreed, would never be left alone whether she was with them at their home or in Tullaree. They did not trust her nephew or his associates.

Three others were, by chance, heading towards Middle Tarwin that night. Against a backdrop of crackling flames and thick smoke a dark car sped along the narrow road. At the wheel was Clem Carnaghan and with him were his friend Alexander Blitz, the jeweller, and a nurse acquaintance, Mrs Anne McCourt, from North Melbourne.

Unaware of the drama of the bushfire, Clem had asked Mrs McCourt to travel with him to Gippsland to look at Margaret because he was concerned she was not well, physically and mentally. He hoped to finally persuade her to return to St Kilda with him, one way or another. He thought, too, he might be able to confuse her with the presence of Mrs McCourt, cause her to believe that the visitor was a niece, or...he glanced momentarily at the medical bag that Mrs McCourt clutched on her lap.

As the car headed towards the flames, for Clem was stunned to see such drama being played out when he expected the night to be calm and still, he saw, as he approached the local community hall, the Livingstones' Land Rover parked at the roadside among other vehicles. In his headlights, he could make out Esme Livingstone and Margaret, who were sitting inside waiting for Stan to return from helping fight the fire. Clem pulled up just ahead.

Esme Livingstone watched as the doors of the other car opened and saw Blitz walking towards her. He put his face through the open side window.

'I see there's a fire on,' he said.

'Yes,' Esme replied, 'and if you and your friends there have any conscience you should be helping.'

As the tense conversation continued, Esme was to claim later, Clem Carnaghan crept up behind the Land Rover, let the tyres down and threw the valves away. Her concern was to get Margaret out of the vehicle and across to the community hall where there would be safety in numbers. She helped Margaret down and began leading her to the men who were working hoses and throwing buckets of water on the flames consuming the nearby scrub. She found her husband.

'Carnaghan's here,' she said. 'I think he's looking for trouble.'

'I can clock him, or I can get the police....' After a moment's hesitation he said: 'I'll get the police.' He sent one of the men off for the local constable, deciding to remain with his wife and Margaret.

Meanwhile Mrs McCourt walked across to the hall and stood close to Esme and Margaret. When she believed that Esme was distracted, she took Margaret's arm. 'Come over with me to the other car,' she said, 'there's someone who wants to see you.'

But Esme had heard and, glancing around to see Clem waiting nearby, said angrily: 'She's not going anywhere near that scoundrel!'

Margaret, confused in the darkness and by the events surrounding her, stared at Mrs McCourt for a moment, then said: 'Do I know you? You're Eileen, aren't you?'

Esme, also mistakingly believing that Mrs McCourt was Eileen Glenny, Margaret's Ballarat niece, asked if she was indeed the relation.

There was a moment's hesitation. Then Mrs McCourt replied: 'Yes.'

Hours later, in the early hours of the morning, Esme Livingstone returned to her diary to record what she claimed were the dramatic events of the previous night. She told of Mrs McCourt's claim that she was Eileen Glenny, then continued in her diary:

'I answered that Margaret had often spoken of her and that I was a nurse also and that we had Margaret with us and she would be pleased to see her.

'While I said this, the woman disappeared to the car. They drove down the road and waited. Our personal impression is that that night they came to get Margaret at Tullaree, making out her sister at Ballarat was ill and asking her to go. This woman very slightly resembled Eileen's build and as Margaret had only seen her about three times, coming at midnight like that in dim light she could have mistaken her.'

Believing it was important to record all events concerning Clem Carnaghan and Margaret, Esme went on to describe how Constable Ernie Collins had turned up, questioned Clem Carnaghan and his companions and then 'sent them on their way to Leongatha.' The firefighters helped her and her husband fix the flat tyres and then, while they were discussing the events of the evening at the roadside 'the nephew's car sidled past on the way to Tarwin Lower.'

The drama of the night was far from over. The local farmers, who had sided with the Livingstones, decided to take matters into their own hands. Esme wrote:

'The farmers got in their cars and chased him, converging and making him stop. Margaret, too, had requested that we let her see this woman. Margaret climbed out of the car and I took her round to where the woman was, who said: "Hello Aunty, don't you know me? Oh, Aunty is getting very old."

'I said "Are you insinuating Margaret is not in her senses?" So we asked her to get out of the car and she replied "Not again". Margaret studied her and she walked away saying "No, you are not Eileen." Then she went to the side the nephew was on and said "I'll thank you to keep out of my affairs." Eileen calls her by her Christian name and is single. This woman had a wedding ring. Next morning Margaret rang Ballarat and spoke to Eileen, who said she had never been away.'

But Esme was not the only one to ensure the events of that night were put on record. Clem went to a solicitor and made a statement, although he made no reference to the presence of Mrs McCourt. But he was eager to record his growing suspicions and concerns about an apparent friendship between Stan Livingstone and the local police officer, Ernie Collins. It was nothing more than a suspicion, but he wanted it officially recorded.

He began by describing how, after seeing the Livingstones' vehicle parked at the roadside, Blitz walked across to it and saw that Margaret was inside.

'Mrs Livingstone grabbed Miss Clement out of the car and took her over to the hall and we could not see her so we went down the road and waited to see if they would go back to Tullaree. After about half an hour Constable Collins came along and pulled up. He wanted to know what I was doing in the district. I told him that was my affair. He said two tyres had been let down. I said I knew nothing about it.

'He ordered me out of the district. I told him I would not go. He ordered Mr Blitz out of the car. I told Mr Blitz not to get out of the car. Collins demanded his name and address. I told Mr Blitz not to give it. He asked my name and address. I told him there was no need for that because he rang us up to ask us about paying for the funeral of Jeanie Swanson Clement [suggesting that the officer already knew who Clement Carnaghan was].

'I asked him what interest he had in the Livingstones and the property as well. He did not answer. I also asked him where most of the stuff had gone from Tullaree. He said he did not know. I told him I would try and find out where it had gone and also what connection he had with the Livingstones. He then hopped into his car and went off.

'We pulled into the side of the road and waited about a quarter of an hour. Later two cars went up and down looking for us. We waited there about an hour and then went back to the hall to see if there was anyone about. As we got near the hall three or four cars spread across the road with their doors open. One was Livingstone's car. I speeded up to go through. There was one very narrow gap. They closed the door and I just got through.

'They hopped into the cars and chased us. I slowed down and let one pass. He tried to stop me and run me off the road. I speeded up and went past him and ran him off to the side of the road. They tried to stop me for about six or seven miles going on towards Inverloch and then my car broke down.

'I said to Mr Blitz: "It looks as if they are going to try and belt us up."

'They pulled up alongside me and got out of their cars. I did not know any of them except the Livingstones. They rushed at us and were going to pull us out of the car. I said "If you are going to belt us up it is not going to do you any good."

Tullaree becomes search headquarters as volunteers and police look for 'The Lady of the Swamp'.

'I spoke to three of them and asked them did they know what was going on down there. I said did they know we had kept my aunty for many years and that the Livingstones were trying to buy the place for next to nothing?

'Mrs Livingstone said to her husband "I think we had better go."

'The two men seemed rather surprised and said they knew nothing about it. They went off after that.'

Shortly after the incident, Clem received a letter from Margaret's solicitors, warning him she had 'no intention of sustaining your molestations further.' She resented his repeated visits to her home and his threatening attitude. He had removed articles from Tullaree and if he returned he would be treated as a trespasser. And his attempt 'to impose upon your Aunt by obtaining the services of a woman to impersonate Miss Eileen Glenny of Ballarat, a niece of your Aunt, was particular despicable. We have already ascertained that Miss Glenny was never absent from Ballarat on that date.'

Clem was appalled by the tone of the letter and what he told friends were unsubstantiated and unfair claims. The deal with the Livingstones was due to go through on 30 March 1951. The Carnaghans had less than a week to stop the sale. On Easter Monday, 26 March, Anna and Clem, accompanied by Phil Ellis, ignoring the warning letter to 'stay away', drove to Tullaree for one last attempt at persuading Margaret to change her mind about dropping the court action against Grey Smith and therefore allowing the Livingstones to handle her affairs and take over the title.

The swamp water lapped at the three visitors as they made their way to the house, hoping Margaret would be there. She was. And so were the Livingstones. Stan stood on the verandah watching them approach, punching a fist into his hand. Dingo was barking at them.

'We're not here to make trouble,' Clem called. 'This is a discussion, not a fight.'

The bigger man stepped back and the group gathered in the musty sitting room. It was a warm day, but a chill hung in the room, causing Anna to shiver. Margaret, in a hand-me-down sweater given to her by Esme, appeared not to feel the cold.

'We'll be settling in four days time,' said Stan. 'And then you'll be out of all of our lives, thank God.'

'Well, I'll fight you all the way – legally,' said Clem.

But he failed to stop the settlement. After a short delay Stanley Russell Livingstone became the official proprietor of Tullaree on July 12, 1951.

Five months earlier, on 1 February 1951, Margaret had drawn up a new will, cancelling out the one she had made in 1925 and which gave Clem benefits from her estate. The only beneficiaries now were three nieces – the children of Margaret's older sister Flora.

Clem was out in the cold. Defeated and frustrated, the radio mechanic and his ageing mother remained in their dingy St Kilda flat, aware that as each day went by the Livingstones had begun renovating Tullaree with the intention of turning it back into a valuable property.

Down on the land, Stan worked away at clearing the drains in the Tullaree region, a job he was doing under contract for the Tarwin River Improvement Trust. But it was for his own benefit too, for the work would help to drain the swamp from his newly acquired property. He and his wife closed down their Middle Tarwin home temporarily and lived in a hut on the Tullaree land while Margaret continued to sleep in the mansion's living room.

The district was alive with chatter about the coup they had pulled off – paying £13,000 for the property, plus agreeing to give £3,000 to Margaret personally, which had been paid into a trust account for her.

In addition to clearing the drains, Stan started work on a small weatherboard four-room house, near the old mansion, where Margaret could live in comfort – particularly during the cruel winter months. It would be her home while they were carrying out renovations to the actual Tullaree building, after which she could live in there with them.

Occasionally Stan and Esme travelled to Meeniyan, a few miles away, where their presence was greeted with mixed reactions. On one visit, Stan became involved in a row with John Buckley, who believed Margaret had been robbed. The verbal stoush turned to blows – and Buckley ended up knocked out cold on the pavement, having been felled by a sledgehammer of a punch from which it took him more than half an hour to gain consciousness.

Esme realised that she would have to keep her diary up to date, for while the controversy over their purchase of Tullaree raged on, she believed it was necessary to maintain a record of all that happened – at least, as she saw it.

All was quiet after that ugly incident in Meeniyan, she noted 'while the dragline worked on the drains and we lived in our hut, closing our attractive new Middle Tarwin home. Margaret came to the hut often and in the Land Rover while I served tea to the boys and State Rivers men, etc., and she thoroughly enjoyed it all.'

Continuing her kindness to Margaret, Esme took her to the cinema and to see the Jubilee Train, a visit followed up by an evening at the Jubilee Concert.

'Margaret admires Stan tremendously,' she told friends. 'She's always saying "He looks like a real Scotsman and the Scots are the best fighters."' Margaret had told Stan that her father came from Scotland and he had fought from virtually nothing to become one of the wealthiest men in Australia.

Esme noted in her diary how much Margaret loved poetry and even made some up as she walked along the road. She even showed it, shyly, to Esme one day and the younger woman thought it was 'really good'. Esme wrote how she cut Margaret's hair and did most things to help her. The old lady had been delighted to receive a cheque book, now that she had money from the house sale, and she had an enjoyable day out shopping for new clothes with Esme.

The swamp waters were dropping, a few inches only, but it was a good sign, as the drainage work continued. Margaret was told that it would probably be a year before Tullaree even started to look better but she should not be concerned – at the end of all the work she would be able to live in surroundings that were similar to those she had enjoyed decades before.

And so the routine continued, with Margaret insisting on spending most of her time at Tullaree, still a dark, damp, and, for those who had no emotional ties to it, miserable edifice. She told the Livingstones that she could not simply walk out of the house after so many years, would not walk out, but she was happy that its new owners had plans to restore it to its former beauty.

But the longer she remained in the months after the sale, the more defiant she became. Doubts about the change that was coming began to overwhelm her; it was a change that was being introduced by strangers. She believed she would rather live in the ruins of what had once been, rather than in a new environment that would be only a copy of past glory.

Esme tried to persuade Margaret to wear the new clothes she offered her, but Margaret, increasingly determined to cling to the past, defiantly insisted on wearing her old black coat with the fur collar. The smells that clung to Tullaree, too, were of comfort to her. Sitting in the old kitchen with Dingo and the cats, swamped in memories, brought her more joy than listening to the radio in the Livingstones' place.

On a cold day in May 1952, Margaret meandered as usual through the once-magnificent Tullaree to the kitchen. She was not expecting any visitors. The Livingstones were busy working on another part of the property and, of course, the days when carriages had clattered up the driveway had long since gone. But she still remembered them. Flashes of those extraordinary days returned from time to time, bringing a smile to the old lady's lips.

On this day, she seemed to feel the chill more as the wind swept through broken window panes that had yet to be replaced by the Livingstones. It had been raining hard for the past week and it seemed to her that the water had risen again. She looked at the pile of legal papers on the table. She was thankful that everything had been finished. She glanced at the document on the top of the stack. It had been signed and that was that. The rows were over with. Now she could enjoy her memories in peace.

Margaret sat for a while as images of the past flashed before her. She was carried right back to her school days and coming home to Prospect, further along the coast, in the pony and trap and seeing big jolly pa on the verandah smelling of whisky and tobacco. There were those evenings when, with ringlets in her hair, she had sat in a long white dress and played the piano for her parents' guests. And then there was Fulham Park, William's place, which held mementos of her travels abroad and the sound of laughter on their return. And Peter…she remembered him with a touch of sadness and the way he had ended his life. But there had been happy times when he lived with her and Jeanie and managed the farm. She could picture it now…Peter sitting with the two of them at the table that gleamed with its silver and crystal while they engaged in spirited conversation. How far away it all seemed. Had it really existed? But of course it had. There were still a few things in Tullaree that were evidence of that.

It was during that stormy afternoon in the autumn of 1952 that she heard Dingo barking furiously from somewhere out the front. She went out and called him in, but could not determine what he had been barking at.

Later that night, as she slept on the couch, she woke to what she thought had been a bark – and was that a splash? – but then there had been silence. Perhaps the sound had been a shriek of laughter from a dreamy flashback of an evening long ago.

It was only when she found Dingo dying on the verandah in the early morning light, a pool of blood around his head, that she realised her fertile imagination had not played tricks. Staring in horror at the clean, straight wound across his throat she knew that no animal had caused it.

Margaret buried Dingo when life finally left him, then walked silently back to the house.

'Now,' she said sadly, 'it is just me and the cats.'

Chapter 14.

~VANISHED~

Stan Livingstone ran into the tiny Meeniyan police station in the late afternoon of Saturday, 24 May 1952. He asked for Constable Ernie Collins, but was told by a member of his family, who lived in the police house, that the officer was on leave.

Stan urgently contacted Leongatha police station. He told First Constable Arthur Bentley: 'Margaret Clement, the old lady who lives at Tullaree, is missing. She's not at home. We haven't been to the place for a few days but when we called yesterday she wasn't around and she's not there today. Something's wrong.'

The policeman filled out Margaret's description on a blue form: 'Date of birth, 1880 (although this was a year out); height 5ft 7ins; hair, dark brown; eyes, grey; complexion, olive; build, medium. Date last seen, 21.5.52.' Margaret's hair colour and her size – for she was just a slip of a woman these days – were inaccurate, but it did not matter. Everyone in the district knew what she looked like.

Constable Bentley realised the necessity to get a search mounted right away and tried to reach his senior officers. But he met a series of frustrations that were to delay the start of the hunt. First, he tried to reach his police colleague Paddy O'Keefe at Korumburra, 10 miles to the north-west – to learn that he was also on holiday and no-one had taken over.

Next, Constable Bentley telephoned Warragul, almost 20 miles away, to be told that Inspector Sammy Williams had retired and a replacement officer had yet to be appointed. Finally, the Leongatha policeman managed to contact an officer, Inspector Albert Dendle, in the Morwell police district, 50 miles from Tarwin Lower. It was now Sunday evening and the 53-year-old inspector, with years of experience of police search and rescue work, realised it was too late in the day to send men out into the soggy wintry wastelands of Gippsland. But he organised a full search for the next morning, Monday, 26 May.

Fire brigade equipment was requisitioned and the district's farmers were contacted asking for their assistance to look for Margaret. Constable Ernie Collins was also reached and he promised to return to Gippsland to help in the search for the old lady.

At first light, at the break of a bitterly cold and overcast morning that was five days before the official start of winter, nearly 100 men, dressed in long mackintoshes, scarves and gloves spread out into the swamp, grimacing at the chill that cut through their bodies. Some had turned up in Wellington boots in a futile attempt to keep their feet dry, but the water poured in over the top and made their progress more difficult than it need have been.

For miles around, the water lay from ankle depth to breast high. The flooding was worse than it had been for years, which puzzled several farmers, for was not Stan working to clear the drains to avoid this problem? Men tripped on stunted tufts of grass and their boots sank into the mud. Two were almost swept away by a roaring undercurrent in one of the ditches and had to be hauled to safety as they yelled out. As the morning proceeded, an icy wind howled from Anderson's Inlet at gale force, carrying bursts of rain. Some of the searchers were on horseback, the animals fighting for unseen footholds. One horse became stuck in the mud and half a dozen men were needed to pull it out.

Inspector Dendle was brought partly through the swamp on a sledge pulled by a tractor. He was accompanied by a group of farmers' wives who, on entering the homestead, set up as the search headquarters, lit fires in several rooms, aware that soon the men would need the warmth. The cats fled, seeking dark corners away from the crowd.

'This,' the experienced Dendle admitted to a group of shivering volunteers, 'is the hardest search in the worst country I have ever known.'

Throughout the day, the swamp waters rose as the rain hammered down and the cold intensified. No-one had experienced anything so bad. There wasn't a man who avoided a thorough ducking as he tripped and plunged forward into the water. Police called in Horrie Vaughan, a veteran bushman, and Charlie Williams, a black tracker, who created a surreal image as he rode in through the lashing rain on a white horse. The Aborigine took one look at the watery surroundings and shook his head.

'A bloodhound couldn't find anybody in this. There aren't any tracks. Where am I supposed to start?'

Clem Carnaghan, summoned by phone by the police, arrived that afternoon, a tractor driven by Constable Dalman of Foster taking him as far as possible before he had to start wading for more than half a mile to the homestead. Not that he didn't know the route through the swamp. He looked around the house, taking note of what he saw in each room. Then he became the first man to use a word which had been on many of the searchers' minds, but which no-one had dared use.

'Murdered,' he said to Inspector Dendle. 'I'm sure my aunt has been murdered.'

'What makes you think that, Mr Carnaghan?'

'Aunt Margaret wasn't the sort of woman to walk out to the store or anywhere without leaving food around for the cats. Nothing's been left out. And if she'd fallen over in the swamp you'd have found her by now. If she'd fallen over in the road, you'd have found her.

Horses flounder in the swamp. One takes six men and a tractor to pull out.

She wouldn't have just got lost in the swamp, either. She knew it like the back of her hand. Bloody hell, she'd been walking in and out through it for donkey's years.'

'I'll bear in mind what you've told me, Mr Carnaghan,' said the police officer.

Stan Livingstone stood at the entrance to Tullaree wearing a trilby hat, hands thrust into the pockets of his mackintosh. He watched as rain lashed the searchers and heard some of the farmers say they would have to pull out soon to move their cattle to higher ground. No-one wanted a repeat of the livestock losses they'd heard about, or personally experienced, during the 1934 floods. Already on the Tullaree property many cattle were standing up to their necks in water.

Inside, Esme, wearing a tartan dress, dried searchers' socks in front of the ornate fireplace. On a bed she had laid a fresh blanket, a nightdress and a hot water bottle in case Margaret was found. Someone had brought in a stretcher as a safeguard should she need to be carried out and taken to hospital. If she was found alive.

Nearly 100 men, dressed in long raincoats, scarves and gloves, spread out into the swamp, grimacing at the chill that cut through their bodies..

Men with sticks prodded the swamp water or poked into the scrub on the firmer ground of the Tullaree property. The trees seemed to be leaking water as drops of rain ran down their branches. Other men threw grappling irons into wells – unused for decades – and another iron was pulled by tractor through the water, hooking up nothing more than bracken.

At the end of the first day's fruitless search, a tired group of searchers lay down on the damp floors of the decayed mansion and the women fed them steaming tea and soup. Most had to stay in their wet clothes because there was nothing else for them to wear. Paddy Brennocks, who knew the swamp well, sat on a Chinese black mahogany chest in his gum boots, shaking his head as he studied a plan of the district.

'If we haven't found her today, we'll never find her,' he said. 'There was no reason for her to stray from her regular routes in and out.'

Inspector Dendle, sipping a mug of tea, had a mind full of theories. But he kept them to himself.

'Quite honestly,' he told the men, 'I don't know what angle we're looking at. It's certainly a mysterious affair. And of course, we can't rule out foul play.'

The searchers themselves came forward with a number of suggestions: perhaps the old lady had gone to stay with friends and hadn't told anybody she was going; she could have had a heart attack and fallen into the water and it was just bad luck they hadn't found her yet; grieving for her sister and Dingo, she had committed suicide out in the bush; she had been murdered and her body concealed somewhere else.

'Could be, could be,' said Inspector Dendle as each theory was put forward. 'But in the meantime, we don't give up. We have to assume that Miss Clement is still alive somewhere and the faster we act the better chance she has of survival.'

The following day, reporters from Melbourne converged on the search area. Barney Porter, who had interviewed Margaret two years earlier following the death of Jeanie, waded through the bog and found Stan and Esme Livingstone among the searchers.

'Doesn't look good for the old lady, Mr Livingstone,' he said.

'Poor Margaret,' said the new owner of Tullaree. 'It's terrible to think something may have happened to her just when my wife Esme and I had planned to make her declining years happy.'

'When was the last time you saw her?'

Stan glanced at his wife for confirmation. 'I called in last Thursday to invite her down for a meal and tell her my wife wanted to go shopping with her on the following Monday, yesterday. She was her usual cheery self and I went back to my wife, looking forward to seeing her.

'The following day Lal Lester, who works for me, took her her supplies and when I went around on Saturday to see her the supplies had not been opened and there was no answer to my call. Margaret was not there when I went through the house. The stick she always took with her when she went through the swamp was standing by the door of her room. Her bed was made and had not been slept in. There was no trace of her about the place.'

'No signs to indicate what had happened to her?'

'She was most methodical in her habits and there was not a clue as to where she had gone. She had not come to our place as she had promised and my wife and I went looking for her without finding any trace of her. The next day we notified the police and we have been looking for her ever since, but without success.'

Barney Porter then spoke to Esme. He wanted to hear her impressions of the missing woman.

'She seemed so forlorn and lonely,' said Esme as she warmed her hands on the fire. 'Such a pathetic figure that I could not help asking her if there was anything I could do. She was brusque, but nice about it. She could get along all right by herself, she said. But I could not help but think of her living alone in that deserted old house and I called to see her. Ultimately we became friends. Slowly, but by degrees, she seemed to come out of herself.'

'She's always been regarded as a bit of a recluse,' said the reporter. 'Would you say that was right?'

'She was a lovely person with a keen interest in life and people that had been subdued over the years. She began to take a fresh interest in things. She came shopping with me. And as the months went on she went further afield to Leongatha and Wonthaggi and even down to Cowes. She talked about books and music and let me put a wireless in for her, though she had refused to have one while her sister was alive. Margaret was a keen reader and interested in music. She even visited our house for meals and she loved to sit back and listen while Stan and I played for her the favourite songs that she loved so well.'

'How long have you known her?' Porter asked.

'It was 18 months ago when we first met her and my husband got a contract to drain the swamps around Tullaree. He brought in a dragline and started to clean up Fish Creek, which had been silted over the last 40 years. Stan and I lived in this little portable shack that moved with the dragline and Margaret used to come and have meals with us.'

Porter, hands thrust into his pockets and wishing that he'd brought gloves, looked out across the grey swamp. 'Do you think she's out there?' he asked.

Esme shook her head. 'You couldn't lose her in that swamp. She knew every square yard of it, no matter whether the water was inches or feet deep. She and her dog Dingo knew their way about. But Dingo was killed. His body was found months ago with his throat clawed and bitten. Still, Margaret used to go her way through the swamps alone, but unafraid.'

'What's been your involvement with her?'

'Stan negotiated with her to buy the property and she waived a caveat which had prevented the property being sold during her lifetime. We took over, but we decided that, as she loved the place so well, that she would have a decent place to live, and when her time came she would not pass away like her sister. So we started to build a home for her. It was almost finished and the plasterers were to come in next Sunday to line the walls. But it looks as if Margaret will never have that home.'

As she spoke those last words to the reporter, Esme buried her head in her hands.

John Maher, a reporter from the *Herald* newspaper also travelled to Tullaree with a photographer, Frank Tolra. It was to be a bizarre experience.

'Neither the bustle nor the fires lit in the ghostlike rooms of the old homestead could shut out the feeling of eeriness,' he wrote of his visit.

'Here was a mystery house that seemed even more mysterious now that its owner had vanished. The roads had vanished. Once, polished buggies used to rattle up to Tullaree when the gentry called, but now the swamp has conquered so much of its broad acres that when Tolra and I got to Tarwin Lower we were told we would never get through. Pouring rain had made the swampland more treacherous than ever. Some of the roads had vanished.

'We drove to within four miles of the homestead and were joined by local farmers. From that point it was "wade if you can". For the first mile, the water was only two feet deep and our first fear was of the swamp snakes we could see slithering in the water. Then the water got deeper and the scrub really rough with ducks and quail in the swamp and rabbits on the few patches of dry land. At one stage our guide, Paddy Brennocks, disappeared for an instant beneath the flood. We came to within a mile of the homestead but could see nothing but stunted bush trees and water. We came to a drain with a current that nearly swept one of the farmers away. And then, at last, dry land and our first view of Tullaree.'

The newspaper men noticed the doors which swung madly in the gale and the windows that were stuffed with mattresses in an effort to keep the storm out. The verandah, Maher saw, was rotten and inside antique furniture, once worth thousands of pounds, was now lying dust-covered and broken. Moths had destroyed a Belgian carpet. Fragments of delicate glass that had once gleamed on mantelpieces could be seen on the floor. Birds' nests and cobwebs were everywhere.

Photographer Tolra lifted his camera to take a picture of the interior of the house but one of the local women, distressed at the sad decline of Margaret Clement's home, decided his actions were intrusive and a photo was not in the public interest. She grabbed at the camera.

'When I tried to stop her,' Maher said later, 'she punched me in the eye and broke my glasses.' Someone told him later that it was Esme who had hit him.

Because the police had an open mind on the disappearance, it was decided to call in detectives from the Criminal Investigation Bureau at the main police station at Warragul, led by Senior Detective Bryan Traynor. Stories, rumours, came at them from all directions. Four men, Traynor was told, had tried to lure Miss Clement into a car six months earlier. And only three weeks before, three men in a big black English car had asked local farmer George Dunlop the way to the 'haunted house where the old swamp lady lives.' For there had been rumours around outside the district for years that Tullaree was haunted not by a person but the spirit of a woman who had lived there years before.

Detectives found the pile of letters that had been sent to Margaret following Jeanie's death. A number of people, they noted, were very interested in the property and they would all have to be interviewed. Someone pointed out three axes that were lying around the house, but the detectives quickly ruled them out of their enquiries. Rusted, they appeared to have been unused for years.

The officers spoke to Stan, asking him exactly when he had last seen the old lady. He recalled hearing his dogs barking during the previous Wednesday night while he and his wife were sleeping in their temporary home, the hut they were using while he was clearing the drains some distance from the mansion, but they thought little of it at the time.

There was one other person they were keen to talk to, following whispers by a number of the searchers. They approached Clem as he returned from a search of the swamp that he was convinced would yield nothing. What did he think had happened?

'Look, she just wouldn't walk out into the scrub and get lost,' he repeated. 'She knew the country too well. She could get in and out in all kinds of weather. She would know her way about even in the dark. My aunt was well educated and the last time I saw her she had all her reasoning powers. She wasn't the type to commit suicide – yes, I've heard that talk – and I'm sure she hasn't just been lost.'

The searchers agreed to keep looking until all hope was gone. So day after day, farmers, police and volunteers from around the district fought through the swamp and the surrounding scrub, calling her name, prodding the water with poles, cutting down branches. But all they heard in reply were the calls and movements of the other men.

Detectives were inundated with a number of false alarms. One day, they found a white, mud-stained woman's handkerchief in the bush about a quarter of a mile from the house, but it was later established it had not belonged to Margaret. It was too new. A blue plastic headscarf found floating in the water interested police until it was claimed by a local woman. Then tracker Charlie Williams and Senior Constable Lloyd of Bundoora found tracks on some dry land they believed Margaret had made in the last week, but they followed them right back to the house and established they were made by the old lady's boots – which were still in the mansion.

Police were puzzled by a Biblical quotation, clipped from a magazine and found in one of Margaret's old handbags sitting on a dressing table. The words read: 'I will rise above my enemies and fools; they will not defeat me.'

In another part of the house they found two other clippings: 'These things I have written unto you that believe in the name of the Son of God; that ye may know that ye have eternal life'; and 'These things I command you, that ye love one another.'

'Do you think she's been kidnapped?' Detective Traynor asked Clem.

'Who'd want to kidnap a defenceless old woman like Aunt Margaret?' he responded. 'What would be the motive of such a fantastic step? Everyone knows how hard it is to get through the swamp unencumbered. It would be a problem for anyone to get through there unobserved with Aunt Margaret.'

Traynor had a reason for asking that question. He'd been told by the police at St Kilda that Clem had once been suspected of kidnapping his aunt and taking her to his flat. He seemed to virtually confirm the claim with his comment that it would be difficult for anyone to get through the swamp with a kidnap victim like his aunt, as if he had already learned from past experience.

The policeman let the questioning go for the time being. In any case, the detective was being besieged by the press. Had the old lady been murdered, he was asked?

'Foul play is a possibility,' he answered with caution. 'But I do not say it is a probability.'

The search was so demanding that some of the men had to drop out after the first two days to take 24 hours rest. The remainder waded, plodded and continued to call Margaret's name. 'Cooo–eee!' echoed across the swamp, but no-one really expected her to reply with a similar call; the men were just anxious to try anything and everything to find the Lady of the Swamp.

Stan Livingstone brought in his bulldozer and cleared the scrub in the dry areas, policemen walking in front and behind looking for a body. Police boats put out to sea at Anderson's Inlet, the men's faces lashed by spray, while other boats went up and down the widened Tarwin River prodding the reeds with poles.

After the fourth day of a fruitless hunt, Inspector Dendle told a conference of searchers standing beside the little weatherboard that Stan had been building for Margaret: 'We must now look for the unexpected.'

By that, the cold searchers understood they had to look for Margaret or her body in places where she would not expect to be found had she just collapsed. The tired men spread out again, covering unlikely areas, even looking upwards into the branches of trees. Across the paddocks the roar of the surf could be heard in Venus Bay and the wind whipped up waves on the surface of the swamp.

There wasn't a man or woman who now believed Margaret Clement was still alive. Stan did not want to give up the search, however. Sitting on his bulldozer, he said: 'It doesn't make much difference now, but if her body is in there I'd like to get it out.'

Inspector Dendle called off the search in June 1952: 'We have no chance of finding the old lady dead or alive in this country at this time of the year. She never could have survived in the open all this time.'

On Friday, 30 May, police contacted every telephone switchboard within 30 miles of Tullaree asking for help in the call for volunteers for an intensified search. It was to result in hundreds flocking to the district, for the story had leaked out through local gossip about the gold that, in the previous century, ship's carpenter Martin Wyberg may have left behind. Bizarrely, casual searchers used the search for Margaret's body as an excuse to also look for possible hiding places for the gold.

Once again, the massive hunt turned up nothing and on Sunday, 1 June, the first day of winter, it was called off.

Inspector Dendle told the searchers: 'We have no chance of finding the old lady dead or alive in this country at this time of the year. She never could have survived in the open all this time. Nobody can suggest that the search has not been carried out to the utmost in the difficult circumstances and I thank you all for your efforts and the sacrifices you have made to us.'

While the search was on, detectives from Melbourne's homicide squad took a close look at the case of the missing swamp lady. They went through the records of complaints made by both Stan Livingstone and Clem Carnaghan about one another. Was there a motive for murder by either man? If anyone was a suspect it was Clem, for he had missed out on gaining anything from the property, whereas Stan had conducted his purchase legally through lawyers. But there was no evidence to charge Clem with anything more than jealousy and finally the team resolved that there was not enough suspicion against either man – or anyone else. However, the official conclusion was that Margaret Clement had not been the victim of foul play. But where was she? Or rather, after all this time, where was her body?

A few volunteers searched unofficially over the next six weeks but found no clues to her disappearance. She had vanished off the face of the earth. Police continued private enquiries in the district but they could gather no firm evidence to suggest the whereabouts of Margaret Clement. Gippsland and Melbourne buzzed with rumour ranging from Margaret dying accidentally to her being the victim of a terrible murder. And although the homicide team had declared Margaret had not been the victim of foul play, they did not close their files. Before they did that, they needed to find the missing woman, dead or alive.

Several weeks after Margaret's baffling disappearance, the Livingstones handed to police a number of letters they said they had received anonymously in the mail. They were handwritten in clear, bold type, one of which read: 'To you who are about to die. We have warned you before. We warn you again. Have you ever placed a wreath on a grave? Have you ever followed a funeral procession?'

This was followed by several hundred words of theological references dwelling on the theme of death and resurrection. Stan and Esme also claimed that two men had been following them during visits to Melbourne and Newmarket.

Was Clem Carnaghan behind the threats and the stalking? One thing was certain, as the radio mechanic's associates were to confirm later, he remained embittered that the Livingstones had taken over Tullaree. He cursed as he went about his repair business.

'I'm not finished yet,' he told his mother. 'We did more for Margaret and Jeanie than anybody, but we're the ones who have ended up with nothing. All we've got is fingers of accusations pointed at us over her disappearance.'

'There's nothing more that can be done,' said Anna. 'The Livingstones have Tullaree and that's the end of it. You tried everything possible to stop Margaret dealing with them and it didn't work. Leave it alone, Clem. It's finished.'

But Clem could not sleep. His hatred of the Livingstones grew. There had to be something he could do. He despised the thought of yet again turning to lawyers, to whom he had paid all his savings, but he believed it was the only course open to him.

One afternoon he returned to the flat to tell his mother that he had taken legal advice. It might be possible for him to continue the lawsuit Margaret and Jeanie had initiated in 1930 when they had contested the sale of the property to Ross Grey Smith while they were in desperate straits in the rented accommodation at Fish Creek. But he could only do that as a beneficiary of Margaret's will. He had been cut out of the last will she had drawn up but he was a beneficiary in the one she made in 1925. The lawyers' advice: prove that the 1951 will had been made while Margaret was not of sound mind and while she was under 'undue influence' by the Livingstones. That would invalidate the latest will leaving him free, as a beneficiary of the 1925 document, to continue the unheard court case.

He accepted that there was little point in contesting the will to gain anything of value from Margaret's personal possessions – her once-valuable collection of furniture and household effects had been priced by valuer David Cooke of Ballarat and found to be worth just £106.5s. To be added to that was the sum of 9s.1d found in the house. What had once been beautiful possessions had simply rotted away – or been stolen by unknown visitors or lost when Margaret and Jeanie moved out for a while.

Clem knew that Stan Livingstone had paid Margaret £3,000, but he had been advised there was no hope of getting his hands on that if he won the fight over the original will. What he had to hope for, he was told, was to get Margaret's old case to court as a beneficiary of the original will, for to win that outstanding action would put the property in the hands of himself and his Ballarat cousins. He would be more than happy to share it with them – anything would be better than seeing the Livingstones settling down happily ever after in Tullaree.

Before he could contest the new will, however, there was a problem: he had to prove that his aunt was dead. Or wait until she was legally declared dead in seven years time. By then, he feared, Tullaree would probably have been sold by the Livingstones and the whole affair would become a legal nightmare. Besides, Clem was not willing to wait that long. It was time to get a private eye working on the case of the missing woman.

On 29 June 1953, he signed an agreement at the Law Courts in Lonsdale Street, Melbourne, with Clarence Sullivan, a former policeman now operating as a private investigator, and Victor Houldcroft, a former investigative newspaper reporter. Their brief: find out what had happened to the old lady.

Eventually Houldcroft met Clem to report what Stan Livingstone had told him, for it was this conversation that the radio mechanic was most interested in.

'He'd agreed he gave your aunt £3,000 and promised her a home for life in return for removing the caveat she'd put on the place years ago – which I think you're well aware of,' Houldcroft told Clem. 'All that's past history now. But what you'll be interested to hear is the next bit – that 3,000 quid was being held by Margaret's solicitors, waiting for instructions to invest it in bonds, but then Livingstone has gone and borrowed back £2,700 of it to develop Tullaree.'

'What!' exclaimed Clem. 'He gives her 3,000 quid with one hand and then "borrows" it back to do the place up? I don't believe this! Pretty funny, isn't it, that he won't have to pay it back now that she's missing?'

'What he is doing, though, is paying interest into her account at Leongatha, even though she hasn't been found. He told me that she could have the £2,700 back in cash immediately if she turned up.'

Clem sat back shaking his head as Houldcroft continued. 'You won't like this next bit. Livingstone reckons that Tullaree's going to be worth £100,000 in five years after he's finished doing it up.'

'The bastard.'

Clem could not contain his anger. He stood up and slammed his fist on a table.

'But there's something funny, too, that I haven't been able to pin down,' the investigator continued. 'Esme Livingstone is a changed woman, according to some of the locals. There's been talk of an incident when she was seen in the Tarwin River.'

'What do you mean?'

'I don't know any more than that. People are talking about a guilty conscience. She had a row with Stan and jumped in the river when she was drunk.'

'She could have been taking a swim.'

'Not with her all her clothes on. People think she's hiding something, but who knows? Sorry Clem but I don't know any more than that.'

On 29 July 1954, Mr Justice Lowe, in Supreme Court Chambers, pronounced that Margaret Swanson Clement was legally dead. Clem's next step was to try to prove that her action in changing her latest will, cutting him out of the earlier arrangement to make him a beneficiary, was invalid because she had been under the influence of the Livingstones. The case was thrown out of court

So his hopes were dashed. He returned home, once more defeated and frustrated. It was the end.

'The only way this whole business could be revived would be with the discovery of Margaret's body,' a police officer told him. 'And if we find the body, it might tell us who did away with her, because that's what we all privately believe. Until then, you'll have to accept that everyone who knew her, everyone who had an interest in the property, everyone who was owed money, remains a suspect in one way or another. Her body will give us the answers, you can be sure of that. Just be patient, it's bound to turn up.'

After the judge's findings, Stan and Esme returned to Tullaree, where they toiled for many hours a day, gradually bringing the mansion back

to what it had been. The swamp waters were drained and the pastures found their lush green. In the mid-1960s Stan sold the transformed mansion for £96,500. With their vastly enhanced bank account, Stan and Esme moved to Cowes, on Phillip Island, south-east of Melbourne, from where Stan told friends that he and his wife were planning to set off on a long overseas trip. He was hoping to buy a trimaran in England and sail it back to Australia.

At his flat in St Kilda, Clem Carnaghan continued his radio business but not a day passed without him thinking of the affair that had consumed him. In Gippsland, people continued to talk about Tullaree and the old Lady of the Swamp. There were only two suspects in her disappearance, it was said – Stan Livingstone and Clem Carnaghan. They hated one another. Each had had an interest in the property. Each had tried to influence Margaret into reaching an arrangement with him. And the word about the district was that each man continued to accuse the other of murder.

On one occasion, in a conversation with a group of local people on Phillip Island, Stan testily answered the questions that were asked of him by those who wondered if he had any thoughts on what had happened to Margaret.

'My wife and I crammed a lifetime's work into nine years,' he declared. 'It was work that not even the pioneers had to face. In the beginning my wife had to wade through the swamp to milk cows and wring out her clothes before entering the house. At one stage I was £45,000 in the red so I had to keep on working. We sold out because we had no children to leave the property to.'

Stan and Esme did not proceed with their plan to sail back to Australia on a trimaran. Instead, after their long holiday, they voyaged on the S.S. *Simba* from Rotterdam to Melbourne and later they invested in a well-known grazing property, Murrundindi, at Yea, Victoria, set in a beautiful valley near the Yea and Goulburn Rivers.

But the spectre of the Lady of the Swamp, as Margaret – now more than ever part of local folklore – was being referred to would not go away. Sometimes bones would be found in the Tullaree district, raising speculation they were hers, but they always turned out to belong to animals.

Esme continued to record events in a black covered exercise book, pasting newspaper cuttings of the discoveries in her diary to add to her clippings about Margaret's disappearance. Many of the articles mentioned her and

Where was she? Or rather, after days of fruitless searching, where was her body?

her husband and it was not long after they moved into Murrundindi that the couple became the focus of local attention again, this time under circumstances that were almost tragic for themselves.

Travelling in their car in eastern Victoria, Stan was forced to swerve out of the path of a driver travelling towards them. The vehicles hit and Esme was thrown through the windscreen.

In a letter to a friend she wrote that 'Stan spent one night in Koo Wee Rup Hospital and I was taken not breathing to Prince Henry's by ambulance. Had five transfusions before they operated on left fractured femur from collarbone, injured hand and ankle, sixty five sutures to face, severed artery under chin, partially paralysed mouth. I looked and felt awful.'

The Livingstones recovered from their injuries and after spending some years at Yea purchased a huge property on Curtis Island, off the Queensland coast north of Gladstone. They planned to settle on the 3,240 hectare Spadeley property and breed Brahman cattle. But their idyllic lifestyle was to be interrupted. Just as Tullaree continued to consume Clem Carnaghan, it was not going to let the Livingstones go, either.

Chapter 15.

~SKELETON~

Shortly before midday on 7 November 1978, Carlos 'Charlie' de Merlo, an agricultural contractor, sat humming behind the controls of a grader as he ploughed into the grass tussocks near Venus Bay. He was clearing lot 367, a site for a new holiday house, working as he usually did, taking off the topsoil in layers and pushing it to one side and then taking the sand out from underneath.

Each layer was about 15 to 20 centimetres deep and about 2 metres wide, and although it was monotonous work, Charlie was in a cheerful mood because the weather was good and so was the pay. He was thinking of stopping for a tea break when he noticed the grader blade pushing aside a dull, yellow object. As it rolled, he realised what it was.

A human skull.

'Bloody hell,' said Charlie, shoving back his woollen beanie.

He stopped the grader, jumped down, and as he bent to examine the skull, which was badly cracked, he noticed other bones sticking out from the dark earth. He stood up, looking for Henry Collins, the architect who had employed him to level the site.

'Hey, Mr Collins, come here quick!' called Charlie.

Collins hurried across the newly churned earth, whistled at the skull, then fossicked around with Charlie. They weren't exactly experienced at identifying parts of the human anatomy but they were able to recognise leg and arm bones, some ribs, vertebrae and a tooth.

'Bloody hell,' Charlie said again. 'We've found a grave.'

Collins told Charlie to move the bones to the side of the site while he went off to telephone the police at Inverloch.

'But don't stop working,' he called back. 'Don't forget, I'm paying you by the hour!'

Charlie climbed back onto the grader and continued his levelling work, making sure he kept the heavy blade away from the grave site. By 12.30pm, Detective Senior Constable James Fary of the Korrumburra Criminal Investigation Bureau and two colleagues, Detective Senior Constable Pavlovic and Senior Constable Kamode, were at the site, a block of land at the corner of the newly named Milky Way and Saturn Parade. A quick inspection of the bones satisfied the officers they were human, but they were unable to find any clothing that may have been on the body. Perhaps it had rotted away, they considered. In any case, the team decided this was a case for the Homicide Squad in Melbourne.

Before leaving for the Tarwin Lower Hotel, from where they planned to telephone the murder squad, the officers told Charlie: 'Don't do any more grading around here until we return.'

But when they arrived back they found that Charlie had levelled off all the area except the spot where the bones had been unearthed.

'Why?' asked Senior Constable Fary. 'Why have you disturbed the area when we specifically asked you not to?'

'He's paying me by the hour,' said Charlie, nodding towards Henry Collins. 'He ordered me to keep working. I didn't have any choice.'

The frustrated detectives could now only question Charlie about the grave site. He'd made such a mess of things that it was impossible to gauge how deep the bones had been.

'I reckon they'd have been about three feet down, judging by the number of layers I'd taken off,' he said.

How were the bones lying – were they all at the same depth?

'Yeah, I'd reckon so, with the feet pointing in the direction I was working.'

Senior Constable Fary gathered up the bones that Charlie had moved to one side and put them in a plastic bag. He then drove to the Korrumburra police station and telephoned the local medical centre, asking Dr Ron Murley to call around as soon as possible.

On inspecting the bones, Dr Murley confirmed what Senior Constable Fary had already concluded – that they were human. He added they appeared to be of an elderly female who would have walked with a stoop. It was the doctor's opinion from a cursory inspection that the woman had not had any children, unless by caesarean section. What he wasn't prepared to do was guess how long the body had been buried, although he suggested that from the discolouration and total absence of any skin or tissue the bones had been in the ground for many years.

Back at Venus Bay, Charlie de Merlo was asked to put in some extra work at the site during the following two days, this time under strict police supervision. The detectives helped too, rolling up their shirt sleeves, taking up spades and digging into the sand and mud. They ran a piece of string across the site as a guide to how far down they had dug. At the end of the excavation work the police had recovered just one more piece of bone.

The bones were reassembled by Detective Sergeant Trevor 'Bill' Townsend and forensic experts at Russell Street police headquarters and the skeleton was then photographed in the hope this would help towards identification inquiries. The detectives, with help from the forensic team, had established the woman had been about 155 centimetres to 165 centimetres tall and possibly aged around 60 or 70 years of age.

Checks were made in the missing persons files but already police were beginning to make guesses. An old woman had gone missing in the area 26 years ago – could this be her?

Then, on the strength of new information that came in as a result of details of the skeleton being published, Senior Constable Fary travelled to Meeniyan on 15 November, where he called at the home of David and Ruth Burnett, in McDonald Street. The Burnetts handed the policeman an old hammer and a spade they had found partially buried in bushland at Venus Bay round about 1965 while they had been out rabbit hunting. They would travel to the area nearly every weekend, pitch a tent among the ti-trees and manuka bush, trap rabbits and do a spot of fishing.

On that particularly morning Dave Burnett was digging a hole to bury rabbit remains when, about eight inches down, he came across the hammer and spade, buried together. The wooden handles were rotted through, so the couple burned those remains in a camp fire and kept the head of the spade and the hammer but neither item had since been put to any use.

But the Burnetts had a further surprise to tell of what emerged from their trips to the dunes of Venus Bay.

Ten years after the discovery of the hammer and spade, Dave Burnett had taken his wife back to Venus Bay to go rabbit hunting again, a pastime they had kept up over the years. As fate would have it, they returned to the very spot where they had once found the hammer and spade. This time, close by, Mrs Burnett spotted a hole in a bank, a fox warren she thought,

that the rabbits were using. She started digging into the hole, shovelling the mud and sand away from the bank in the hope of frightening out a rabbit. Then she saw something green. Wiping away the mud, she realised the object was a handbag, crumbling with age. Clearing away more earth, she pulled out what appeared to be a crocheted shawl. Mrs Burnett carefully opened the handbag and spread its contents on the sand. Two 2s pieces with the dates 1946 and 1947; a penny dated 1939; and four halfpennies, two of them dated 1914, one 1916 and the fourth 1927.

The items, which the Burnetts handed to the police, had been found just four metres from where the spade and hammer had been located more than a decade earlier.

Senior Constable Fary asked the Burnetts to go with him to Venus Bay and point out the exact spot where they had found the items. They walked across the mud that Charlie de Merlo had recently excavated.

'Round about here,' said Burnett, pointing to the area where the hammer and spade had been found. The spot was just 25 metres from where the bones had been unearthed eight days earlier. Then the Burnetts took the police officer to the old fox hole where the handbag and shawl had been uncovered. They did not have to walk far – just four metres.

With the evidence of the bones, the hidden hammer and spade, the handbag and the old coins so close to where the skeleton had been found homicide detectives were convinced they had evidence of a murder. Either that or the bones and the other items lying so close to one another was just an amazing coincidence

Coincidence or not, each member of the homicide squad was handed copies of documents in a file. Its title: Margaret Clement.

But they still needed proof the bones were indeed those of the old woman known as the Lady of the Swamp. Then they could start looking for a murderer. And there were a number of residents in Tarwin Lower who, knowing the strange twists the course of Gippsland's history had taken, the hardships, the crime and the deceit, believed the police task would be far from easy.

Detective Chief Inspector Paul Delianis, head of the homicide squad, sat at his desk, the missing persons file open in front of him.

'I don't like making assumptions, but it looks like it's her, doesn't it?' he asked Detective Sergeant Townsend.

Murder squad detectives dig for clues after a skeleton is found in Venus Bay in 1978.

'It's a strong possibility,' said Townsend. 'Those bones were only 13 kilometers, or eight miles, from the homestead called Tullaree where she lived – about 10 kilometers or six miles in her day, as the crow flies.'

'Well, we must investigate every possibility. Let's check through all the other missing persons files while the forensic team continues their work. I want to see the site myself, so I'll go down there in the morning.'

Standing in the mud the next day, Chief Inspector Delianis held a conference with his men, who included a photographer and forensic experts. He made a detailed examination of the area, then issued operational instructions.

First, detectives checked with local people in Venus Bay to establish that the body had been deliberately buried – and that it was not someone who might have died from a sudden heart attack or misfortune like a snake bite and been covered by sand blowing in the wind. Several local people had died in paddocks or around the coastal region over the years, but they had always been found after their families had raised the alarm. Useful information continued to pour in from members of the community.

There was Lawrie Sutherland, aged 62, who said the lay of the land had not changed in the 40 years he had lived in the area.

'If those bones were a metre deep, then I reckon they were put there,' he said. 'Nothing gets buried that deep by the sand, no matter how strong the wind. It was pretty isolated around here many years back and you didn't get all that many people wandering around. But somebody could have been brought here in a four-wheel drive.'

Detectives, unable to link the bones to any missing person other than Margaret, drew up a list of all who knew her, or who had been associated with people who knew her. Almost from the start they realised it was to be a frustrating task, for as they checked out the list they found that many who could have helped with information had died.

Somebody told them they believed Margaret had had treatment once by a dentist called Shea. After numerous enquiries, Detective Fary traced Mr Shea, but he was to meet with more frustration. Shea had suffered a mental breakdown, was vague and could not assist. Fary then went to the dental clinic but was told that all the records before 1952 had been destroyed just 12 months earlier.

Identification, then, depended heavily on what experts could establish from the bones. Neville White, lecturer at the School of Genetics at LaTrobe University, Melbourne, was called in to Russell Street headquarters to examine them.

White pondered the skeleton that had been assembled by Detective Sergeant Townsend, considering the police officer had done a reasonable job.

His conclusion was that the bones were of a European woman who was probably more than 60 years old but the possibility of her being of Aboriginal descent could not be ruled out.

In order to continue their inquiries on the basis that the skeleton was that of Margaret Clement, detectives needed to hear more positive evidence. They called in Geoffrey Quail, a senior lecturer in anatomy. He concluded from examining the teeth that the bones were more likely to be those of an Aborigine. But he did agree that no matter what the origin of the skeleton, the person would have walked with a marked stoop and had never given birth.

Gerald Dalitz, Doctor of Dental Sciences at Melbourne University, also considered that the bones belonged to an Aborigine when he examined them on 15 November. From the state of the bones, he estimated they had been buried for a very long time – certainly in excess of 30 years. The murder squad team, anxious to clear up the mystery of the bones, the hammer, the spade and the handbag – and finally the baffling disappearance of the Lady of the Swamp – were disillusioned by the findings. They went back over the experts' summaries, one believing the bones could be of a European, two believing they belonged to an Aborigine. Police needed another opinion, one that might swing the bones back to being those of Margaret Clement, for that was the gut feeling many officers had. Without an added possibility of the bones being Margaret's it was likely her file would be closed yet again.

There was an added disappointment in their investigations. The handbag that several detectives were convinced was from the Victorian or Edwardian era turned out to be far more recent. Police Sergeant Hubert Peters, from the Field Investigation Section of the Forensic Science Laboratory, established that the style of bag had first come onto the market in about 1953 – a year after Margaret had disappeared. It had also been designed for the 18 to 21 year age group. But there was a possibility the bag had been manufactured a year or two earlier than 1953, in which case someone could have bought it for the old lady shortly before she disappeared. And there was a slim chance that the bag had been made as much as five years earlier because the bottle green plastic material it was made of had actually come onto the market in 1948.

Could there have been an 'early edition' of the bag that was later produced for the 18 to 21 year age group? That would explain the presence of the old coins, the latest of which was dated 1947.

The shawl, made of a material the sergeant established was known as guipure cotton lace, had been on the market for at least 40 years. So Margaret could well have owned that, although no-one could recall her wearing it.

It was puzzling – a handbag that did not seem to be Margaret's, unless it was bought for her very close to her death, containing coins that could have been hers, buried with a shawl that could also have been hers.

However, it was at the National Museum in Russell Street that Detective Sergeant Bill Townsend found the encouragement police needed to continue investigating a murder. Archaeologists Daniel Wilter and Ian Stuart agreed to examine the bones and later Stuart said: 'We're of the opinion these are the remains of an elderly white woman. She'd have been about 70 years old, shortish and suffered from arthritis. She probably had a stoop, too. We don't think they're Aboriginal.'

They also agreed it extremely unlikely for the Aborigines who lived in that part of Gippsland to have dug a grave as deep as one metre.

'Let's go ahead on the basis that it's Margaret Clement,' Delianis told his team. 'Time to continue our inquiries.'

There were two men who were at the top of their list because they had figured so prominently in the last two years of the old woman's life – Clement Carnaghan and Stanley Livingstone.

Townsend went to Clem's address in St Kilda and was told he was no longer there – he was now in hospital, a sick old man suffering from Parkinson's disease. The policeman drove to Melbourne's Austin Hospital, where doctors took him to Ward 11. Clem lay back on his pillow, his face grey, eyes fixed on the ceiling. Townsend introduced himself and told him about the discovery of the bones.

'Are you up to talking to me?' Townsend asked.

Clem tried to sit himself up further, but there was no strength in his wasted arms. When he spoke, his voice was an indiscernible whisper. Townsend realised that this might be the last chance he ever had of getting anything out of Margaret's nephew. He put his ear very close to the old man's dribbling lips but could not catch the words he spoke. Clem's hands were shaking, making it impossible to write. Townsend stood up, nodded goodbye and left.

He realised that Clement Carnaghan, who could have provided some vital information, would not be of any assistance – ever.

The policeman consulted his list. There was a Mrs Maisie Wyatt, who needed to be spoken to. She and her husband had once lived in the Tarwin area and had become friendly with the Livingstones early in 1952 while Stan was working on the Fish Creek drain.

On 18 November, Detective Sergeant Townsend drove to Lalbert Crescent, Armadale, where the Wyatts had moved to and was invited into the front room by the elderly housewife. Yes, she recalled, she had had several conversations with Esme while Stan was working on the drain. Years later, she recalled having another chat with Esme when the other woman had said she and her husband were going to America for a trip.

'There's something I have to tell you,' Mrs Wyatt suddenly told the policeman. 'I haven't known what to do about it, so I did nothing.'

'What are you talking about?' asked Townsend.

Mrs Wyatt left the room for a short time, then returned with a sealed envelope.

'Esme gave me this before they went off on their trip. There was a letter inside, but…well, I don't have it any more.'

Townsend saw the concern on Mrs Wyatt's face. He told her to relax and start from the beginning.

'When she gave me the letter,' Mrs Wyatt began, 'she said something that really worried me. It was along the lines of "If I disappear suddenly, hand this letter to the police. He's not going to knock me off like he did the old girl." I said to her "What old girl?" and she said, "Poor old Margaret."'

Townsend was stunned. This was explosive.

'Go on,' he urged.

'I didn't take much notice of what she said and just hung on to the letter. In fact I didn't open it for about 20 years, that is, this year. What are we now, 1978? The letter was not addressed to any person and the envelope just had "Police" written on it.'

'Well, where is the letter?'

'I'm coming to that. I don't have it with me any more. Just let me tell you what happened.'

'OK, go on – try to give me the gist of what it said.'

Mrs Wyatt took a deep breath and stared at the policeman for a moment. Then she said: 'It was obviously meant for me and the police. It read something like "In case I disappear suddenly when I'm on my way back from America or go overboard, would you give this letter to the police because he is not going to push me over like he did the old girl. He was in a temper as usual and he killed her in a rage as usual. He got rid of the body easy and the grave is not very far from the house.'"

Townsend stared at her, astonished. 'What did you think about that?' he asked.

'I got a fright when I read it and put the letter back in the envelope and kept it for safekeeping.'

'But you said you don't have it any more. Where is it?'

'I'll try to turn it up. I've sold a lot of books to a man in St Kilda and it's possible the letter could have been in one of the books. I can't say who the books were sold to because I can't find a phone number.'

Townsend wondered if the purchaser had been Clem (although in later inquiries he was unable to establish this). He continued with his questioning. 'Where were you when the letter was handed to you?' he asked, taking notes of the conversation.

'She gave me the letter at Fish Creek. I parked the car at about the fruit shop and she came over. She was very upset. She was really drunk. She was worried about Stanley at that stage. The letter was written in ink. She must have had it on her before then because she would not be able to write the letter at the time because she was drinking.'

On his return to headquarters, Townsend reported all that he had learned to Inspector Delianis. Had guilt consumed Esme in the four years since Margaret Clement had died that she felt compelled to write the letter and give it to a neighbour? The homicide team had had two men as suspects, Clem Carnaghan and Stan Livingstone. Clem could have killed his aunt in anger, or by accident in a kidnap attempt. Stan Livingstone could have killed her although they could find no immediate motive, but the letter, if its contents had been correctly recounted, was damning. Yet, Livingstone had bought Tullaree from the old lady quite legally and there were no loose ends apart from the fact that she was still living in the mansion at the time of her death. Could that have been a motive for murder? That she refused to move out even after the place had been sold?

There were many more inquiries to make. But one thing was certain. With the story related by Mrs Wyatt, even if there was no letter to back up her comments, the pendulum of guilt had swung towards Stan Livingstone.

The following day, Townsend drove to the country, to Yea, where the Livingstones had been living before moving to Queensland.

The dunes of Venus Bay – was Margaret's body dumped here?

There was another elderly woman on his list he was anxious to interview – Mrs Jean Sharp of Yea-Yarra Glen Road. Her husband had once worked as a general hand for the Livingstones at Murrundindi Station and Mrs Sharp had become friends with Esme.

'Yes,' she said, 'I've been to the property when she invited me, but I've never become friends with Stan. During our conversations she talked sometimes about the old lady disappearing. Her name was Margaret, she told me, and she lived in an old homestead and Stan had been buying it.'

Mrs Sharp recalled that on one occasion, when she and her husband were living in a cottage on Murrundindi, Esme came to see her.

'As we were chatting I could tell that she'd been drinking and she said something like "Stan's going to get rid of me and I don't know what to do." I offered assistance to her if we could give it.'

Another witness pointing the finger at Stan through his wife's drunken words, thought Townsend.

'She said that at Tullaree Stan used to leave her and sleep with the old lady and this had upset Esme greatly,' Mrs Sharp went on. Townsend was astonished. It seemed an unlikely scenario and he thought that perhaps what Esme said when she had been drinking was nonsense after all – but he let his host continue with her comments.

'She said that Stan had been standing over Margaret, the old lady, until she would sign some document. Esme said she finally signed under threats of being shot and then suddenly disappeared. Esme said that Stan paid two men from Melbourne the sum of £500 to get rid of the body.'

'Names?' asked the detective.

'I think from memory the names of the men were Bradshaw and Bradley. I don't know how the actual matter was handled but Esme said the two men had taken her away. She did not indicate how Margaret Clement was actually killed but it seemed to point at Stan, having got the property, now wanted her out of the way.'

'And Stan Livingstone himself – what did you think of him?'

'During the time we knew him he was a very violent man and would not hesitate in beating Esme. I've seen him holding her arm up her back and pulling her hair. Another time I saw him holding her on the floor by his foot on her head.

'At one time Esme showed me a book. It was the form of a scrapbook and was quite thick. It contained photos of her family and then newspaper cuttings regarding the disappearance of Margaret Clement. She told me that should anything happen to her to get the book and take it to the police.' Townsend made a note to try to track down the book.

Mrs Sharp was speaking again: 'One day, Esme showed me a pistol she said belonged to Stan and said it was a German Luger. She said he kept the pistol under his pillow and that he slept with one eye open.'

Detectives were moving fast, taking statements from everyone who knew Clement Carnaghan and the Livingstones. The answer to Margaret's disappearance, they were convinced, was between those two groups – and the evidence was piling up almost daily against Stan Livingstone.

In Frankston, on Victoria's Mornington Peninsula, pensioner Phyllis Roberts recalled the voyage on the S.S. *Simba* she had taken from Rotterdam to Melbourne during February 1965, 13 years after Margaret had disappeared. It was on the voyage that she met Esme and Stanley Livingstone.

'Mr Livingstone,' she said, 'did not mix with any of the other passengers and would not let his wife socialise. He was a very unsociable man and if he saw his wife speaking to me he would order her away. He was a nervous and jumpy person and I have seen him jump in fright.'

Mrs Roberts' mind went back to an evening in the ship's lounge when, she said, Mrs Livingstone appeared to have been drinking.

'She indicated she was a very worried lady and in conversation said she had a lot on her mind. She said they had bought a property for a song and sold for a huge amount. She said to me that she was frightened and that her husband had killed once and he would kill again. I can recall that she was wearing a red dress at the time. She indicated that when she said he could kill again she indicated herself and said "It could be me."'

Detectives were astonished that people like Mrs Roberts and the others they had spoken to had kept so much information to themselves. Not one of them had been to the police during all the years that had passed. But was it hearsay? Had the years in fact tainted their memory? Had their recollections been influenced by general gossip, by rumour put about by people who suspected the Livingstones were involved in Margaret's disappearance when the reality was that there was not a scrap of evidence against them?

'Esme did not enlarge on her comments, but I believe she was sincere and truthful,' said Mrs Roberts. 'The actual conversation about getting the property was that he worked on the old lady until he got the property. The words "having murdered an old lady" were used by Mrs Livingstone.'

In Benalla, Sam Rogers, a retired handyman, was also talking to the police. Round about 1973, he remembered, he went to work for Mr Stanley Livingstone at Murrundindi Station as a general hand, gardener and cook.

'I was employed there for about two months and then went to Curtis Island with the Livingstones, when they moved there – off the Queensland coast,' he recalled.

'I worked at Curtis Island for about a month until I had an argument with him and he paid me off. At one time at Curtis Island I saw Stan dragging his wife Esme by the hair up the stairs of the house. This is the only time I have actually seen him using violence on her but frequently saw her cut and bruised and her clothing torn.

'The day after I saw her dragged up the stairs I saw Esme had a black eye, her lip cut and swollen and some marks on her face. Several times at both Yea and Curtis Island she said "He's going to kill me like he did the other woman." She wouldn't tell me any more about this other woman, who she was or when it happened. She would have told me this at least half a dozen times at Curtis Island.'

Another witness to Esme's claims…another witness who had not reported her words to the police. Rogers said that while he was at Yea, Mrs Livingstone gave him an exercise book in the form of memoirs and a scrapbook. It had, he said, a black cover and gave details of a case known as the Swamp Lady.

'When Mrs Livingstone gave it to me she said to keep it and not let him, Mr Livingstone, see it under any circumstances. She indicated that if he knew she had given it to me, he would kill her.'

A black book. A black book of secrets. Detectives would need to find it. They established that Rogers had loaned it to a Dr Banks at Myrtelford, Victoria.

While other officers tried to track the book down, Detective Senior Constable Alan Gray and Detective Sergeant Townsend flew to Queensland. Their mission: interview Stan Livingstone, who had now become their prime suspect. They quickly established from their colleagues in Gladstone and Rockhampton that talking to the grazier would not be an easy task – Spadeley, his $1,500,000 property, which covered the northern half of Curtis Island, was completely isolated, with no easy road access. To reach the island by boat meant waiting for the right tide and no vehicles would be available to take them to the house. In addition, the officers would have to wait several hours for the tide to rise again before they could leave the island.

Understanding the lie of the land would be helpful, they agreed, so with the assistance of Queensland police the Victoria detectives were given access to an Army helicopter to fly over the Livingstones' sprawling property.

Spectacularly beautiful and stretching 40 kilometres from north to south and 19 kilometres wide, Spadeley had been used as a cattle grazing property for almost 100 years, but it was clear to the two visiting officers that reaching Stanley Livingstone would not be a simple task.

So rather than go to him, they decide to wait until he came to them…

Chapter 16.

~INVESTIGATION~

Once a week, the Livingstones took a boat to the mainland where they left a car parked. On Sunday, 26 November 1978, the couple moored their boat and climbed into their vehicle. They were followed by a police car as they headed for Rockhampton. Close to the city's police station, they were waved to a stop.

Stan was taken to an interview room where Detective Sergeant Townsend and Senior Constable Gray and two Queensland officers were waiting for him.

Townsend did not waste any time. Sitting opposite Livingstone, now white-haired and balding, the officer said:

'I'm making enquiries into the disappearance of a Miss Margaret Clement from a property known as Tullaree near Tarwin Lower in 1952. Recently, human bones were located near Venus Bay, which we believe are the remains of Miss Clement. I believe that you can help me in my enquiries. However, you do not have to say anything unless you wish to.'

Stan smiled slightly. 'I thought you blokes would have been up here before now,' he said. 'I've been expecting you.'

Townsend did not return the smile. 'I take it,' said the detective, 'you knew Miss Clement quite well.'

'Of course, but I bet you don't even know how she died.'

'Do you know how she died?'

'That's for you to find out and prove.'

'Then would you tell me where you were on the night she allegedly disappeared?'

'At home all night. You can ask Esme.'

'What about the next morning?'

'I forget.'

Detective Sergeant Townsend looked through some papers in front of him, then said: 'I have information that on that day you organised a shoot on the property. Do you recall that?'

'No.'

'Who actually realised that she had disappeared?'

'I'm not sure. But Lal Lester who had the next property to us reported her missing.'

'Is it correct that Miss Clement lifted a caveat in your favour?'

'You should know.'

Stan was confident to the point of being arrogant. Townsend realised he was up against a man who was not going to confess to any wrongdoing – that was if he was even guilty of any wrongdoing. There were still many questions begging answers.

'Therefore,' he continued, 'her disappearance would have been of benefit to you in that you gained the property?'

The police officer had not fully realised that the property was already in Stan's name at the time Margaret disappeared. The grazier did not correct him. He merely replied:

'I didn't do anything to her.'

'But you did gain possession of Tullaree?'

'I bought it fair and square – and I'll knock the head off anyone who says otherwise.'

Detective Sergeant Townsend paused before bringing up the next topic. This would go straight to the heart of the inquiry.

'It is well known that your wife Esme has frequently stated that you killed Miss Clement. Do you deny this?'

Stanley Livingstone sighed. 'She's an alcoholic and will say anything to try and hurt me because I wouldn't give her more to drink.'

The detective then hit Stan Livingstone with the vital question he had been leading up to.

'I believe you became upset and knocked Miss Clement over. It may have been an accident that she died, but you then panicked and hid her body near Venus Bay. What do you say to this?'

Stan's face hardened as he looked directly at the policeman.

'You go ahead and try to prove it,' he said.

'Is it a fact that at that time you used to agist cattle near Venus Bay?'

'I don't remember.'

'At that time in 1952, did you own a four-wheel drive vehicle?'

'Probably. I had one around that time. So what? A lot of people own the same things.'

He was belligerent, thought Townsend. He clearly wasn't going to co-operate. The detective sat back in his chair.

'It would appear,' he said, 'you don't wish to assist us in this inquiry.'

'That's your job,' said Stanley Livingstone. 'I've got to where I am on my own.'

'Is there anything further you wish to say that would assist me?'

'No.'

'Do you wish to make any written statement in relation to this matter?'

'I will make a statement that I don't know anything about her death.'

There was nothing further that Townsend and his colleagues would be able to extract from their suspect. They eventually allowed him to rejoin his wife, who had been waiting in another part of the police station. He had put up simple defences to the questions – he didn't know this, they had to prove that. He was confident. And he had the passage of time on his side: 26 years. What police needed were written records – not just memories – put together by people at the time of Margaret's disappearance. And there was one record the homicide team were looking for in particular. The black book Esme Livingstone had compiled and which had been passed on to a doctor for his reading interest.

A few days later, at Russell Street headquarters, Chief Inspector Paul Delianis held a conference with his men. They could not prefer charges against anyone until a coroner's inquiry had been held into the identity of the bones and a verdict given on how the deceased had met her death – unless someone came forward and owned up to murdering Margaret Clement and burying her in the place where the bones had been found.

'It looks like we'll be relying heavily on the verdict given at the inquest,' said Delianis.

But he had one more piece of valuable evidence to place in the jigsaw puzzle of mystery. After his men left, the homicide chief picked up an exercise book with a black cover – Esme's book. It had been collected from the doctor to whom it had been loaned. He had flicked through it and found its contents fascinating. Esme had written numerous clues to Margaret's disappearance.

On the inside cover, tantalisingly, was a poem by Arthur Hugh Clough:

Say not, the struggle naught availeth,
The labour and the wounds are vain,
The enemy faints not, nor faileth,
And as things have been they remain.

If hopes were dupes, fears may be liars;
It may be, in yon smoke conceal'd,
Your comrades chase e'en now the fliers,
And, but for you, possess the field.

For while the tired waves, vainly breaking,
Seem here no painful inch to gain,
Far back, through creeks and inlets making,
Comes silent, flooding in, the main.
And not be eastern windows only,
When daylight comes, comes in the light;
In front the sun climbs slow, how slowly!
But westward, look, the land is bright.

What did it mean? Why had Esme written it in her black book? Was there a hidden message?

Chief Inspector Delianis turned the pages, reading references to strange cars being seen in the district shortly before Stan bought Tullaree. There was mention of the day Esme's husband punched Clem Carnaghan in the St Kilda flat…and notes about the times Margaret came to visit them and sat listening to the radio, intrigued…the occasions when Margaret had ventured out to go to the pictures and sit in cafés…

The policeman pushed his hand back through his dark hair, then read Esme's summary of Margaret's disappearance. He had read it once, twice, before. Could he – should he – believe what she had written?

'…Then came the day when Stan reported she had not opened her stores left. I could not believe it and went down with him and after a thorough search of house and nearby scrub immediately reported it to the police. To Stan and I it was unbelievable. She was so bright when Stan saw her and her last trip out with me on the Monday we shopped, had morning tea at a café and she bought a new rain coat and told me after she had really enjoyed the outing. That is the last I saw of Margaret.'

Then came her personal thoughts – and they pointed the finger of suspicion towards Clem, his visits, the aggression…

'As a nurse, while fully aware of the possibility of a heart turn at her age, these glaring incidents which happened before, I'm afraid, have made me very suspicious of the fact that she had been taken away. The police say there is no motive, but jealousy can be a serious motive.

'It is with a feeling of horror you realise you are suddenly involved quite inadvertently in a mystery that has not yet been solved. Public opinion is very varied, yet we put ourselves in their position and would probably feel the same while it remains unsolved.

'Knowing Margaret's feelings, there is much she could say and would gladly verify all I have said and how often I have wished for her appearance.

'We have been annoyed with police because at the start of the search we thought the CIB were investigating in Melbourne while the search was in progress and found out later they did not start until the search was finished, thus losing much time.

'Then they seemed to be surprised at the amount of water and seemed to disregard these other incidents that had happened as unimportant. That exasperated us.

'Farmers would come to the search early in the morning and police did not come until 11 and 12 when days were short. They would not consult Stan much and he could have shown them around much better – even their last search they were all too close together to do any good and although they have maintained they have searched thoroughly, we both maintained they have not.

'I am hoping the future will reveal the truth. We have undergone much tension with questioning, but it does not worry one when in the right but only we can certify this until Margaret is found.'

Her record did not square with comments she had made later to neighbours – comments in which she had blamed her husband for Margaret's death. Having written one version of events in her black book, which pointed the finger at Clem, had a guilty knowledge, fired by her drinking, caused her to start blabbing the truth? That her husband was the killer? Or were her words to neighbours the fantasies of a woman whose mind was unbalanced through the effects of alcohol? They were questions to which police needed to find answers before any action could be taken against anybody. Clem Carnaghan was still alive…just. His mother Anna, the last of Peter the Packer's children, had passed away. Stan Livingstone was alive and, it seemed, in the picture of health. His wife was now frail – and what of her mind?

Delianis continued reading. In further notes at the rear of the book, after the pages of newspaper cuttings, Esme wrote that Margaret had mentioned her main boyfriend in the early days – Willie. And in an added paragraph, written at Murrundindi Station in December 1970, Esme described how busy life had been since she was admitted to hospital clinically dead after the car crash six years earlier. She concluded: 'I have been surprised and disappointed no news of Margaret over these years. Perhaps even when we both pass away. But I sincerely hope it is not another of those unsolved tragedies…'

Chief Inspector Delianis closed the black book. He sat thoughtfully in his chair for a while and then he went home.

Police scientists had by now examined the old hammer and spade found in 1968 by Mr and Mrs Burnett some 25 metres from where the bones had been unearthed. Because of their condition, reported the forensic men, it was impossible to find anything on the tools that could link them with the bones. Particularly, there was no blood or skin attached to the metal. Nevertheless, a skeleton with a cracked skull lying close to a hammer and spade seemed too much of a coincidence to ignore.

As did the added curiosity of Mrs Burnett finding the remains of a handbag in the same area in 1979. The latest date on coins in the bag was 1947 and detectives were certain the evidence of the money was strong enough to convince a coroner the bones were those of Margaret Clement, who disappeared five years after the date of the most recently minted coin – except for the problem of the handbag. Unless Margaret had acquired it soon after it had come onto the market, very close to the time of her death, it was probably not hers, police concluded.

More work needed to be done on the skeleton itself. Detective Sergeant Townsend made further inquiries about Aboriginal burial methods, consulting the best archaeological brains. He learned that long before the holiday homes had sprung up in Gippsland, hundreds of years before the pioneers had thrashed through the thick scrub and fought the swamps around the banks of the River Tarwin, the Aborigines of the region lived happily with the mud, carving stone axes made with red flinty stone. Fishing for the Boonurrong tribe was easy on the neap tide and there was abundant wildlife to be hunted around the marshes; Cape Barren geese, ducks, swans, teal, pelicans and penguins.

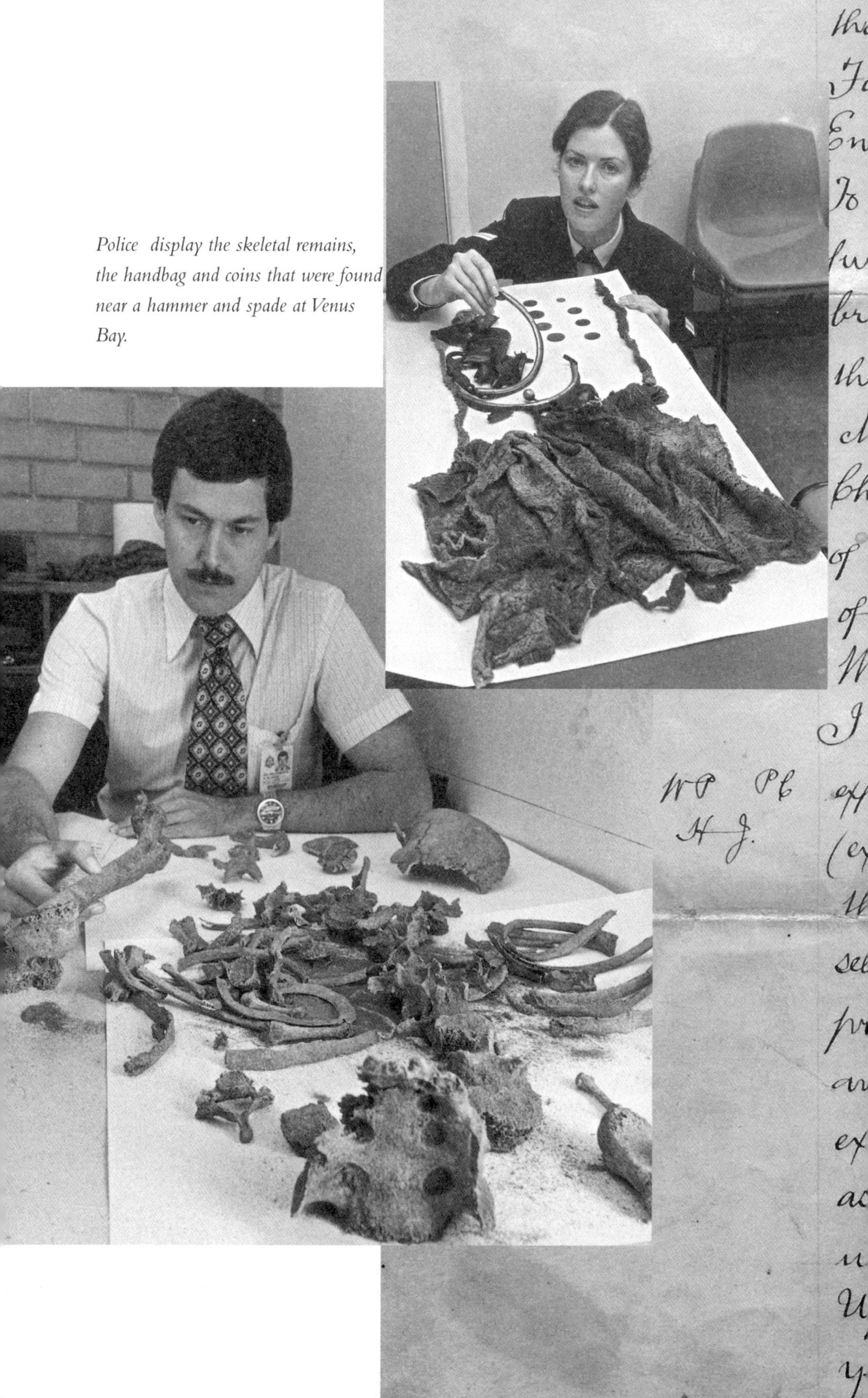

Police display the skeletal remains, the handbag and coins that were found near a hammer and spade at Venus Bay.

There were battles, though, with surrounding tribes. In the early 1950s hikers found 70 stone axe heads at nearby Stony Point, believed to have been left by the Omeo Aborigines in about 1840 as they returned home from a raid into the Tarwin region. The bodies of those killed in battles were buried in the area and several graves had been unearthed by farmers over the years. The skulls of Tarwin Aborigines were similar to those of the Tasmanians, revealing that the race was Negroid, with curly hair. Their heads were long and the mouth projected forward.

The area was steeped in history and there could be bones of European explorers and Aborigines everywhere.

Detective Sergeant Townsend spoke to numerous experts on Aboriginal traditions and burial methods. He confirmed that it would be extremely rare for Aborigines to bury their dead in a horizontal grave and certainly not as deep as one metre. The few graves that had been uncovered with bodies lying horizontally had been just below the surface. But most importantly, the body would in almost all cases be buried in an upright position.

Townsend double-checked the files into missing people. No-one of a description who could have matched the bones had disappeared. Certainly not with a handbag containing coins from so long ago. If the handbag had indeed belonged to someone else, why on earth would they have stuffed it into a foxhole with money still inside? While there had been no cloth found with the skeleton he was still inclined to believe that this was the old Lady of the Swamp.

Chief Inspector Delianis studied all the reports his men had brought to him. He believed it was enough.

'I think,' he said, 'we are ready to report to the coroner.'

Chapter 17.

~INQUEST~

Many of the people the police had interviewed were so old and infirm that they were excused from attending the inquest into the skeletal remains that was held at Wonthaggi Court in July 1980, nearly 70 years after Margaret Clement had visited the town in her gleaming carriage. Now modern vehicles passed through the main street, lined with shops that had replaced the simple stores that she knew.

Aside from those who were able to attend, the coroner, Mr Kevin Mason, had a number of statements that had been taken from the older witnesses. Clem Carnaghan was far too ill to attend – although now back home from hospital he could not even leave his bed – but Stanley and Esme Livingstone made the trip from their remote property on Curtis Island. They had no choice, for they were the key witnesses. It was the first glimpse of the couple the Gippsland people had had of them since they had left the district 16 years earlier.

Now in his early 70s, Stan was still a towering, powerfully built man. Wearing a dark grey cardigan, cream trousers and a pale silk tie, he was a contrast to the dusty grazier and horseman that his neighbours remembered. He clutched his wife's hand as they walked into the courthouse for what he expected to be a grilling over Margaret's disappearance. Esme, wearing a spotted blouse, a zig-zag patterned dress and a silk scarf appeared much more frail. Her smile as she entered the court was tinged with nervousness.

The witnesses, most of them white-haired, could not help but to mix with one another as they waited for the inquest to begin. Many had not seen each other for years.

Eventually, Chief Inspector Delianis called a very important, witness on his list: Mrs Esme Livingstone. She smiled briefly as she stepped forward, all eyes upon her. She knew that the questioning would be relentless.

Her voice firm, she recalled for the inquest how she had first met her husband of 41 years in 1938 in the Riverina district of northern Victoria and told of the work they had done improving properties. She agreed they did well from buying and selling. Then she described her meeting with Margaret Clement, when the old lady had called at the Buckleys to notify them of her sister's death. Margaret had become 'a great friend'.

Asked whether Miss Clement was much like her property – run down – Esme replied:

'Her intellect was good. You could hear her speaking of operas like *Faust* and *Aida*. If you were sitting next to her at the table you would be really surprised. The property was badly run down. The neighbours – there was a boundary fence – had been grazing cattle on her property for a long time. When my husband bought it some of them refused to believe it had been bought. There had been six farms draining into Tullaree which had blocked up all the drains. You could not drive a bulldozer across it and also the water was over the road.'

When she first went to Tullaree, she was asked, how high was the water?

'Up to here,' she said, putting her hand on her waist. She was 'rather scared' about going in there but she walked through the water and became lost. 'I ended up miles away from the homestead and I had to walk back… when I came back there was a window missing and I could see Miss Clement there where the window was.'

'Did it impress you as being a home that had had magnificence in the past?'

'Undoubtedly. The kitchen had no stove left. Just cavities. And there were a lot of floorboards which had gone at the back door, but right up the hall was quite solid. Apparently the brickwork had been done exceptionally well because the doors fitted perfectly.'

The first time she had heard about Tullaree was when she and her husband were at Middle Tarwin – everyone was talking about it. Her main thrill was befriending Miss Clement and getting her to go to the shops, the pictures and theatres. Things she had not done for years.

'She had been living virtually as a recluse?'

'Yes. She read extensively but she had been made a recluse. She had no choice but to confine herself to the homestead. She had no radio. We gave her a radio and she was very thrilled.'

Asked whether she thought of Tullaree as a place she would like to own, she replied: 'I did not think of it at the time but I knew my husband was so obsessed with developing properties and he was the one person who could do it – and I believe that Miss Clement thought that, too.'

Esme remained composed as she added that, naturally, she had spoken to her husband about restoring the property and he had said one of the obstacles was that Miss Clement's nephew had been dominating her for some years and he, the nephew, had wanted her to sign the Power of Attorney. But Miss Clement would not do it.

'He took her to a flat in St Kilda and tried to force her to sign a Power of Attorney which she would not do,' said Esme.

'Why,' asked Chief Inspector Delianis, 'do you say the nephew was trying to dominate her?'

'He tried to dominate her once before at St Kilda when he had a solicitor and tried to get her to sign the Power of Attorney. She escaped from the flat and caught the train back to Gippsland.'

'It is quite clear, is it not, that right from the beginning you saw the potential that there was in the property at Tullaree, the potential for improving it?'

'Yes, I think anybody would see that. There was an enormous amount of work to be done.'

She was asked about Margaret's general condition – was she frail in her later years?

Esme shook her head. 'She was extremely strong. She told me that she used to swim for a mile and a doctor told her she had abnormally large lungs. I am quite sure that Margaret Clement would have lived for another 10 or 20 years. She was quite happy with my husband and I. I'm sure Margaret would have lived for a long time. She used a walking stick for probing her way through the water and she also carried it in case it was necessary to hit any snakes. But she was very much against hurting animals. She had large knuckles on her fingers. She used to carry a bag of stores through the swamp on this one finger. She gave us the impression she would be very happy for Stan to restore the homestead. She used to inspect the cottage we were building and she planned the rooms; what she was going to put in them.'

Those present in the court sat fascinated to hear these impressions of Margaret's life, even though many had been witness to the old lady's habits.

Esme was asked why she had been so friendly with Margaret – was she sounding her out on whether she would sell the property?

'No, I never sounded Margaret out with anything to do with the property. When she was driving around to Middle Tarwin one day with Stan and I in the car she turned to Stan and said "Do you think you can buy the property?" He replied "I don't think so – I have all my money invested in Middle Tarwin."'

The former nurse agreed that £15,500 had been paid for Tullaree – made up of £12,500 for the discharge of the mortgage and £3,000 to Margaret for the withdrawal of the caveat. Twelve years later she and her husband had received back something like £126,300.

'It was a pretty gigantic profit?'

'Yes, and an enormous amount of work was put in. There was the draining of the property, thc road to be built up and the land to be cultivated; fencing, sheds and the homestead restored.'

Asked if they were wealthy now, she replied:

'We're comfortable.'

'Millionaires?'

'Well, I suppose you could class my husband as a millionaire.'

Delianis paused, keeping his stare on the woman in the witness box. Then he said: 'I put it to you, Mrs Livingstone, that Tullaree was a stepping stone towards you and your husband becoming millionaires.'

'No, Tatura [an earlier property] was a stepping stone.'

She was asked how she and her husband got on with Margaret's relatives. Had there been a public feud with them?

'Her nephew was very much against my husband. Miss Clement was very much against her nephew. Actually, when we befriended her she told us she was very much annoyed with her nephew and the way he was dominating her and the fact that he took her away.'

She recalled that when they went to St Kilda they decided to tell Margaret's relatives about the sale of the property.

'We took her there. My husband waited in the car.…We knocked on the door and Mrs Carnaghan came out. She took Margaret by the wrist and dragged Margaret inside and slammed the door in my face. I called out to Stan and he got out of the car.'

'He put his foot in the door?'

'Yes.'

'He forced his way into another person's property?'

'Yes.'

'And it finished up with him hitting Mr Carnaghan in the face with a punch?'

'I don't remember him hitting him, but he told him to get out of the way of the door.'

'Do you deny he hit Mr Carnaghan in the face with a punch?'

'He could have done.'

Now the questioning was becoming far more serious. Esme was asked whether she had used any 'brainwashing process' on Margaret.

'I took her up the street and bought her things she had not tasted for years, like cakes and bananas. I also gave her food I had baked at Middle Tarwin.'

Detective Chief Inspector Delianis turned his questioning to Esme's relationship with her husband. She was asked if she was frightened of him and when.

'We had our upsets.'

'Had he ever struck you?'

'Never to hurt me.'

'Ever hit you?'

'Not violently.'

'Has your husband ever hit you in an unfriendly manner?'

'No, he was only trying to stop me if I had been drinking.'

Esme said she had had a couple of minor bruises, not serious ones. She revealed that she drank beer years ago and perhaps half a glass of wine or a gin and squash.

'Has your husband been involved in fights in the Gippsland area?'

'When he was to take possession of Tullaree he bought the cattle to put on the property and held on to the Middle Tarwin property. Buckley had cattle and refused to take theirs off so Stan had to bring his cattle in the back way of Tullaree and impound theirs. When we came in there were five horsemen trying to block Stan. He kept going with some men he had. They tried to gallop to scatter the cattle. Stan asked me to go to the police in the car.'

'Your husband had a fight with Mr Buckley and broke his jaw?'

'Oh no, never broke his jaw.'

If anyone had expected Esme Livingstone to give up terrible secrets of her relationship with her husband, they were disappointed by her answers so far. Everything she said was in defence of Stan. However, her answers had caused several people, including police, to ask later whether she had been warned by her husband to be careful about what she told the court.

She agreed he was a very strong man and he did have a temper – but it was very slow to rouse.

Under further questioning, Esme told the inquest about their property on Curtis Island, which covered 3,240 hectares. It could be worth $1,500,000.

Then she was suddenly asked if her husband had any guns.

'He had a gun, which he still owns now. He won the Riverina Championship once for clay bird shootings. It's a big long gun – I don't know the name of it.'

Esme was asked if she had been to the Tarwin Lower Hotel on a number of occasions with people. She agreed she had.

'Did you ever get under the influence down there at all?' asked Chief Inspector Delianis.

'Yes, I was very upset once.'

'You can recall it, being upset down there?'

'Yes, I was.'

'Why were you upset?'

'It had nothing to do with Miss Clement. It was a personal matter.'

'An argument with your husband?'

'Not an argument but something I was upset about personally.'

'In fact an argument developed with your husband to the extent that there was an incident involving the river outside the hotel?'

'Yes. I swam the river.'

'Because you were afraid of your husband?'

'No, he wasn't there. I was upset after having a few drinks.'

She was asked whether she had ever said to the licensee, Goff Jongebloed, something like: 'What do you think of a man who would kill and bury a woman and run cattle over the grave to disguise it?'

'Never, ever.'

Delianis continued to probe Mrs Esme's relationship with her husband.

'Has your husband ever hit you?'

'It depends what you call hit.' Pressed further, she said: 'He is only trying to stop me if I had been drinking...he would see I was upset.'

'Has he ever caused bruises on your body?'

'I have had a couple of minor bruises, not serious ones...I bruise very easily...he might have just grabbed my arm, something like that.'

Asked about the letter that Mrs Wyatt had spoken of, the one in the

Above: Stan Livingstone and a neighbour inspect Tullaree, hidden behind thick blackberry bushes in 1952, months before Margaret's disappearance. Right: Stan and Esme Livingstone, by now white-haired millionaire retirees, attend the inquest into the skeletal remains in 1980.

envelope marked 'Police', Esme denied she had written it. 'That letter has been made up,' she insisted.

'Did you or do you categorically deny that you have ever said to anybody while you were sober, jokingly or otherwise, that your husband killed Margaret Clement?' Delianis asked.

'I do,' she replied firmly.

'Do you categorically deny that you ever said to anybody, jokingly or otherwise, that your husband had something to do with the disappearance of Margaret Clement when you were perhaps under the influence of liquor?'

'No, even if I was under the influence of liquor I would not be saying such a thing.'

'So not only has Mrs Roberts (who had given a statement about comments Esme had made on the cruise ship) lied, but so has Mrs Wyatt?'

'Apparently.'

Delianis pointed out to Esme that the court had heard, in varying words, what boiled down to claims that her husband killed Margaret Clement.

'Can you tell me,' he asked, 'how three different persons could come to this court – three strangers could come to this court – and make accusations? Perhaps you could give me some explanation. Can you give His Worship some explanation of how this might occur?'

Esme turned to the coroner. 'Your worship, I would not say that my husband had killed Margaret Clement to any person, because I was with him all the time and I would have had some indication…I can only think that they were against my husband and that they wanted to incriminate him instead of the nephew.'

'Three persons who are strangers,' put in Delianis, 'strangers to each other, have been hostile to your husband and have come to this court to deliberately commit perjury and implicate your husband in relation to the killing of Miss Clement – is that what you are saying?'

'They are.'

He wanted to know if Esme could give any reasonable motive why Clement Carnaghan would want Margaret Clement dead. In an answer that was confused and had to be repeated, she suggested that if Margaret was dead, it would be easier for Carnaghan to argue that she had been insane when she had lifted the caveat which had allowed the sale of Tullaree to go through. If she was still alive and a court saw that she was in possession of all her faculties, he would not be able to prove that she had lifted the caveat while she was not of sound mind.

Asked why she was blaming Clement Carnaghan for killing Margaret Clement, Esme replied: 'Well, if you were sitting in the car with Margaret Clement and Mr Carnaghan came down the road waving a gun and letting the tyres down…'

It was the first time anyone had spoken of Clem having a gun. But at that point Esme trailed off and the police officer had no further questions to put to her.

It was the turn of Sergeant Bill Townsend, who had already outlined the general circumstances of finding the bones to the court, to be recalled to the witness box. He was asked about the interview he had had with Stan at Rockingham police station. He then went on to read the lengthy observations Esme had made in her black book, written in sloping, blue ink under the title 'Impressions Gained from the First Time I knew Tullaree Existed'. The reading completed, the detective was asked whether he formed the opinion that Miss Clement never left Tullaree without her walking stick.

'Yes, I conducted extensive inquiries and spoke to people who knew Miss Clement personally…It's well known she would take a walking stick which was used for probing the swampy areas. She would not leave the house without it.'

'There was a walking stick discovered in the house after her disappearance?'

The police officer confirmed that had been the case.

Finally, it was time to summon the key figure. Stanley Livingstone strode purposefully across the courtroom to the witness box, confident, smiling slightly, just as his wife had. He, too, knew he would be questioned at length about Margaret's death and he expected the worst kind of accusations to be made against him. But he had lived with gossip and innuendo for what was close to 30 years and nothing was going to shake him now, whether he was in a courtroom or in the street.

Chief Inspector Delianis began with some general questions, asking how Stan had first become aware of Tullaree. The former footballer described how his wife had called at the Buckley homestead to fetch horse straps and it was there that she had met Miss Clement. It was about a month later that Miss Clement had asked him if he could buy the property. He ultimately paid some £16,000.

'Did you sell the property later for £126,000?'

'Yes.'

'That's a bargain for a property for which you paid £16,000?'

'We did a lifetime of work in 10 years. That was a recognised thing by my wife and myself. We did not do seven days a week. We got eight days a week in.'

What he had paid to Margaret was put into her trust account.

'So the only monetary benefit she got out of it was £3,000?'

'No, she got a house to live in.'

'Did she?'

'It was not quite finished.'

He pointed out that he and his wife had built a small four-roomed house on the Tullaree property. They thought they would be able to drop the stores there easily enough and also take Margaret into town. The house would have been finished within six weeks.

'She used to come to me and ask me what she would do with the will, how she could make a will out. I said "I think you should include the nephew and Eileen, the two closest." She said "No, I am going to cut him right out. He is always domineering."'

Stan was then asked about personal rows he had been involved in. Describing his clash with Clem in St Kilda he said: 'He was coming at me. He ran up the corridor at me flat out and I said to myself "I had better stop this fellow."'

'Is he the only person you have ever hit?'

'No, I've had to fend for myself against a few people.'

And what of the incident involving John Buckley?

Stan replied: 'He and I were having a bit of a row on the street. We had a bit of an argument and we were going to have a fight. I got in first.'

'You king-hit him?'

'No, I hit him in the face. My wife brought a pillow out and put it under his head.'

What of a Mr Curtain, of Yea?

'He bought some property off me and he did not treat me very fairly. I hit him in the chest.'

And a Tom Bell?

'I didn't hit him really. I just grabbed hold of him and stropped him.

He had had a few drinks.'

'Whether it was founded or unfounded,' Delianis put it to him, 'you had a reputation of being a man of violence?'

'If you give a dog a bad name, it sticks with him.'

Yes, he had 'slapped' his wife, but not very often. 'About half a dozen times in my life, all about drink. I have never marked her at all very much.'

Stan said he had not struck his wife 'for ever so long. She has been like gold to me really.' He insisted it was untrue to say it was well known in the district that he was often 'belting' his wife.

He showed a flash of anger when Delianis asked him if he did in fact belt his wife. 'Not belt. Cut that out! There's a bit of a limit to this. A slap is as much as I've given my wife.'

Asked about his height, Stan told the court he was 6 foot 3 inches. He had played football for Port Melbourne, Footscray and Melbourne.

'You are a person renowned for feats of strength, are you?'

'I am a little bit above the average.' Then, with a touch of sarcasm, he added: 'I was not good enough to go to the Moscow Games.'

Delianis ignored the remarked and continued with his questioning. 'It is well known in the district you were capable of picking up a 44-gallon drum and putting it on a truck.'

'I think you have better cut that in half and divide it by 10.'

But he finally agreed that when he was 28 he had indeed picked up a full 44-gallon drum and walked five or 10 metres with it.

He and his wife continued living in a hut while he was working on the drainage in the area, while Margaret remained in Tullaree.

'Are you aware that the caveat was on the property taken out by Miss Clement and it was along the lines that she was to live there until such time as she died?'

'That was my agreement with Miss Clement.'

'Did you discuss with your wife that she [Margaret] would live another 10 or 20 years?'

'If she lived another 10 years, we would be quite happy. It was not hurting at all.'

Stan was asked about Clem Carnaghan and he said that the nephew had been trying to prove Margaret was insane because that was the only way he could upset the sale to him.

'Do you believe that Mr Carnaghan had anything to do with her disappearance?'

'I'm pretty sure that somebody did…those three associates. I did really think that.'

Asked what motive Carnaghan had for killing or arranging the killing of Miss Clement, Stan said: 'He could not have a big court case and prove her insane while she was alive.'

'Have you ever heard of the expression "brainwashing"?'

'Yes, I have.'

'What do you believe that means?'

'Saying the one thing over two or three times until you think you believe it.'

What about the 600 per cent profit he had made?

'I don't think I made a hell of a lot of money out of it after 10 years and all the work we put in. I did have an overdraft and I have to pay that off so that I did not really get £126,000.'

Stan was questioned whether he had walked up to any strangers outside the court the day before the current hearing and said: 'They're not going to pin this on me.'

He stared back at the detective. 'Well, I naturally think you are trying to.'

'You went up to absolute strangers outside the court, did you?'

'Yes, I might have done. They can't pin this on me.'

The homicide chief asked about the letter that made a reference to Esme's worries about 'going overboard' on a voyage. 'You would agree this is a terrible accusation to make against you, is it not?'

'Yes. I'm not worried about that because I'm not doing anything and did not do anything like that to Miss Clement.' If his wife had written that, it was when she was upset, had been drinking and wanted to hurt him…'just an ordinary upset that comes along.'

Referring to Mrs Roberts on the boat, Stan said he did not have a friendly relationship with her because 'she is not my class of woman. She used to be drinking a fair bit.'

'You kept a bit aloof from her?'

'Yes, I was. I did not like the woman. I thought she had had a facelift. She had a lot of wrinkles under her neck and I did not like the idea. Very common.'

People in the public gallery wondered if Stan's judgement was an admission that he aspired to greater things in life – that he considered himself one of the landed gentry, the likes of whom Margaret Clement had mixed with in her heyday.

The grazier agreed that Murrundindi, which he had acquired after

Tullaree, was one of the best properties in Victoria. He had owned it for nine years. He had paid £150,000 with stock and he had sold it in small pieces; five different lots for a total sum of £590,000.

He was then asked whether he knew a Jean Bell. Yes, she used to work for him – 'Jean and Tom. They were big drinkers. They used to swim in it.'

'You have something against women who drink?'

'No. That's the truth. That's their business.'

'Do women who drink upset you?'

'No, not at all. It's their business and they can do what they like.'

The name of Clive Sherry was put to him – a name he did not recall. But Chief Inspector Delianis said that Mr Sherry had told police of meeting Mr Livingstone at Murrundindi and Mr Livingstone had then 'said something about coming into money and that was how he had bought Murrundindi.'

Did he, Stan was asked, tell anyone he had come into money?

'No way. Anyway, I do not tell people my business.'

'If you had not bought Tullaree, you could not have bought Murrundindi?'

'I could have bought another place and gone on to make some money. I did not make all the money on Tullaree. I made a lot of money on the other three farms.'

'Did anyone say to you, "It's a real mystery that they never found the body of the woman?" Do you remember?'

'A lot of people have said that to me.'

'Did you say to anybody "I'm damn sure they won't"?'

'No, never.'

'It is all invention again?'

'Never came from me, oh no.'

'And your wife is supposed to have said, "They never will find the body"?'

'No, I don't remember anything what my wife said. I do not remember the man actually coming to the place.'

Delianis continued the visitor's statement: '"Mr Livingstone then repeated he was damned sure they wouldn't."'

'I would not be sure of anything.'

'Do you suggest this is also an invention?'

'It is my word against his, you know, and I have never met the man.'

He was then asked whether he thought his wife had written to Jean Bell making certain claims.

'No, I don't think so. It was a mistake.'

'It's a serious sort of mistake.'

'It's not a serious mistake, either.'

'To accuse you of killing Margaret Clement is not a serious mistake?'

'It's not serious when Jean Bell is a drinker. It used to get that bad drinking with Tom, and I had a drink with Tom one day. I had an argument and she took the axe to both of us. She brought the axe to us when we were drinking. She would not be responsible for her actions in lots of cases.'

Questioned about the claim that he had been sleeping with the old lady, he screwed his lips into a mocking smirk. 'That's laughable,' he said.

Did he have guns at Murrundindi?

'Only a shotgun – it could be a pea rifle. Definitely nothing else.' He had never had a handgun. He told the court he was always sorry for himself when he hit his wife. He had a little bit of a temper through drinking sometimes and he regretted it afterwards.

'Do you think you bought Tullaree fair and square?'

'Yes I do. Legally fair and square.'

But Delianis was not going to let it lie there.

'You did use undue influence, did you not, Mr Livingstone?'

'Only by meeting Miss Clement and being kind to her. That's not undue influence. I was the only one prepared to give her £3,000 and none of the other people would.'

Miss Clement, he told the coroner, never used a walking stick except when she got into the bush. She would leave it on the bridge. She used it as a sort of probe to see how deep the water was. He did not think it was significant that on the day she disappeared the walking stick was found at the house.

'I did not put any importance on it because I did not find the lady gone. It was Mr Lal Lester who found the lady gone.'

Stan said he had made the report to the police because 'Lal could not go in there.' There was no significance in the stick, he said, because she had two or three.

When he first heard she was missing he thought she might have had a heart turn while picking up wood in the bush or when she had gone to the lavatory 'and we would find her dead or something.'

He continued: 'As soon as I went to look through all the home and looked around the side of the house where she generally gathered wood, we set out to town to report to Mr Collins.'

Satisfied that she had not died of a heart attack he believed, naturally, that she had been 'taken'.

'We went to her room. Her room was quite tidy. A couple of blankets she used to lie down on the couch were tidily put away and she never did that. We knew she was taken.'

He said 'taken' because 'she would not leave the homestead without seeing me or Esme. We think she was taken by the associates who were giving her so much trouble in the early part before the sale.'

'Did that not provide for you a beautiful false trail – the fact that there was this altercation with Mr Carnaghan?'

'No, never gave it any thought like that. I was quite certain that somebody had taken her away or that she had wandered away in the bush somewhere.'

'Are you suggesting that Mr Carnaghan came down and took her away?'

'Yes. Margaret Clement often said that Knobby had hit her over the head. That is a fact.'

'Did she go to the police?'

'No. She would not go to the police.'

'A 70-year-old woman being hit over the head?'

'With their hands, not a stick. They hit her over the head and tried to dominate her. Her words were that they had bully ragged her.'

Chief Inspector Delianis suggested that, assuming he had killed Miss Clement, these claims were a good way of shifting the blame to accuse Clement Carnaghan. Stan replied:

'Listen, I have got to explain again to you: we had given her £3,000, we had built a home for her and we had bought the property.'

He added that although he considered that Clem Carnaghan and his associates had not kept Margaret prisoner, 'we thought that, if she was missing, they might have done something to her because they had to get her out of the way.'

'Killed her?'

'Yes, we think so.' He repeated that this was because she would not be able to appear in court and reveal that she was of sound mind and had not been under undue influence when she agreed to sign the property over to him.

Finally, on what was the second day of the inquest, the questioning of the Livingstones was over. There were no more witnesses to be called. Stanley Livingstone stepped from the witness box. Still confident. Still proud.

Coroner Mason shuffled his documents together and adjourned the court while he considered his findings, which, he said, would be pronounced shortly. Police, witnesses and casual onlookers stepped outside to smoke or talk in small groups.

Who was it then? It was a question several thought but did not ask out loud. Was it Clem Carnaghan or Stanley Livingstone who had killed Margaret – for no-one had ever been in any doubt that she had been done away with by someone she knew...someone who had a reason for wanting her dead. Who else would want to sneak in there, murder the old lady and then hide her body?

On his return just 20 minutes later Mr Mason looked momentarily at the pile of statements in front of him, then raised his head to glance around the courtroom. This was the moment when the mysterious case of the disappearance of Margaret Clement, former wealthy socialite who had ended up a pauper, would have a line drawn under it. A guilty person might now be named. Face charges. Face a court. Face life in jail, although Clement Carnaghan and Stan Livingstone would not have so many years left.

But Mr Mason had a surprise verdict to hand down.

'It is unfortunate,' he began, 'but I think I can only come to a finding which is an open finding as to the identity of the person and the manner of death of that particular person.

'I think that the evidence is insufficient in any event to say that the skeletal remains which were found and Miss Clement are one and the same person.

'There is no doubt Miss Clement disappeared from Tullaree homestead in May 1952. How she came by the manner of her death, as indeed she did, the evidence disclosed does not enable me to say.'

Mr Mason added that there was 'no positive conclusion' that the bones were Aboriginal or European. There was no evidence to link the bones with any outstanding missing person other than that of a woman 60 to 70 years old.

'Of course, that fits the description of Miss Clement,' he said. But he was not prepared to state officially that the bones were of the Lady of the Swamp.

He then pronounced his official verdict:

'I find that the skeletal remains found buried at Venus Bay Housing Estate, Tarwin Lower, South Gippsland on the 7th November 1978, are those of a female origin.

'I further find that the evidence adduced does not enable me to say who the deceased was or when, where, or by what means the deceased came by her death, whether such death was accidental or otherwise.'

Having handed down his finding, he had more to say – about the Livingstones. He was, he said, far from satisfied with their evidence.

'I think they were, in their answers, in a number of ways, far from frank with the court.'

The verdict was a blow to the police. Had Mr Mason decided the bones were those of Margaret Clement, they could have taken their inquiries further. But the coroner had not been convinced. The experts had cast too many doubts on the origin of the skeleton.

There was no question that 28 years after her disappearance, the Lady of the Swamp was dead; a judge had already decided that two years after she went missing.

But without an official decision that it was her skeleton that had been found at Venus Bay, police could not proceed against anyone.

The case was closed.

Chapter 18.

~AFTERMATH~

The photograph, taken with an old Box Brownie, is beginning to fade and the features of the six people smiling in the sunshine are better seen through a magnifying glass. There is some camera movement and the focus is soft. The group is squinting in the glaring afternoon light and a hot wind in their faces is blowing back their clothes.

The only known picture of the Livingstones with Margaret Clement in 1951, a year before her disappearance. From left: Esme Livingstone, Margaret, Stan Livingstone, Jim Cope Snr, Harry Pride and Lil Cope.

The three people to the left of the group are significant. For it is possibly the only photograph in existence of Margaret Clement with the man who may have murdered her in the coming months. A tiny figure in a wide-brimmed summer hat, a blouse and a long skirt, Margaret stands between Esme Livingstone on the left of the picture, while towering over her on the other side, nearly half as tall again, is Stan, hair tousled, arms folded behind his back. The picture was taken on dry ground amid the sun-whitened swamp grasses of Tullaree in February, 1951 – five months before the Livingstones became the official owners of the property – by Jim Cope, a farmer's son, then in his early 20s. His dad, also called Jim, stands next to Stan and then there is Harry Pride, an Englishman whose job had been to kill a sheep a week for the mansion's cats in earlier years. Finally to the right of the picture is Jim Cope snr's wife, Lil.

'I can still remember that day,' says old Jim's son, who is himself now in his mid-70s and still working the land a few kilometres from Tullaree. It is 27 years since Stanley Livingstone walked from the coroner's court with his wife, a man free to enjoy his remaining years.

'It was blowing hot but as there was a gathering of us we thought it was a good opportunity for a photo. There was, of course, no hint of what was to happen the following year, when Margaret vanished off the face of the earth.

'We all went for a walk around Tullaree that day, pushing our way through the long grass. I remember staring at the blackberry bushes that had almost swallowed the house. I took a picture of my father and Stan staring at the bushes because all you could see of the house from that angle was the roof and the chimneys. There was a pile of empty tins of cat food near one of the windows because all that the sisters used to do was toss them out once they'd fed the cats. At least one of the other windows was broken and the birds were flying in and out.'

Jim's second photo appears to show Stan discussing the state of the blackberry bushes. Examining the picture with the knowledge that he was at that time already talking to Margaret about buying the home, his body language appears to suggest he was detailing plans he had for the property.

'You know, I can't honestly think of a reason why he would want to kill the old lady,' says Jim, sitting with his family and a neighbour who has a house on the Tullaree land. 'If he ended up buying it, why murder her after the event?'

But Esme had told many people he had indeed killed her.

'Yes,' put in the elderly neighbour. 'We've all heard about that. There was that letter she gave to Mrs Wyatt addressed to the police. I can tell you for a fact that that bit's true because Mrs Wyatt told me about it to my face.'

Did Esme's drunkenness turn her mind, cause her to take vengeance out on a husband who used to beat her by making false accusations? A former neighbour, George Shand, living in a hostel for the aged in northern New South Wales, had told a local newspaper in 1999 that Esme was 'as silly as a buckled wheel.' I ask Jim about the day when Esme, for reasons she refused to disclose, had become drunk at the local hotel and tried to swim across the Tarwin, a distance of some 30 metres.

'Oh, she didn't just try,' he replies. 'She really did it. Fought off two strong men who tried to restrain her, went across the road, jumped in with all her clothes on and swam across to the other side. She could swim like a fish. There were a lot of witness to that at that time. We never did find out what it was all about. But what we mustn't do is just pin Margaret's murder – assuming it was murder and I think we have to – on to Stan. That nephew of hers appears to have been a very dark fellow and we mustn't forget he had as much interest in Tullaree as Stan.'

Stan Livingstone or Clement Carnaghan – who did kill the 'lady of the swamp'? The question has lingered for more than 50 years as I head now along the road that Margaret once trudged to pick up meagre supplies for herself and Jeanie – and finally just herself – from the store at Buffalo, a 24-kilometre return journey from Tullaree. I have driven past Tullaree, unsure whether to enter and intrude on the McRae family who now live there. Time has moved on. The swamp has been drained, their cattle graze peacefully. How receptive would they be to a stranger turning up at their door to ask about the misery and murder that has enveloped their home in years past? Word around the district is that the McRaes have had enough – that they want to get on with their lives.

I drive on to Buffalo, past a sign that warns 'Water Over Road', although it will never be as bad as years gone by. Neal's fibro and wooden General Store that Margaret walked to is still there in the small community, perched at the side of a slight incline. Inside are the original wooden floors that she stood on and so are the counters, shiny with age, on which she scrawled her pleading penciled letters to her mother and her sister Anna. The current owner, Mrs Leonie Margetts, on duty as grocer and local postmistress, searches through some old historical magazines on a shelf and finally produces a black and white photo of Mr Neal. He is seen holding a credit book he kept when he was providing Margaret with groceries in the hope that one day she or her mother would be able to pay him. The book's contents tell of the basic foods Margaret collected in the last few years of her life….oatmeal 3s 11d; tea 1s 11d; eggs 2s 11d; butter 1s 7d; candles 1s 3d; matches 8d; milk 1s 7d; sardines 1s 6d.

I ask Leonie if she knows the McRaes – and whether they would be happy to welcome questions about their home. I wonder at that moment why I am so troubled about going to Tullaree.

'Why don't you ask Glenda yourself?' Leonie has interrupted my thoughts, nodding towards a woman who has just entered. 'That's Mrs McCrae who's just come in.'

It is an extraordinary chance. Of all the scores of people who come to the store each week, Tullaree's owner, the only customer, should walk in at the very moment I am asking about her family. Wrapped up in woollen clothing against the winter winds, she has lived with the story of Margaret Clement in the near-20 years that she and her husband Rod have lived there, having taken it over from Rod's father. He had purchased it from Reginald Reschke, the father of the 1963 Miss Australia, who had acquired it from the Livingstones.

'I've lived with the Clement women, if you know what I mean, from the day we moved in,' says Glenda. 'People have come from all over Australia to stare at the place. Sometimes when we've been away, we'll come home and find people wandering around taking photos. One man came all the way from Western Australia just to look at Tullaree and he had the cheek to tell me that he'd picked up my mail and put it on the window sill. Another couple of families were even having a picnic on the lawn when I got home one day, can you believe?'

'But it must be a happy place now, compared to the time when Margaret disappeared?' I ask.

'No, it's not a happy place. It's fine when there are lots of people there and there's life and movement all around you, but when you're in there on your own it's spooky. That's the only word I can find for it. We're moving out soon, passing it on to other members of the family, and I can't wait to go.'

The spectre of Margaret Clement was so near that one night her entire family thought the ghost of the old lady had returned to haunt Tullaree. But it was only one of their cattle dogs which had broken away from a post and was running around the veranda dragging his chain. Glenda, though, relates a more tragic incident, too personal for public disclosure, which emphasises her reasons for wanting to turn her back on Tullaree, the setting for so much joy and misery.

I drive to Tullaree with her blessing to meet her husband Rod. There are only the dogs to greet me at the end of the white-gravel driveway, two tiny animals barking from the verandah, just as decades earlier Dingo had watched strangers wade through the swamp towards the mansion. There is no-one to be seen. Perhaps I am influenced by Glenda's words, but the desertion encourages a feeling of sadness. Then a four wheel drive comes in from a paddock and out climbs a big man in a soft bucket hat and a woolen pullover. With a powerful handshake Rod McCrae invites me into the house, through the rear kitchen where a sheep once stood in the 1934 storm. We sit in the living room where the sisters entertained so many wealthy guests in their heyday, where Rod says he remains open minded about Margaret's death.

'Perhaps she is around here somewhere but if she is she won't be found now,' he opines. 'The ditches have been cleared, there's new topsoil everywhere and the years have drifted by. I don't reckon Stan did it. He bought the place, so why would he kill someone after he'd bought it from them? But those are just my thoughts. I don't think we'll ever know.'

We leave the room, with its framed montage of yellowing newspaper stories about Margaret's disappearance and walk down through the wide hallway, Rod throwing open doors to empty rooms. Then we stop at a doorway towards the rear, on the right hand side. It is a narrow room, the dark blue of the walls emphasising its gloom. 'It's in here that Jeanie died, so I've been told,' he says.

There's a chill in here but that's just the winter cold that has seeped through the glass into this unheated part of the mansion. Isn't it?

Outside I brace myself against the icy wind sweeping across the paddocks as Rod points to the drains that Stan cleared in the distance. 'The drag line had a huge bucket on a crane that could be flung a far as that fence and scoop up the earth,' he says, indicating a post perhaps 10 metres away.

'He did a good job. The whole point was to speed up the flow of water through the creek and on down to the Tarwin River, preventing any more flooding. Then, when he got this place, he cleared all the brush and got it into really good shape. But it was all done after he'd bought it. Doesn't make sense to me that he'd kill someone after he'd bought it from them. No, that doesn't make sense at all.'

Stan Livingstone has been dead since 1992. The man who lived for many years fighting the spread of water after purchasing Tullaree died by fire – collapsing while fighting a bushfire that ran out of control as he was clearing land on his more recently-acquired property near Mt Larcom, a sleepy town between Rockhampton and Gladstone on the Queensland coast. He died at the age of 79 in hospital and was buried, according to his wishes, in the Traralgon Lawn Cemetery in Gippsland. His wife was by then lying seriously ill in the Morwell Hospital in Gippsland, passing away two years after her husband. Esme took her secrets to the grave. But were they secrets?

Were her claims about her husband killing Margaret credible? Or were they the ravings, the wild imaginations, of a woman who could not hold her drink? The old folk of Gippsland who can remember Margaret and the Livingstones are split. Mrs Dorothy Davies, whose late husband worked for the Livingstones at Tullaree after Margaret vanished, believes Stan is the only possible suspect, pointing to his wife's constant references to him killing her. Yet she has a good word for them.

'They were very good and kind to my husband,' she recalls at her home at Lakes Entrance. 'He didn't have a bad word to say about them.'

Len Nelson, who helped in the search for Margaret, has told of his conviction that Stan Livingstone killed the lady of the swamp. He repeated his beliefs in a 1997 newspaper interview when he was 78. He was with the Livingstones in the kitchen of Tullaree while police searched the swamp and, he recalled, 'Esme kept getting up and going out to the back verandah. She'd come back, sit down and say nothing. But as her drinking became more frequent, she'd return and report on where the police were looking. Then she had said: "They'll never find her. They're looking in the wrong bloody place."' The house that Stan was building for Margaret, Len remembered, 'was just a shell. There were no windows and it was cheaply constructed. I believe it was never going to be completed.'

Clement Carnaghan has been spoken to by the police, but his illness has always prevented him from talking to them for more than a few minutes each time. I have also sat with him on several occasions, the only visitor, aside from detectives, he has allowed in to his gloomy flat in St Kilda. On my last visit in the early 1980s, with his death not far away, he was slumped in a chair in a room piled high with old television sets, wirelesses from a bygone era, valves, wires, batteries – the trappings of an electrical trade to which he would never return. His once-dark hair now grey and thinning, his cheeks sunken and hopelessness in his dark eyes, he was being cared for by a female friend who confirmed that he knew he was a dying man. Clem's body shook with the disease that had taken over his body. His voice was a harsh whisper. He asked his friend to pass me a pile of documents. The papers were everything he possessed relating to the Clement family, for, he said, there was no-one left in the immediate family and he did not know what to do with them.

I was handed the original will that Peter Clement had drawn up, bequeathing his wealth to his wife, sons, daughters and the poor of his birthplace in Crieff, Scotland. There were letters that Margaret had written to her mother and original court documents touching on the bitter fight for Tullaree. But what Clem also gave me was not written down. It was his whispered claim of innocence.

'I had an alibi for the time she disappeared,' he said, his bony hand reaching out for mine as if to emphasise his words. I had to put my ear close to his lips to catch what he was saying:

'If there was a time to confess something wrong it is now, but I can assure you I was here in St Kilda and the police knew it because the local police officer was a friend. My mother was also here. People reckon I was involved because I'd been left out of the will and got nothing out of Tullaree. Fair enough, I can see why they'd think that. But I don't hit old ladies. I don't kill them.'

He paused to take in breath.

'I hate Livingstone, I'm not going to hide that. He was a brutal man and he was determined to get that place by fair means or foul. He could put a man down with a single blow and we all know how capable he was of doing that. He floored me right here in this flat with a backhander and knocked me silly. Imagine that happening to an old woman. She wouldn't have a chance.'

And Margaret…what did he feel about her?

'She frustrated me. Everybody knows that. But it wasn't her fault. Once the Livingstones saw that property and realised she had lost control they made up their minds to get their hands on it. The police asked me if I thought they'd brainwashed her. How else do you look at it – she clung on to that place all her adult life and then, within a few months of them making friends with her and taking her shopping and things like that she changes her will, refuses to have anything to do with me and lifts the caveat so that the Livingstones can have the place. And then, when I reckon she refused to move into the poky place they were building for her, he knocks her on the head, one way or another. Doesn't matter where he put her. But there's one thing I'm certain – it was he who put her in the ground.' I didn't see Clem again. They took him to the Austin Hospital, where he died in 1982.

Where are you, Margaret?

A late burst of afternoon sunlight casts an orange glow on the dune brush as I now walk along a narrow trail over the hillocks at Venus Bay. The sea is roaring. The beach is empty. The wind is strong enough to whip up clouds of sand and blow it onto the tussocky mounds. At the junction of Milky Way and Saturn Parade, where the bones were found in 1978, the road still has a soft surface. It is easy to imagine how it would have looked in 1952, a no-man's-land of thick brush and sandy hillocks...

Headlights rise and fall as a vehicle lumbers over the darkened dunes. It stops right here where the holiday homes will rise. A man gets out and begins to dig, confident there are no witnesses as he works away in the headlights. He lifts the body of a small woman from the vehicle, strips her of the clothes that could identify her and drops her into the grave, sweeping the mud and sand back over her.

Margaret Clement has not died in her home. She's been clutching a new handbag as she travels in the vehicle. There is only her and the driver. A row has erupted about Tullaree. An angry blow is struck. She's been injured – very badly injured. Her attacker finishes her off with a hammer. The clothes he can burn. The handbag he'll hide in the dunes. And the hammer. And the spade.

His work done, he drives away. It's a box-shaped vehicle, a four-wheel-drive, and he doesn't have all that far to go. The next day he runs his cattle over the area, the pounding hooves disguising the newly-dug grave.

Then he gets on with his life, never imagining that nearly three decades later the developers would move in and start digging it all up.

Is that how it was?

The sun is almost gone now as I walk through these dunes, but I recall the words of Sergeant Bill Townsend, to whom I spoke several times after the inquest. He had no doubts that Margaret had been murdered by Stanley Livingstone, giving her a backhander in a fit of anger.

But why hit her after he had acquired the property? Was he furious that Margaret had told him that, even though he had bought the homestead, she would never move out, that she would never take up residence in the small house he was building for her?

Whatever Esme's kindly feelings for the old lady were, was Stan appalled at the thought of an old woman, heading towards eccentricity, wandering around the newly-restored home – his home – for perhaps years to come, carrying with her all the misery that had engulfed her in more recent years?

Did he tell her she must move out – and did she say, as she had said so many times in the past: 'No, I will never let Tullaree go'? Was it then that he had struck her, a blow delivered, accidentally or deliberately, with fatal force?

Bill Townsend had spent weeks reading and re-reading everything that Esme had written, and, with his boss, Chief Inspector Paul Delianis, was convinced that she was a woman with a terrible secret. But he had wanted to hear it from her own lips. And she had admitted, after he had interviewed her husband in Rockhampton all those years ago that yes, Stan had killed Margaret – but she refused to make a formal statement that would condemn him.

'When Stan discovered she was dead after he hit her, he panicked and buried her away from the homestead,' Esme told the detective. The words of a woman who had earned a reputation as a drunk were not enough to charge and convict Stanley Livingstone.

Were they even Margaret's bones that were unearthed here beside the sea? Police, weighing up the varied opinions of the experts, including those with great knowledge of Aboriginal burial customs, remained convinced that the skeleton was that of the lady of the swamp. The hammer and spade and then the coins found in the handbag discovered nearby were an added clue, although, to add to the mystery, the bag itself might have been manufactured after Margaret disappeared.

Over the years, several sets of bones have been unearthed, creating a stir in the local community, but they have been false alarms – one cluster uncovered on the beach belonged to an albatross, while others were quickly identified as those of a rabbit.

Now it is twilight in the dunes and time to leave this place and its mysteries. It is in this windy half gloom, where ancient warriors fought and died and explorers perished that the imagination runs wild, when branches become beckoning arms, bushes the rustle of a dress. The undergrowth is alive. Is she still here? Was she ever here?

What happened to you, Margaret…where are you?

ACKNOWLEDGEMENTS

I originally wrote this story in 1980. Since then, new information has emerged which has shed further light on the mystery of the disappearance and death of Margaret Clement. Several people who helped me with my research at the time have died; others have come forward with new information that has enabled me to compile this present version of the incredible story of the riches-to-rags recluse known as the Lady of the Swamp. I am grateful to those past and present who have helped and I apologise if there is anyone I have inadvertently overlooked. I would particularly like to thank the following people for their ideas, help and inspiration:

Rod and Glenda McCrae of Tullaree, Gippsland; Susan and Peter Lendon, Yarragon Book Shop, Gippsland; Jim Cope, Gippsland; Brian and Stan Fitzgerald, Dumbalk; Lyn Skillern and members of the Leongatha and District Historical Society; Clement Carnaghan, St Kilda; Detective Sergeant Bill Townsend, formerly of the Melbourne Homicide Squad and his colleagues; Sid Castle, secretary, Sale Public Cemetery Trust; John and Kathleen Buckley, Camberwell; Matt Gleeson, Ennisvale, Victoria; Leonie Margetts, Buffalo Store, Gippsland; Methodist Ladies' College, Melbourne; Registrar-General's Office, Melbourne; Tarwin Lower School; Peter McFarlane, Lang Lang; Bryan Fitzgerald, Dumbalk; La Trobe Library, Melbourne; Mitchell Library, Sydney; *The Age*, Melbourne; *Herald Sun* (formerly *The Herald*), Melbourne; former *Truth*, Melbourne; former *People*, Sydney; *Gippsland Times*, Sale; Michael Downey, researcher, Sydney; Peter Gill, researcher, Melbourne; Victorian Public Records Office.

I would also like to thank my agent, Mr Tim Curnow, for his encouragement and guidance and, of course, the team at New Holland, who have supported me in their usual professional and friendly manner and made the production of this book a pleasure.

Finally, I would like to say another thank you to my wife, Isobelle Gidley, my most severe critic, whose suggestions and vision are always spot on.

New Holland Publishers
Sydney

newhollandpublishers.com

This is a revised and enlarged edition of the book entitled *The Lady of the Swamp* first published in 1981 by Sphere Books. Newspaper clippings reproduced with permission *Sun-Herald.*

A record of this book is held at the National Library of Australia

ISBN: 9781760792671

Managing Director: Fiona Schultz
General Manager/Publisher: Olga Dementiev
Cover Designer: Andrew Davies
Production Director: Arlene Gippert
Printed in China

Keep up with New Holland Publishers:
NewHollandPublishers
@newhollandpublishers